DEATH
WITH
UNDERSTANDING

RELIGIOUS RESEARCH
WRITERS GROUP

RELIGIOUS RESEARCH PRESS
Box 208 Grand Island
Florida 32735 U.S.A.

i

DEATH WITH UNDERSTANDING

Typesetting by Marlene Hassell
Cover by Cotty Kilbanks
ISBN 0-915151-10-3
Library of Congress card # 87-61427
Printed in U.S.A.
9 8 7 6 5 4 3 2

Religious Research Press
Box 208 Grand Island
Florida 32735 U.S.A.

DEATH WITH UNDERSTANDING

The sponsors of the first publication of this book,
William and Myra Cook, lovingly dedicate it to their mothers,

MURIEL THOMPSON ADAIR

and

DESSIE MULL COOK

DEATH WITH UNDERSTANDING

INTRODUCTION

For years I waited for the right person to write this important book. My Religious Research staff and I had gathered much material – on death-and-resuscitation experiences, out-of-body experiences, near-death experiences, authenticated cases of psychic communication with the dead, dreams and visions, Kirlian photography with its still unknown reaches and meanings, a three-year locked laboratory research into the prayer-effect upon plants (published in the 1959 Doubleday bestseller *The Power of Prayer on Plants*), etc. I personally have interviewed 54 persons from various parts of the USA, Canada, and England who had been clinically dead and then returned to life. In taking hundreds of persons into thousands of pastlife recalls I have taken perhaps 500 through the death experience of a pastlife, and in our 5,000+ Loehr-Daniels Life Readings we have well over 1,000 cases where the death and the life after death had been brought through. I wrote from this *Diary After Death*, the account of a man who dies and does not come back.

But I knew I was not the one to write the longer, more comprehensive, more difficult and important *Death With Understanding*, the book you are reading now. I read the Egyptian *Book of the Dead* (fascinating and noble in its way), and the Tibetan *Book of the Dead* (more primitive and in some

v

parts quite disgusting). The Chinese have several books describing death and how to meet it. It certainly is time for a modern *Book of the Dead* to gather what science is finding out about the death experience and the life after death, so that people today can themselves face death without fear, and experience much less grief at the death of loved ones.

Finally I found the right person to write this particular book. Approaching 60 herself, she had cared for older people and had written a short essay on "Death With Dignity." We talked for months, and other staff members shared their material with her. Finally she joined our Writers-in-Residence program and undertook the project. She is not a professional writer, and I worked closely with her throughout the two years she was with us. She left before the final year of editing and re-write but she had mothered this book through nearly to its birth. She prefers to remain nameless so we shall call her "Pilgrim," but the life experiences she shares, particularly in the opening chapters, are her own and in her own words.

I think you will see that the thousands of hours of work and the contributions of all concerned have made this a most worthwhile book — indeed, a book much needed today. And the excerpts from the Loehr-Daniels Life Readings and Teaching Readings have been carefully selected.

Really, there is no reason anymore to fear death. Even as smallpox, tuburculosis and polio have been conquered in our time, so also ignorance of death will be conquered. I hope that your attitude toward death and your living of your life now, will change for the better as you, too, now come to know *Death With Understanding*.

Franklin Loehr, Director of Research
Religious Research Foundation of America, Inc.

CHAPTER ONE

A TRIBUTE TO THE PAST

DEATH is the harshest reality of all to face. It is a matter of major importance both in our personal living and in any philosophy which seeks to understand and explain life. It is of particular importance to religion, where death is in effect the great attack upon the religious teaching that man is an immortal being.

But despite the universal fear of death, the subject has received scant attention in our own culture. The ancient Egyptians, the Tibetans, and the Chinese each had a "Book of the Dead." These books gave specific instructions to the dying person and to the living, in preparation for death. In our culture, the only preparation we have for death is the grim knowledge that all must die, contemplated in the private fears, wonderings, griefs, and rebellion or resignation of our individual hearts; and the religious teachings of survival, usually linked with a teaching that death brings us into a certain judgment upon the life we have just lived. Thus the religious teaching of survival is used to inculcate virtues or spiritual values during our earthliving.

It seems incredible, when we stop to think of it, that a subject of such major significance in life as death should have received so little attention in our culture, since it is the very end of earthlife as we know it. It is of continuing imminence throughout all our living, as death can come unexpectedly from a multitude of causes and at any moment, and we all know and accept that everyone and everything that has lived either has died or will die.

Perhaps it is our ignorance primarily, and our fears secondarily, which produce this conspiracy of silence and evasion. The true place of death in our thinking and in our living awaits the true knowledge of death. And this true knowledge of death is being made known in our generation, even as the true knowledge of space travel and medicine and so much else awaited the findings of this Age of Science.

Death has been referred largely to the general field of religion, and scientific research in religion has only now begun. But despite this lack of scientific knowledge, of facts, religion has one very important positive factor in preparing us for death, which is its historic insistence that WE DO LIVE AFTER DEATH. Let us pay tribute to the religions that have valiantly and stubbornly brought to all centuries of man a definite and insistent teaching that the physical death of the body is not the end of life. This teaching has been amazingly consistent considering the multitude of centuries and cultures and religions through which it has been proclaimed. Religion has held stubbornly to the non-dying nature of man despite all material evidence to the contrary. If ever an institution or an article of faith deserves the support now beginning to come from scientific research, it is the religions of the world and their teaching of the survival and immortality of the human being.

Survival of death is at the very heart of Christian history and faith. The physical resurrection of Jesus Christ is the foundation, the great fact, that validated His teachings and His life. It is not His teaching, it is not His life, it is not His death upon the cross, that is the central point of Christianity. After all this had taken place, at His death His disciples scattered, convinced that Jesus and what He stood for was at an end. The electrifying events of the Resurrection, the triumph of Jesus over death, is the central point in Christianity, the very foundation of the Christian religion – and a major reason why Christianity has become the largest religion in the modern world.

The resurrection of Jesus, His coming to life again after undisputed death, is firmly established as historic fact by two major evidences: first, there is the attestation of various historic witnesses and the reports of those who personally saw the risen Jesus. More importantly, there is the impact of the resurrected Jesus upon the lives of those who saw, heard, spoke, even ate with Him. This changed their lives forever. Vacillating disciple Simon became Peter the Rock. The fishermen apostles who had returned to their old trade upon His crucifixion, left it to become full-time fishers of men. Those who had gone over the hill toward Emmaeus, saying sadly, "We had hoped that it was He who would restore the kingdom to Israel," hurried back to Jerusalem after He appeared to them, there to join the other changed men and women who had seen Him. Indecisive, frightened, ordinary men and women, after seeing the risen Jesus became fearless preachers, unshakable teachers, healers, foreign missionaries, and unflinching martyrs. What changed all this was the factual demonstration by Jesus of the victory of life over death. Henceforth the ultimate threat, death as the end of our lives, had lost its power over them. The last frontier of fear – the fear of dying – had lost its hold on the followers of Jesus, and when they lost their fear of death, they lived courageously and fully in the present.

The highpoint of the Christian message is not Christmas, the birth of Jesus. The highpoint has always been Easter, Jesus' survival, His victory over death. And because of this triumph over that last fearful enemy, we too know that we will live after the death of our bodies. This is the Christian message.

Other religions express in other ways their comprehension of life after death. But all religions have kept alive for all these many centuries this insistent message of the undying nature of Man. The one thing that damns a person after the death of the body is not knowing that there is another realm of life. If, at death, the person does not know that another realm of existence exists, if the mind of the person is earthbound, that person is not freed from earth by the death of the earthbody.

On the excarnate side there are persons whose bodies have died, but who do not have an enlightened comprehension of either the death of the body or of any real existence after death. They are like a rocket where the first booster worked and fell away, but the second stage failed to fire, and the whole thing is still held in earth's gravitational pull. These unfortunate persons wander around in a place of shades and shadows until they literally wear out. They briefly haunt the earth, particularly the places where they had lived; and they may haunt the person or persons upon whom their earthlife centered. They are pulled back and do not escape earth. Expending without replacing the energies of their being, they quickly exhaust themselves and die the second death without ever experiencing the second life, the excarnate life of their personal beingness upon astral and then etheric planes.

If the earthbound "dead people who do not know they are dead" are alcoholic, or sex-centered, or if in some other way their thinking and living was totally involved in the physical life of the body and its sensations, or if thoughts of revenge or hatred fill their thinking, they may try to reach back through the body life of some person still "alive" to experience vicariously that which they seek. The alcoholics, the drug addicts, the sex-centered and the criminal in our society often support these invisible parasites. They work their evil of seeking gratification by subtly urging and influencing the decisions and experiences of their incarnate hosts. Then rather quickly, their energies expended and not replenished, they sink into this second death of personal extinction without ever experiencing their immortality.

Any religion that teaches a life after death does bring its followers into the first step of salvation. The fact that their religion plants firmly in their consciousness an expectation of living after the death of the body, does prepare those persons to be open to the next step in their progression. They will enter into the next stage of growth after the death of their body rather than deny it or in ignorance miss it entirely. That part which lives on after the death of the body is the spirit, the mind, the emotional nature, the personality of man. If the mind, which is the consciousness instrument, has never been opened to a life beyond the body, it does not comprehend the new place and the new state of being into which it has come.

There are various ways in which many of these persons can be reached even though they do not know they are in a new state of beingness. Sometimes these disembodied non-believers are reached by a still-incarnate person, one they recognize. A good deal of "psychic rescue work" can be done in this way. Another way of helpfulness is for loved ones who have gone on before to be used to reach into the consciousness of the materialist who has died. The prayers of those still on earth can sometimes be used to convince a deceased loved one that he has made the transition onto another plane of life. Still another method sometimes used is for the materialist to be put to sleep and dream-impressed that he is no longer an earth person, and that he is now in a new and different state of being.

The death problem with the materialist could have been prevented if he had learned while still in the physical body that there will be on-going life and growth for him after his physical body dies. Until the mind is opened to the reality that there is a life after death, immortal life does not become a reality for that person. Every religion which teaches the survival of death brings to its followers that very first step needed in order to be saved from a final death. The person's understanding of the after-death state may or may not be correct, but this is not decisive. What is important is that one have some tentative expectation of a life after death, or at least be open-minded to that possibility. Once the person is safely, consciously, knowingly on the other side, there will be plenty of time to explore that new world and find out for himself what it is like.

Grateful credit is given to the spiritual teachers of the past who taught (1) that Man is not primarily a physical being, but that we are essentially spiritual beings even while in the physical body; (2) that death simply ends the temporary association of our spirit with the physical body; and (3) that following the death of the body the spiritual part is free to go on into other exciting, meaningful planes and realms of expression and experience. This essential message that man has a spiritual nature is the most important message of the many spiritual teachings and religions in human history. Now the tool of science is coming to their support, adding facts to this valiant faith of the past.

CHAPTER TWO

MY SEARCH

My intense interest in the subject of death and life after death is not just a current research project, not a passing curiosity. On the contrary, the subject has been of continuing interest to me most of my life. It has been a constant and unrelenting need to discover the facts, the truth of God's reality in this area so vitally important to us all.

From an early age I found it difficult to accept the teachings in the many churches I attended while growing up, especially in this area of life after death. My father was an oil driller, and we moved once or twice a year – after the wells were drilled – and each move meant a new school and a new church. My mother was very religious, so attending Church, Sunday School, and Summer Bible School were absolute musts. The after-death teachings in the various churches seemed to me vague and negative. Heaven, presented in the way sometimes caricatured as "floating on a cloud and playing a harp," at best seemed pointless and silly. And hell, sending people to hell because they were not perfect, and babies because they were not baptized, was unacceptable to me even when very young, as a contradiction to their teaching that God was a wise, just and loving Father. I saw little evidence of even human kindness in many church teachings, let alone divine love.

So up until I was fifteen I was sent to a succession of Methodist and Baptist churches, whichever was close to where we lived. Then I set out on my own search. At fifteen I became for two years a Mormon, and in my way studied it in depth. At seventeen I became a Roman Catholic convert, reasoning that since it was the oldest Christian church, it had the answers; I found it did not, for me. As with so many Catholic girls, I thought seriously of becoming a nun, and went on retreats at various convents. At 32 I turned to Unity, studied it, thought of taking training to become a Unity minister; during this period I also attended other metaphysical churches and groups, such as Religious Science and Science of Mind. In 1960, at age 38, I turned to "Eastern Thought" for eight years, at first Astara, then the Yogananda teachings through the Self-Realization Fellowship, and I became a direct disciple of Kriyananda. In this period I also studied such bodies of teachings as the writings of Alice Bailey and the Tibetan master, Djwhal Khul, in the teachings of the Arcane School.

During these years of my seeking, the teachings became a little more believable, more expanded. But still there was much unacceptable and much left unexplained. The only teaching I could always accept with a sure knowing was that there is indeed a life after death, and with it a more expanded consciousness. Even in the physical with the five senses, I could easily perceive God's order, beauty and love everywhere. Surely when the physical body, this limited instrument of perception, is dropped at death, my understanding of reality would be expanded to where I could see more of what God's reality actually is. I acknowledge with gratitude what I learned from each group, and each was a part of my growth. For many of their members, these fine churches and organizations do provide all the answers they need. But always I came away unfulfilled.

I did not begin my long search for truth with any altruistic desire to serve mankind. My impetus was to alleviate my own anguish, my doubts and fears when looking ahead to my own eventual old age and death. What about life after death? I knew I wasn't perfect as my Heavenly Father is perfect, and if there is only heaven and hell — and nothing else — where did that leave me?

It has been reported that Freud, the father of the new science Psychology (the first scientific discipline to venture into the area of the non-material), initially entered into that field of study and research in order to better understand himself, to discover what was normal behavior and what was not. Many have benefited from Freud's lifetime of study and his search for truth. It opened up this first non-material area to scientific scrutiny. Freud made a major contribution to scientific inquiry, and fathered this infant science, Psychology. But his impetus in the beginning, and at the end, was his own search for truth, for reality, in order to alleviate his own fears and doubts as to the normality of his own thinking-feeling nature. Just so my search for true knowledge of the nature of death and the life after death was to answer my own questions, my curiosity — yes, and sometimes my fear.

I started each and every new study with the high hope that it would lead to the knowledge of all truth, the "ultimate" truth. But after a time I would be dissatisfied, disappointed with the teachings. Invariably I reached a saturation point where I wearied of the struggle to accept the unacceptable and became bored with the repetition of the simplistic teachings. Then I would leave that group, that church, that organization. Many of the teachings I felt maligned my concept of a loving, wise and just God. Others were more in line with a wise and good God, and I could not quarrel with what they had, but what they had was so limited. Yet each one characteristically maintained it had all of truth, or at least all that was important. It was difficult to comprehend this degree of arrogance, this lack of open-minded humility to reach out for further knowledge.

Each time I came to the end of a particular path, and had not found the "ultimate truth," I became despondent for awhile until another path caught my attention with a renewed hope. Finally, after repeating this search over and over again for many years, I just gave up and sank into a deep depression, feeling, "If this is all there is to spiritual knowledge, then life holds no further interest. Why go on?" This was unrealistic of me, I now recognize, and life held much of other activities and distractions. But at heart I had searched and not found.

During the darkest hour of this, my "dark night of the soul," I had the first of a series of waking-visions. Two of the visions stay with me to this day, the others have faded. The two remembered visions I will share with you.

In the first vision, a kind and wise Teacher came and showed me a long flight of stairs leading as far as the eye could see, with the clear knowing that beyond that point were more steps as far as the eye could see, and then more, and so on and on. I was so awed by this new (to me) concept and insight into spiritual progression, I exclaimed to my Teacher, "My God! There is no end to it!" To this, the Teacher smiled, "Yes." I was told that when I came to the end of a particular path or course of study, it simply meant I had finished that step and was reaching toward the next one in a succession of spiritual steps that never end. This first vision pulled me out of the deep depression, and I never again fell into despondency when I had finished another step in growth.

This vision gave me a measure of comprehension of the magnitude of spiritual progression. But in spite of it I could not completely give up the notion that somewhere there must be a group that possessed a body of teachings that was the ultimate spiritual knowledge of our day, a group to whom I could give my whole life in service.

Twenty years later I was introduced to the Religious Research body of spiritual teachings, and received my own Loehr-Daniels Life Reading. Dr. John Christopher Daniels is the chief spirit guide of Religious Research, Jesus Christ is his and its Master. Dr. John, who also is the akashic record reader in the life readings, helped me transcend the foolishness, really, of my (or any) personality demanding the ultimate in spiritual knowledge. He showed me instead a free-flowing growth, ever upward and onward. I share this part of my life reading with you:

Dr. John: We offer this as a contribution of thought to the whole truth. There is no one school of teaching in the earth, there is no one school of teaching in the other realms, there is no one individual soul, whether in personality expression or in soul expression, who expresses all truth and from whom another soul can learn all truth.

We have used somewhere in our teachings the picture of truth as a rather long, wide stream stocked with many fish. Many fishermen are standing up and down the banks of the stream throwing in their lines, catching a fish and then only too often calling out to the other fishermen, "I have a fish! See my fish! This is the place to fish! Come and join me here! This is where the fish are!" But the many fishermen who hold their own place on the bank, catch their own fish – and all of the fish come from the same stream and live and move and have their being in that stream – and this is true of truth.

Do not seek for the ultimate truth. This will bring confusion and bewilderment, sometimes disillusionment. Let the seeker for truth expect to find different portions in different places. Wade up and down the stream, cast in your line at different places. Or, to change our illustration, remember that truth is a multi-faceted diamond. Don't become so enamored with the beauty in one facet that you forget to turn the diamond around and see the beauty in many facets. When the study of truth is approached in this way, then it is an adventure

and one does not become disillusioned or discouraged or
despairing when one seems to come to the end of what
one felt to be a particular course or path of truth and
still feels unfulfilled.

Of course there will always be a certain nature of
unfulfillment. If all truth could be found in earthliving,
what would the other realms of continuing experience
and growth be for? Search and rejoice in the search for
truth on many pathways. And rejoice that when the
incarnate life is complete, the search for truth will be
expanded. (B2296:7)

The second remembered waking-vision addressed another
pitfall which was also an obstruction to greater growth. This
obstacle was my propensity to get constantly bogged down in
negativities with relationships and experiences. This over-
reaction took a heavy toll in suffering, in psychosomatic
illnesses and the building of wrong attitudes. At my present
point of progression, I can easily see how that could negate
the larger purpose.

In this vision the Teacher showed me a much larger picture
of progression, and of how the little self of the person relates to the larger self of the soul. In the larger picture of
the soul these experiences and relationships of the person,
taken now so seriously, are trivial in comparison. I was
shown how these experiences and relationships were merely
the "vehicles of transportation" carrying opportunities for
new learning and growth, and that once the growth within
it has been achieved the vehicle can be discarded. I was
further taught that in view of this the vehicles can be for-
given for their limitations and with gratitude for being so
used. This brought fresh insight into the Bible's admonition
"love your enemies. . . and pray for them which despitefully
use you." With this understanding of why, it becomes easier
to do. Dr. John addressed this area of not giving undue attention to the negativities of life with the encouragement of,
"Yes, life is serious business, but live it with a light touch."

This is an excellent attitude in which to approach all one's experiences and relationships, no matter what the life purpose may be.

The crystal clarity of this second vision imprinted itself sharply and showed me the utter absurdity of my petty concerns, and this lesson was shown to me in such an amusing way that I came out of this altered state of consciousness laughing hilariously. And each time during the days and weeks that followed, when the memory came to mind, I would again laugh heartily at my foolishness.

The teachings in the Loehr-Daniels Life Readings brought me further comfort and ease, for Dr. John addresses this area of pain and suffering many times when asked by a client, "Why have I had so much pain and suffering in this lifetime?" The basic response is, "Pain and suffering break the shell which encases the understanding. This is one of the purposes and a usefulness of experiences of suffering — to allow the understanding to expand and mature."

The seeds planted as a result of the visions, and the deeper insights given in my 1970 Religious Research life reading, helped me to mature spiritually. The learning within the visions was absorbed in consciousness, and I never again allowed myself to become overwhelmed by any "vehicle of transportation." There was pain and suffering, yes, but never again any feeling of being overpowered, nor over-reacting and falling into a hopeless state of despondency. And when the preparatory stage for my service was completed and I finally came into the usage of that preparation, I had the spiritual maturity to understand larger and deeper levels of Truth — knowledge that had been built upon knowledge. Without this firm foundation of knowing, I wonder if my personality could have survived.

As I have said, it was twenty years between my experience with the visions and my finding Religious Research. Twenty years — observing, exploring, experiencing, learning, growing — studying on many pathways both secular and spiritual, learning from each with gratitude with always knowing that, "Yes, of course, I've found grains of truth here and there, but oh! what foolishness and ignorance I had to wade through first before I found it." And I often wondered if I would ever find a body of teachings I could accept in total without inner resistance. In my heart, I doubted very much that such a body of teachings existed.

Dr. John explained this long and difficult search in a supplementary reading I received when I had finally come to the end of my long search and had found the best source of spiritual teachings for me, the Religious Research body of spiritual teachings of Dr. John Daniels (excarnate) and Dr. Franklin Loehr (incarnate):

> Dr. John: Deliberately she has been led into a number of channels of seeking, partly to let her develop discrimination that she may see the teachings, the amount of truth, the direction of spiritual thrust and advance, in various branches of teaching.
> She has found that which we bring is good. (A3151:3)

What an understatement!

I was first introduced to Religious Research in the spring of 1968, and the introduction came about in a rather strange way. "Mysterious are the ways of God!" I came into Religious Research mainly to please a friend who felt I might be interested in this group. She had ordered lessons from Religious Research, and after reading them found they were not in her area of interest. She then was mainly interested in the general psychic field. She was just on the verge of tossing those lessons in the trash when a strong feeling came over her that she must give them to me. She did not understand it, but obeyed the prompting and gave me the lessons, with her explanation of this experience.

Upon this, my introduction to Religious Research, no light suddenly went on to announce "Finally! This is it!" On the contrary, my feeling was more like, "Oh well, here we go again." I embarked upon this new path of spiritual study with serious misgivings — waiting, expecting that familiar inner-resistance to build up, waiting for the usual unacceptable teaching to emerge.

Gradually, and with much surprise, I found that resistance did not come! I found no unacceptable nonsense along with the teachings. My goal of finding truth, after my long and painful previous searches, seemed too good to be true — of finding, really finding, a body of advanced spiritual knowledge I could indeed study with constantly growing enlightenment. I found myself evaluating each and every new step in the teaching, and I still do, but with the joy of discerning that to me, at least, "This is true. This is all true." This is true, I think, not only because Dr. John Daniels is, in my opinion, the most advanced spirit guide now bringing through teachings to earth, but also because Dr. Franklin Loehr, the earth-head of Religious Research (and according to Dr. John, his soulmate) is so solidly grounded and well-rooted in both science and religion.

In my opinion, this body of teachings indeed does teach the true value-system of God for planet earth. In my judgment this is the reality of God as He has ordained it, not as man has proclaimed. And these beautiful truths are clothed in clear, modern-day language, easily understandable to all true seekers. This is not everyone's experience, of course, but it is mine. Dr. John speaks to this generation in this generation's vocabulary — even as the Master Jesus spoke to His generation in their common language. Not that we equate Dr. John with the Master Jesus, but we can learn from his manner of teaching, so that the seeker of truth really understands that which is being taught.

It took two years of study with Religious Research, two

years of testing and waiting for the resistance, before I became confident that probably I had found my earthly spiritual home. Now after fourteen more years of study and research, I have yet to feel any resistance to any teaching here, and I have yet to be bored. How could one, when experiencing this exciting phenomenon of constantly expanding spiritual horizons of new knowledge, deeper knowledge, with the resultant growth and expanding consciousness? And with this a great joy, a renewed commitment to this body of teachings, and the desire to play a part in the wide dissemination of this material to as many people as possible.

Within this body of teachings, I found my answers to death and to life after death. Answers I can believe. Answers that satisfy my concept of a wise, loving and totally just God. Answers that comfort. Answers that enabled me to finally and completely release all fear of death and of what happens to me after the death of my physical body. Knowledge that has indeed set me free.

In the myriad paths of spiritual study I was drawn to before Religious Research, the teachings on old age, death and life after death were, on the whole, negative. During much observation, I saw the wholesale loss of dignity and independence of the elderly, and it was fearsome to contemplate my own inevitable old age. And what of life after death? The teachings of "eternal bliss and oneness with God," with the implication of a loss of individuality, gave small comfort. I was not at all sure I wanted any part of that.

I had been exposed to many experiences of seeing the elderly, in nursing homes and in private homes, living in disabled bodies, with disturbed minds, some in a non-human state — alone, unwanted, a burden to themselves, to their families, and to society. The experiences were chilling. But in spite of this, there remained a glimmer of hope and faith that it should not be this way. Surely in God's wisdom, love and justice, there had to be a great dignity, a Divine Purpose,

and positive progression in the progression of old age, death
of the body, and the continuing life after death. Surely a
God who created the flowers and birds and all things beautiful, had not forsaken us who are made in His image and likeness. And in this great plan of God, death would hold only
good for those on the spiritual path, and we would go "from
glory to glory" as St. Paul saw. But I needed this glimmer of
hope and faith backed up, substantiated in no uncertain
way, with a body of teachings I had tested and found true.
This now I found.

So many years ago, I started this search for God's reality. I
had a driving desire to understand myself better, and to find
answers to death and life after death. Now, during sixteen
years of studying and assimilating the Religious Research
material, brought through by the spirit guide and teacher
Dr. John Christopher Daniels, there slowly grew within me
the intense desire to share with others what I have found to
be most good. And with the sharing, the hope of bringing the
same light and comfort to others who are now seeking where
I have searched.

I hope to bring a measure of comfort to those who have
lost a loved one or are fearful of their own impending death,
and who need words that are believable and which strike a
responsive chord of knowing within their hearts. With this
knowledge of truth they can be truly comforted in their
grief. We can let go our fear of death, and we can release our
fear and grief for loved ones who have gone on before us.

I share joyously and gratefully my own experiences in this
long search for the truth. As we start this New Age, this
glorious New Age for Mankind, the timing is now right for
these advanced teachings to be brought to earth consciousness. I share with humility what I have found to be good. I
know this is not the ultimate knowledge, not all of truth,
but it is a contribution to all truth, an important contribution. This is a step we can take right here, right now, to slay

this "last enemy," death, and the fear of what actually happens to us when our physical body, like a booster rocket putting a satellite into orbit, drops away.

CHAPTER THREE

THE SOUL AND THE PERSON

In order to understand death and the continuing existence after death, it is basic to understand what a soul is, what a person is, and the relationship between the soul and the person.

The soul is the continuing part of us, the Child-of-God part. God in His wisdom and love has patterned the soul's development through a series of separate incarnations, each one a different person. Thus the Biblical teachings, "Every man is a new creation" and "It is appointed unto man once to die," are literally true. At the death of the body the person comes into the excarnate part of his/her personality life (much more on this later), but the soul is free to have a new incarnation. That new incarnation is as a different person, living at a different time and place, having different personality traits and experiences and problems and relationships and learnings. Thus the soul, which usually has between 60 and 100 significant incarnations all told, has all these different opportunities for experience and learning which the different personalities provide.

We note another thing also: Although the first reason for each life reading is that the person getting it has discovered the readings and decided he wants his own reading, there also is a buildup through the many readings of a body of spiritual teaching. Thus the Religious Research spiritual teaching is not something drawn up by some individual or group in some "ivory tower" and then promulgated to us, as most bodies of spiritual teaching are. Rather, this is life-centered, reading after reading bringing out spiritual principles which apply to that particular person in that particular life. Gradually from them all emerges this life-centered group of spiritual principles. A similarity is noted here with the Judeo-Christian Bible. The Bible is not like the Koran or the Baghavad-Gita or the teachings of Confucius. The Bible is a life-centered book, following for 1500 years the course of the little Hebrew nation and drawing from their doings and experiences the spiritual principles thus brought to light. So also the Religious Research body of spiritual teachings, built from this study of thousands of lifetimes, is a life-centered body of spiritual principles.

The soul is the continuing unit upon which these different lifetimes are strung one by one. Each separate incarnation is a separate person, with its own nature and forces and experiences and decisions. No one needs to do everything and be everything in one lifetime only. Each person is tailor-made to be the person to have the experiences, cope with the problems, have the relationships, of that particular person, that specific lifetime.

Dr. John: The — well, perhaps it is time for me to sum up what I have been bringing, which is a teaching, but a teaching that is applicable to Ryan. The teachings which I bring in these readings are an important part and reason of these readings, but each one is applicable to the person getting it. The teachings I bring, and the team that works with me, are not brought in the framework of a pre-conceived philosophical system. They are brought in terms of life principles, which apply to specific individual human beings right where they are, and this matter of the growth of consciousness is certainly applicable to Ryan. (A815:8)

We start this chapter with a good comprehensive teaching on the soul, the person, and the relationship between the two in earthliving. It teaches the significance of God's purpose in the individuation of the soul out of God-Beingness, and of the soul's extension of different parts of itself into incarnate persons such as you and me.

The one getting this life reading asked the question, "What is the essential nature of human life on earth?"

Dr. John: We will begin with a little basic theology, laying the basis for information of the beingness of the individual soul:

In the beginning was God, or Cosmic Love, or Divine Intelligence, or Divine Love, or Cosmic Energy; call it by whatever term you wish to use. From that central Beingness were individuated portions partaking of the very nature of that central Beingness, but without the self-knowledge of their own nature. These portions have come to be labeled 'souls.'

The soul is not a single unit, not just one kind of energy or expression of beingness. The soul is a complex of energies engaged essentially in the task, the fulfillment of the purpose, stated by Jesus the Christ in the words, 'Be ye therefore perfect as your Father in heaven is perfect.' The soul is to grow into knowledge, self-knowledge, of its divine beingness.

The methods, the ways, the paths leading to the knowledge of self-divinity, are many. And they involve the incorporation of various portions of the soul at various times in various frameworks of incarnation. The soul sends out portions of itself, part of its bundle of energies — much like antennae — to experience that into which the part is sent; and then the part is drawn back with its portion of learning into the whole, and what it brings with it as it returns is added to the whole. And in this manner it can be said that the soul grows.

There are various realms of existence, planes of

learning, provided for the soul. One is the earth realm of experience. It is only one of many realms of experience, but it is a very important one. The soul, in certain stages of its learning, follows a pattern which can be likened in concept to the pattern of a student of science. The student of science will enter a classroom where he listens to lectures by experts in the particular fields of knowledge being studied. To him in these lectures are being given certain basic principles and laws. After the period in the classroom the student is given the opportunity of going into the laboratory and using various test tubes, crucibles, and other equipment. The student experiments in the laboratory with the laws and principles which have been taught him in the classroom.

Earth experience for the soul is related to this laboratory experience. The soul, as it progresses in its learning and growth, is presented with the various cosmic principles which underlie beingness. It is given the cosmic laws by the following of which it can come into full expression of its divine beingness, in a true sense of its original and real beingness. Then it is given the opportunity to go into the laboratory of earthliving, using the test tubes, crucibles, and equipment of various personalities and bodies, to experiment with the cosmic laws and principles, to see if they work – or, more properly, to see if the soul can work them properly and get the right results.

So, as you see, it emerges that the earth realm of experience, although it is only one of many realms of experience, is a very important realm. It is a time of the soul actually working, personally, creatively, learningly, with cosmic laws and principles.

As we pointed out, the soul is a complex, a many-faceted, richly endowed individuation of cosmic beingness. It is a grouping, a 'corporation,' as opposed to the idea of single unitism. And a soul sends only a portion of itself into any given, specific earthlife. Never is all of the soul incorporated into one particular earthlife;

for one thing, the total beingness of that individuated portion of God we call the soul is simply too big to fit into a personality vehicle.

The amount or percentage of a soul's beingness that is incorporated in a personality, varies. It varies according to the particular lesson being learned in that personality, and it varies according to the soul's adeptness in earthliving. There are various factors that govern the degree of soul involvement in a given earthlife through a given earth personality. And although the soul has only one incarnate earth personality at a time (except in the case of identical twins), other portions of the soul may be having experiences elsewhere while the incarnate portion is having experience on earth.

Experience in the earth realm, through the instrumentality of an incarnate personality, is a major undertaking for the soul. Earthliving is in general a strenuous experience. There are lessons to be learned in earthliving which can be learned only on earth. There are no other realms of experience that duplicate exactly for the soul the expressions of earthliving, and the soul has to experience these learnings in earth or not at all.

The soul experiences its earth lessons through a series of incarnate personalities. The personality is a tool the soul uses, just as the physical body likewise is a tool which the soul uses. In time the physical body tool wears out, and then there is the experience known as death for the physical body. The personality tool has a longer usage period than the body tool. The body tool wears out first, but the personality tool can still be used. The personality survives the death of the body. The personality has continuing expression in planes above or beyond the physical earth plane. The soul continues to use the personality tool after the body tool is no longer usable.

So the personality survives the death of the body. The soul will go on experiencing the learnings and the growth of other planes through the personality tool which is given its first expression (usually) in incarnate earthliving, and then is carried on to be used in non-carnate and non-physical planes.

But the soul does not use that given personality tool a second time in incarnate earthliving. The personality does not reincarnate, the same *person* does not come into a new body for a second earthlife. The personality, after the death of the body, goes on learning, growing, being used as a tool by the soul in other planes of existence. It goes on, as your scriptures say, 'from glory to glory' – although of course it does not progress in glory until it is on the path of spiritual progression. Simply to die physically does not in itself put a personality on the 'glory road.' There must also be a certain attainment of understanding and character, and a continuing growth in consciousness and in beingness.

While the soul is using that excarnate personality tool in the ascending planes of personality expression and experience, it may also have a new tool, a new personality, or a number of such successively in incarnate earthliving. This is not too difficult to understand if you put it in the framework of a family with several children. The mother and the father don't need to get rid of one child in order to have another child. Yet in a very special way the parents' concentration and attention in the family is focused for a time upon the baby, as the baby is the one who is apt to need the more immediate attention.

The incarnate earth personality of the soul is the baby of its family. And the soul pays particular attention to that baby. But it keeps an eye on the continuing growth pattern of its other children, too, which in this case are the excarnate personalities of that soul. And all of the personalities a soul may have are extensions of its own beingness which, as we have said, in time are recalled into itself, the soul's total self. That is what the oriental scriptures designate as 'nirvana,' the end of separateness for the personality and its reinclusion into the whole of its own soul.

The soul in its total beingness contains those dissimilar elements, those individualized qualities, identified in the earth phrase of 'polar opposites.' As one example and expression of this, the soul has what earthbeings call a basically masculine side and a basically feminine side. In other realms of expression and experience the soul operates with a balance of these polar opposites. But when it is prepared for earthliving, the soul, as it were, is split down the middle, polarized, into the basic masculine half and the basic feminine half. This is for personality experience only, both incarnate and excarnate.

The basic masculine half proceeds into earthliving, has experiences in both masculine and feminine earthlives, and grows, learns, expands in its beingness by all those experiences. Likewise the basic feminine half of the soul will have incarnation in both masculine and feminine frameworks. Then in time these two halves reunite, bringing to that union all the learning that each has had and the greater beingness it has thus developed.

When one portion of the soul is having a particular experience in earthliving, other portions are withheld. If the soul is having the experience of a humble serving maid personality, it does not need – and indeed would be quite hampered by, and discontent with – the sharp mental tool that it may have developed in an earth experience, say, as a scientist. When the soul is having the experience of earthliving in the framework of a feminine being as a wife and mother, it does not need, and would be quite hampered by and discontent if it did have, the strong competitive masculine approach to earthliving it may have developed in masculine expression. When the soul is developing masculine strengths and courage as a sailor or a professional soldier, it does not need the retiring and devotional qualities of a self-effacing, prayer-centered, contemplative nun.

These portions of the soul that are not incarnate in any one lifetime, and all their learnings, are not lost. The learnings of the various portions are, as it were, put into a bank. They are put on deposit, they are held for the soul. They build up the account of the total soul.

The span of experience the soul has in earthliving is sometimes spoken of as the age of the soul in earth, in its earth experience. For purposes of convenience we divide this span into five major sections. We speak of the soul as being just-started in earthliving, well-started, around-the-midpoint, well-along, and nearing-the-end. These are not mathematical divisions, as we use them, but refer more to the particular stage of the soul's attainment of its earthlearnings than to an arithmetical division of the mere number of earthlives.

This is briefly the overall framework of thinking, of theology if you will, or of philosophical approach, that we use in presenting the life readings. When we speak of the past lives of an individual, we are speaking of various portions of the soul which are not incarnate at the present time but which have been in earthliving, and what those portions of the soul learned. This gives then a birdseye view of the total learning of the soul to date, and helps to make clear the framework and place and purpose of the present personality incarnation and its life pattern. (AB920:2-5)

There is a fear among many that immediately after death we are so totally different as to be completely foreign to our incarnate selves, unable to relate to our earth thoughts, desires, feelings and relationships. We are afraid of losing most, if not all, of what we now are. Many people have communicated this dread to me. They worry that after death they may be just a floating light of some sort, with only a dim awareness of who and what they are. Even the concepts of peace and bliss seem to carry the connotation of losing that vital, self-aware, individual spark of the incarnate personhood.

But this is not true at all. You are the same person the day after death that you were the day before death, only set free to discover and grow into a new freedom and a much larger area of experience, knowledge, spirituality, and joy. Death is only the dividing line between us-in-the-body and us-out-of-the-body, and out-of-the-body proves, as we become acquainted with it, a much larger state of beingness. Just think what a wonderful new freedom this new state of beingness gives us! The freedom to leave this gross, heavy body behind, and to be subject no longer to the strenuous physical conditions, stresses, disease, and limitations of the earth body! Haven't you often thought of things you would like to do, places you would like to visit, things you would like to learn, if only you had the chance? Death gives you the chance! And no more taxes, also! Sometimes death seems almost too good to be true. But we must not cut short our work and responsibilities and learnings in the body simply to come more quickly into the better out-of-the-body stage of our personal life. It is as we live our incarnate life well that we are truly prepared for greater excarnate life to follow.

This earth realm of incarnate life has its divine and cosmic and personal purposes. But it is difficult and it is not our true home. We are spiritual beings, and earth is alien to our basic nature. We do not lose ourselves at death, we find ourselves:

> Dr. John: In death, persons are freed from the physical portions of beingness, of body and such. Then as they learn in the lower astral realm, they can free themselves from the limitations of concepts of physicality.
>
> But when they do so, they do not lose themselves. They do not lose their individuation. They do not lose their particular nature. They do not lose their personification. They are still persons, excarnate persons. They are not souls. But the person is actually a spiritual being, even as the soul is. The soul is a much greater complex of energies, a greater spirit being, than is a person.
>
> But as in our book *Diary After Death* the characters, after learning to stop thinking of themselves in earth

terms, discovered they still existed, were still individuated, were still distinguishable. They could distinguish
each other, know each other, love each other. They were
very much themselves, and freed from the limitations of
physical concepts. They had greater expression, greater
communication with each other. (A8024:2-4)

The ones on the spiritual path, those seeking sincerely to
align themselves with spiritual realities and forces, can look
forward to their excarnate stage with a joyous expectation of
continuing spiritual progression. Awaiting us is an ascending
pathway into many new and exciting planes of experience
and growth, well beyond the earth realm of incarnate life.
St. Paul alluded to this progression when sharing his own high
out-of-the-body experiences in his letters to the early Christian churches. In II Corinthians 3:18 is his famous and
exciting description of righteous (spiritual) progression after
death as "transformed. . . from glory to glory." In I Corinthians 2:9 is the beautiful passage, descriptive of the post-
death state, verified by near-death and out-of-body experiences before death: "Eye hath not seen, ear hath not heard,
neither hath it entered the heart of man (to even imagine)
the richness of glory which God hath prepared for them that
love him" – for those who, with free will and by choice,
happily live within God's value-system.

Just going through the death process itself does not auto-
matically put one on the glory road. The "glory to glory"
is for those who on earth have reached a level of spiritual
knowledge where they put themselves very definitely in the
camp of spiritual awareness and seeking. Certainly those
with openminded outreach to new and expanding spiritual
knowledge have nothing to fear. For those who are not
spiritually aware, for the materialists who hold to their
materialism, the excarnate stage may be brief, or not at all
if they cannot relate to any kind of existence other than the
physical earthlife they left behind. They do not have the
non-material concepts in consciousness as a foundation for

further growth, and are not potentialed to go on. These persons can be rather quickly absorbed into their whole-soul:

Dr. John: It is such a head start when one comes to the other side if at least a start, an opening of the door, has been made in the incarnate earthlife. If the person has heard on earth that there is life after death, and if he at least is open to the possibility that there may be life after death, then there is a contact point where those waiting for him on this side can reach him, can make contact with his consciousness.

True, when there is this beginning in the incarnate phase, there can be many frustrations, there can be glimpses without full sight, there can be momentary whiffs of a fragrance without the great experience of inhaling deeply the wondrousness of the other realms, there can be brief tastes flitting over the tongue without the full savoring of that which is so tantalizingly tasted.

However, the start is there. The first taste has been had. The first smell of the fragrance, the first opening of the eyes. This is tantalizing because the human consciousness is limited in what it can achieve in this way, simply because it is on the incarnate plane as a human earthbeing. It can be frustrating; however, let me say, 'All things in their own time.' If a flower bud has started to form, it may take some flowers much time to become ready to open and the bloom to appear. And if an impatient gardener were to assist it in opening, he would not find the flower within and he would possibly destroy that bud. Now Ryan is not going to destroy the flowering of his spiritual consciousness by wishing that he could do more, but let him be content with doing what does come to him.

Now what is it that comes to him? Well, whatever does comes to him of spiritual door-opening, of spiritual studies in which he finds himself challenged, in which he finds reward for his attention and effort, in which he finds growth of consciousness, let him enter into it. Let him push himself slightly to understand it. But let him not chide himself if he senses that there is more than he can possess now in full consciousness, for I assure him, there is more than any incarnate being can possess in full consciousness.

But this taste, this glimpse, this whiff of a fragrance, this first taste, is the beginning point from which, when the excarnate phase of life comes, he can make great progress. (A815:7, 8)

The excarnate (out-of-the-body) person is not eternal. It does not go on forever. It has duration, duration being the continuation of time, or the equivalent to time, on the lower astral and some other planes. At some point in that duration the excarnate person is absorbed back into its own soul. But the duration of the person does exceed the mortality of the body. We as persons have immortality beyond the mortality of the body, but not equal to the eternality of the soul.

Your first reaction to this teaching may be the same as mine, one of dismay that the person (you and I) is not eternal. This was, at first, an extremely unhappy teaching for me to live with. What sustained me was the knowledge that it was only my ignorance that brought the pain, and that once I learned the truth, the sadness of "losing myself" would dissolve.

In view of this, it was a very happy occasion when finally the opportunity came to ask Dr. John for light in this area of my darkness, my unhappy disquietude. Dr. John's answer was straightforward, simple, and sensible. For me it brought truth and light, and dispersed my residual sadness — actually leaving me with a joyous anticipation for that time ahead when the little me joins the larger me.

I asked the question, "After the potentialed excarnate

person has gone as far as it can go in the higher realms with its personal instrument of consciousness, at what point, is the person aware that it is going to be absorbed into the whole soul? And is it ready and willing to be?"

Dr. John: Usually it is ready and willing, yes, if it has come far enough. Usually, yes, it is happy because it has achieved a lot, it is happy because it knows it has fulfilled its destiny, completed its beingness, and it is supremely happy because it knows its own beingness is now going to expand.

How can you break through the barriers of personal beingness? By entering into the impersonal, the super-personal, the larger beingness. So it is glad to give up its own beingness because it becomes a part of a larger beingness which is really its more true self. Here is why it is so important, as early as possible, for the person to know it is a part of a soul.

You *are* a soul. As a soul, you *have* a person, a number of persons, one at a time, called incarnations. One of the key elements in almost every system of spiritual study is the teaching of the person to identify with soul beingness as the background and basis of his personal beingness. You are a particular person, yes. But back of that, and more fundamentally, you are an individual soul.

So to identify with your soul in this way while you are a person opens the door for that time ahead when, after an extended period of happy and growing fellow-ship of your soul and your person, the good of the person is absorbed into the soul and has a larger being-ness. The person does not lose anything. It gains.

Pilgrim: It still has its 'I am?'

Dr. John: Yes, but the 'I am,' the little 'I am' of the person, merges into the great 'I am' of the soul. When it merges, it can still carry its memories of its 'I am' as a person, its memories and experiences and developments, and it contributes that to the larger 'I am' of the soul.

You see, the soul would not have the experience that the person has had excepting through the person, and the person brings those experiences as its fruit, its gathered treasure, to the soul, its own soul.

Pilgrim: The portion of the soul that's in the personality is the 'I am?'

Dr. John: Yes. Then as it fashions its instrument of consciousness and goes through its personal experiences, it is a very personal 'I am.' You might say the soul gives to its personhood a portion of its 'I am-ness,' and then the person develops that and makes it what it becomes. This is then the treasure that you as a person bring to your soul, and through your soul to God, for the soul is an individuated portion of God. God will grow as God's individuated portions grow.

Pilgrim: This takes away a great deal of sadness.

Dr. John: Oh yes, and replaces it with a great gladness! Nothing good is lost. Only littleness is lost, but why hang on to littleness? Littleness is a prison, littleness is a restriction. 'Don't fence me in!' Don't fence the you-ness of you in, it is to become bigger. It must operate within whatever realm the person operates, incarnate and excarnate, and operate effectively.

Don't aspire to other planes and realms so soon and so much that you do not do a good job as a person; and yet know that there is more. You can grow and grow and grow as a person in beingness, and people will know this. They will say it's your character, it's your spirit, it's your joy, it's the light in your eyes, it's your competence, and other things. Inwardly you will know, yes, that you are growing beyond the littleness of being a person into the bigness of being the individuated portion of God that you are, with infinite potentials. For God is infinite, and infinite lies beyond the mortal, beyond the immortal, beyond the eternal. (A8032:3)

During this same teaching session one of the staff members asked Dr. John to explain the difference between the first and second death. She was confused by what the different groups had taught, and in what she had read. Dr. John took this opportunity to clearly explain his terminology, and to bring an interesting and educative teaching on the misunderstood concept of nirvana:

> Dr. John: In the scriptures, the term 'the second death' has got its own particular meaning, into which I shall not go at the present time. But let me point out that the personality, the personhood of the soul, is immortal but not eternal. As you know, in order to get a certain gradation of duration indicated by the terminology, I have spoken of *mortal*, referring primarily to the physical, the incarnate period of a person's expression, and then *immortal*, referring to that which comes after and extends beyond the mortality of the physical body, the excarnate period of the person's expression.
>
> But then there is a longer duration term, *eternal*; and beyond that, *infinite*. These are the values I give these terms for a purpose of communication, you see. Perhaps someone else would use a different term; and possibly immortal, eternal, and infinite should be synonymous, and are in some usage, and that's fine. But I want you to understand my usage of the terms, so that we can communicate.
>
> In this usage we speak of the person as being immortal. The body as mortal, the person as immortal, going from the body stage to the out-of-the-body stage, from the incarnate to the excarnate stage. And the soul as being eternal, beyond the immortal. And God as being infinite. The soul does not necessarily go very far in the eternalness of its being, as it can be recycled quite early if it is defective. But the extension of duration for a soul is to be considered as more than that of the person, and the person has duration beyond that of the body. Although some persons do not continue very far at all beyond the duration of the body, they are the sad exceptions to the general rule.

This means, you see, that the person in the excarnate phase will come to an end. This actually is the truth in the concept of nirvana. It might not be what is the 'true concept' of nirvana, depending on what the person speaking of nirvana means by the term. His 'true concept' of nirvana may be something quite other. But there is an aspect within the nirvana concept (and on the whole, I believe this is the truth leading to the nirvana concept) of the realization that the time comes when the person, the personal expression, will end, and then that which the person was is absorbed back into its own soul.

The typical popular teaching of nirvana in India, as well as in this country, is that the person is absorbed back into God. There is not in popular thinking too clear a distinction between soul and person. Not very many spiritual systems of teaching know that only a portion of the soul incarnates at any one time. It's there for all to see with just a little bit of digging, a little bit of careful observation, a little bit of research. But very few have it.

Actually, we are quite dismayed at the shallowness of so much of what passes for spiritual teaching. Yes, we can say, 'Well, this is better than nothing' — but it isn't very much better. It is simply opening the door to the realization there is a non-physical component. That is the start, because if that door is closed, then it is pretty hard for the person to go in consciousness beyond the death of the body, and particularly beyond the lower astral stage when the thinking is still confined to earth terms, bodily terms, you see.

So to open the door is the first step. But the shallowness of so much spiritual understanding and teaching on earth today! Just as in the science of biology, to simply say it is possible to study the life stream of the equine animal species, for instance, and to study the bloodstream genetics and so forth. That opens a door. But then if not very much study is made, not very much is learned.

So in so-called spiritual teachings and spiritual systems, so many have so little and they talk so big and so much. (A8032:7, 8)

The absorption of the excarnate person back into the soul can be more acceptable when one understands that there are personal and impersonal realms of beingness. The excarnate entity (you and I out-of-the-body) has a *personal* instrument of consciousness, which is not potentialed, and indeed would be quite inadequate, for operation in the impersonal realm. It is the *soul* in its beingness that can partake of the impersonalness. The excarnate person cannot. Dr. John touches on this aspect briefly in the first paragraph of the next teaching.

He also touches on the mystifying Biblical teaching of the Day of Judgment, when "the graves open and the dead will come forth." In light of this deeper knowledge Dr. John brings, the Biblical teachings now fall into place and become comprehensible to earth consciousness:

Dr. John: The person does not exist forever, and there comes a time when even the most potentialed and most energized person – who has gone through the lower astral, through Post-Mortemia, into the higher astral and 'over the mountain into the land of lights,' into the more spiritual realms often called etheric – will come to the end of its usefulness and of its life. It is not potentialed to go on forever and be useful. It is coming into realms of – well, let us simply say the impersonal, where the personal cannot be used because its instrument of consciousness is completely inadequate for further operation as it comes farther and farther into the realm of the impersonal. This is one illustration. So, finally, it is not potentialed or energized to go further, and then it ends.

As it ends, it is absorbed back into its 'seed atom,' which is not God, the great God, but the soul, the God-child, the individuated portion of God, you see. At this point, the person ceases to exist. But all that the person was is brought into the larger entity of which the person is only one expression. So it is like a drop of water re-joining the ocean, although there isn't that much differ-ence. I mean, a drop of water and an ocean, there is such a tremendous difference in quantity as to be almost a difference in quality. Not quite, but almost. The person and its soul are not that far apart!

The person which has gone far has much more of a quantity of personal and spiritual beingness to it. The soul might be thought of as a large pitcher, from which a cupful is poured forth to be the person, has various substances − flavors, qualities, experiences − added to it. Then, eventually, it is returned back to the pitcher, poured back into it. Thus it adds its contribution to the whole, and takes on the larger beingness of the whole from which it originally came.

If there is reason for the person to be continued it can be reformed, its energies regrouped and given further personal expression. Very seldom will an excarnate per-son continue for ten thousand years of earth time. That is a long time, and very seldom will that take place. How-ever, there can be the manipulation of time so as to come back to where the energies of that person, with its characteristics, its qualities, its personal beingness, is reconstituted, if you will. It is reconstituted by coming back into its own beingness at that former time. This is important.

This is the way in which judgment can be and will be rendered upon the dead. This is the way in which the 'graves are opened and the dead come forth' at the day of judgment. It is not that you are going to see the ground open and beings appear. It is not like that. It's on a different dimension, on a different plane. It is in their time, not in your time. But it will take place.

So I am bringing to you some further understandings here, you see, of the duration of the entity of the person. The term entity usually refers to an excarnate person rather than to the soul. So for 'soul' we use the term 'individuality.' (A8032:4, 5)

Dr. John touches on three interesting aspects of man, the earth human animal (homo sapiens) in the physical realm of beingness. First, the teaching of the interaction of two dissimilar realms of being, the physical and the spiritual, to produce the human being. Second, that as far as Dr. John knows, only earth supports incarnate life. Third, the important teaching that God does nothing without a purpose, a value, behind it. Incarnate life is not accidental. There is a definite God-purpose in the drama of the physical evolution of man:

> Dr. John: The incarnate human being is an inter-action between two dissimilar realms of being. One is the soul, which is a spiritual form of life and is native to spirit and not to matter. By spiritual, here, I refer to the functional and the first definitive meaning of 'spiritual,' which is simply that it is non-physical, non-material. Earthlings live in the material, the physical, universe, but the soul lives in a very non-material and non-physical universe.
>
> The second major component of the human being is of course the physical portion, which is an earth animal which has been adjusted, or purposefully evolved, for the role of interaction with a soul to produce a person. The earth-animal part partakes of the physical realm and of the unique nature of earth.
>
> I repeat what I have said before, that I do not know of any other material place, planet or otherwise, upon which life has entered into matter. Yes, there may be planets in other solar systems which have physical and chemical nature similar to that of planet earth. Thus, theoretically they could support life such as it is found incarnate upon planet earth. But incarnate life did not arise on planet earth spontaneously. It is not a spontaneous event coming out of chemical and physical interactions.

There is no form of life without there being a purpose back of it. It took purpose, not chance, to bring
life, which is native to spirit, into incarnate form, meaning into matter. (A3208:1-2)

You may at first assume that the term Dr. John uses in the
next teaching, "Individuated-God-Being," is another word for
soul. This is not true, and the difference between the two
needs clarification.

The pattern of energies drawn forth from God-Beingness to
beget the individual "I-am" of you is termed by Dr. John
Individuated-God-Being or God-child. Soul is the childhood
stage, the kindergarten stage, of this Individuated-God-Being.
The earth incarnations take place during this soulhood stage.

In this beginning stage, the soul must develop its individual
integrity and be able to hold to it sufficiently in the time-
space and doingness realm of earth to be allowed to gradu-
ate and go on into the next realm of being. In the next
realm, beingness is emphasized rather than doingness, and the
God-child must be able to hold to its individuality while in
the realm of beingness, otherwise it will be taken out of
existence.

The great demandment upon every God-child at whatever
stage and in whatever expression it may be, is to increase, to
grow, in compatibility with God. That is, to discover what
God's way is – and then of our own free will and choice,
choose to align ourselves with it. The Biblical admonishment
to "love the Lord thy God with all thy heart and all thy
soul and all thy mind and all thy strength" addresses this
requirement for *all* God-children to find out what God's
way is, and then learn to live happily within it. This is the
only way a God-child, expressing on any realm or any plane,
will be able to survive, let alone develop, as an Individuated-
God-being. There is no other way.

Dr. John: The Individuated-God-Being is possessed of God-potential for growing in compatibility with God, and hence companionship and partnership with God. Compatibility requires both intelligence and alignment. The second major purpose of the soul, in addition to getting the Individuated-God-Being off to a good start, is to establish upon planet earth the knowledge of God's ways and the following of God's ways by individuals and by the collection of human individuals known as the human race.

There are other realms and planes, and I use those two words to indicate *realms of beingness* and then *planes of expression* within realms of beingness. For instance, and these do overlap and interweave, there is the spiritual realm, which means essentially non-physical, non-material, and there is the material, physical realm. There is the realm of separation into which the soul enters as it takes on personality expressions in incarnation. Within this realm there is the incarnate expression of the personality and then the excarnate expression of the personality, excarnate and incarnate being planes of expression within the realm of personal beingness.

Following this, there is a realm of cohesion. That may not be the best term for it. It is a realm of non-separation. This is difficult to explain and really rather impossible to comprehend with the finite human mind, which is an instrument of consciousness geared to be effective for understanding the realm of separation. (A4534:3, 4)

Next Dr. John answers a question I had asked in my earlier years of spiritual seeking. I was curious as to what his answer would be to this query: "Where in the body is the soul?"

Dr. John: There is no answer and yet there is an answer, and in fact there are several answers. The soul does not reside in the body. The soul does not reside in space as you know it. The soul has existence, yes, and it has duration, yes, but it does not *reside* in space or in time. The *person* and the *body* reside in space and time but not the soul.

Now the soul brings life to the body and, of course, the soul is a vital portion of the personality. Since in one sense life is in the blood, you may say the soul has a close vital attachment to the body via the blood.

Sometimes the soul has been thought to reside in one of the glands, such as the pineal, or in one of the organs, such as the heart or the liver. Sometimes we think some earthlings place their soul either in their stomach or in their genitals, but we would rather question that placement.

I will attempt a little more: The soul is a complex of forces, of energies, and energies have their own ways of making themselves known and of making contact with other energies. This can be somewhat as the gravitational field around an object influences other objects. Gravitationally, every object influences every other object in the physical universe, and the well-known equation for that is 'proportional to its mass and inversely proportional to the square of the distance between them.'

The soul/body relationship can be thought of more along the line of the magnetic field around an electrical current. This may indicate a little more of the relationship of the soul to the body.

Now actually the person is likewise immaterial. The person, an expression-point of the soul and an experience-point in earthliving for the soul, is not material. So the materialists really have to fall back only upon the body. Both the person and the soul are not material, not physical. They are of the spiritual realm; using spiritual there in its definition of being non-material and non-physical. (A3116:6,7)

This chapter would be incomplete without touching briefly the teaching on judgment.

There is a source of energy in the universe which is intent on bringing about separation between the Creator and the created. It has its own will, which is not the will of God. This other source of energy, generally termed "evil," is a self-evident force in our lives and often is mentioned in the Bible. The Book of Revelation tells of "war in the heavens," where this force warring against God's will lost and was cast out. God's creation is a universe, not a multiverse, and as the philosopher Manly Palmer Hall has said, "God does not allow discord in the causal realm."

We are now coming into the period in earth history when we, each one, must either choose to align ourselves with God's will, God's way, and grow in it, or face the judgment. This judgment is whether we as individual souls will be allowed to continue or will be "recycled" — our Individuated-Soul-Beingness terminated. This is not a new teaching. It is found many times in the Bible:

> Dr. John: If you will read the gospels again, read them with an eye to the prevalence of the matter of judgement in the Master's utterances. I think you will be surprised. Usually, of course, the matter of love and brotherhood and such are emphasized as preachers and others quote Jesus. But He stressed again and again that the great day, the time of His next coming, is a time of judgment. The New Testament writers caught this emphasis as central in His teachings, His understanding of God and man. (A3151:2)

Being raised by a fundamentalist mother, the subject of judgment came up many times while I was growing up. But it was such a frightening teaching I refused to even think about it. It was not something I was prepared to deal with until I finally came into my studies of the Loehr-Daniels Life and Teaching Readings. Then, here again, the truth set me free — free from the fear of judgment.

I hesitated to include this teaching. But the major purpose of
this book is to set us free from fear, not only the fear of
death but also the fear of judgment – a fear brought on by
ignorance. Only the truth can set us free.

> Dr. John: Now, don't worry, any soul that has pro-
> gressed far enough for its personhoods to have a con-
> sciousness of spirit beingness is well on its way to really
> establishing itself as a spirit being, a child of God.
> We have had some who came to some of our meetings
> who have been very deathly afraid of being recycled.
> No. Those who are on the upper path will make mis-
> takes. All do. But the great, gracious spirit of God, the
> love of God reaching to all of us, all of His children,
> brings us back into line, gently but firmly corrects us in
> our mistakes, that we may learn the more correct way
> and become more deeply, more clearly, more passion-
> ately children of the living God. (A8034:8)

Not all souls are good. The soul that becomes infiltrated by
evil to the point where it cannot be reclaimed and made
acceptable to God, will lose its selfhood. These are the souls
who not only refuse to align themselves within God's structure, but work actively against it. These souls will lose their
individual beingness. Their energies, the energies that make
up the Individuated-God-Beingness of that soul, will be
taken apart and returned to the general reservoir of God-
Beingness for use in some other way. And that individual
God-child will be no more.

The basic energies of life that were drawn out of God-
Beingness to make up that God-child will first have to be
cleansed of the evil consciousness that has been imprinted
upon them, before being replaced or reused. If this cleansing
did not take place, God's reservoir of Beingness would become polluted. This cleansing of the energies *not* of God, and
the suffering it causes the one being cleansed, is the "hell-
fire" of Biblical teaching. Dr. John terms this process re-

cycling since the God-energies of that one, after cleansing, can be reused.

The God-child does not get to the point of damnation and recycling as a result of just one lifetime of evil. It is the result of repeated lifetimes where evil was allowed to invade and take over the person, as is brought out in the next teaching:

> Dr. John: The soul that ultimately, irretrievably chooses darkness instead of light, that soul shall be taken apart. The energies within it can be used elsewhere, but that soul in its own individual beingness shall be no more. And the Father will weep for every one such. And so will you, as you come into your perfection of Christhood.

The question was asked if a series of suicides, lifetime after lifetime, and a soul constantly refusing to live within the light, would cause that one to be recycled. The answer given:

> Dr. John: Yes, but I think the key factor perhaps should be viewed a little differently, understood a little differently. It would be the infusion of a soul by evil, by darkness, to the extent where that soul could not be reclaimed by the light. (1975 Thanksgiving teaching session)

I can relate to this fear of being recycled. Probably most of us can, feeling that because of our many faults we are somehow "missing the mark" (which is the Biblical meaning of the word "sin"). How reassuring to know that when we finally come into the knowledge of our spiritual nature and work consciously within the spiritual values of God, we are home safe and free. Simply to know we are spirit-beings, children of God, puts us on the right path, then God's truth and grace and love keep nudging us back when we get a bit off the track, and we thus are constantly cleansed as we live our lives. There are two basic, simple guidelines for this requirement of finding, and then staying on, the spiritual path:

> Dr. John: To become a fully developed Individuated-God-Being requires intelligence, and it requires the alignment of will and of nature-of-beingness as well as doingness with the structured universe of God, staying within the lines and purposes of God and having enough intelligence and good sense to know what those lines and purposes are. (A3425:7)

Destiny of the Soul, an early 1987 publication of the Religious Research Press, contains a more detailed treatment of judgment and the recycling of souls that repeatedly and finally fail. But the great emphasis of that inspiring book is upon the souls who succeed, the glorious adventures, the greater self-hood, the enlarged consciousness and beingness of the soul which does work and grow in the framework of God's truth and purposes. What tremendous further attainments await us as we grow in God's way!

The major purpose of this chapter is to clearly differentiate between you as a soul and you as a person and to show the interaction between the two. This understanding is basic for the understanding of death.

You are so important. First, you as a soul have the responsibility to your person-self to help the person discover and experience the realities that lie beyond the reach of the senses. Second, you as a person have the responsibility of being a good expression- and experience-point for your soul in learning the lessons only earth can teach. You have the responsibility of living this lifetime well, to build character, for it is the character you build that is carried over from one lifetime to the next.

As a soul — you ARE. You have beingness. You introduce your person to the secret of *being*. As a person — you DO. You act in a way that teaches your soul what it needs to learn in earthliving. Being and doing — as you ARE and as you DO, you and your soul join hands in a holy partnership.

CHAPTER FOUR

THE DEATH EXPERIENCE

While we are "alive" there are three parts to us: We are a SOUL. We are a PERSON. And we have a BODY. These three are decidedly not the same. Death — and by death we mean the death of the physical body — takes this three-fold, individuated, interrelated unit of human beingness apart.

It follows naturally that death affects each of the three parts differently. Each part of this trinity has its own unique beingness, each part makes its own essential contribution to the whole, and each part reacts differently to the death of the body. So we need not one but three answers to this question of what happens at death.

What effect does death have on the body?

The answer here is easy. Death to the body is death, the end. There may be a slight, brief psychic carryover, even as with other earth animals, but for all our purposes the body ceases to be a living organism and soon nature reclaims its various parts unless man embalms the body for a longer preservation before its component chemicals disperse.

What effect does death have on the soul?

The death of the body frees the soul to have another incarnation. The responsibilities and involvement with that body are done, and the excarnate person makes far fewer demands upon the soul's energies than the incarnate personality did on earth.

To the extent the soul identifies with the body, it can experience the body's death and learn from that experience just as from any other experience. For a young soul, the death of the body may be quite a major learning experience. For the older soul, although the body is valued for what it is, death can be almost casual.

The incarnate personality, with all the strenuous experiences and demands of earth life, is like a child in the womb. Once the person is "delivered" — by death — into the excarnate plane, the soul, like an earth mother, can become pregnant again with another baby, another person, another incarnation. This can happen quite quickly, but usually there is a suitable period between, perhaps a fewscore years, usually a century or more. There can be occasionally a thousand and more years between incarnations, for souls have activity and learning in other cosmic schools in addition to the cosmic school of earth.

The soul has only one incarnation at a time. To maintain the life force of an incarnate person and to lead it successfully through its experiences, all the time learning from those experiences and gaining mastery in guiding its incarnations well, can easily take twenty-five to fifty percent or more of the soul's own life force and beingness. There is simply not enough left over, nor is there reason, for so-called multiple incarnations, more than one at a time. The only exception we have found is identical twins, which is a special case of a soul taking one life in two manifestations; the fact that identical twins are from the same soul is the explanation for the strange phenomena — parallel life patterning, extraordinary ESP between them, etc. — observed so often in identical twins, even those separated at birth.

The soul does not continue indefinitely to have incarnations. As Dr. John has observed, God is frugal in all He does,
including bestowing incarnations upon His children. A child
which does not learn what earth has to teach it, in perhaps a
maximum of 100 incarnations, just isn't going to learn it
and gets recycled along with other souls which more deliberately "miss the mark." We are not to dawdle, for there
are other stages beyond this early stage when we have our
incarnations.

What effect does death have upon the person?

What death does to us as persons is our primary interest
and immediate concern. We live our lives primarily in the
consciousness of being persons. Our names refer to us as
persons, our relationships are as a person with other persons, our consciousness is a personal consciousness. Body-
consciousness and soul-consciousness can at times be reached
through the person's subconscious, and in rare cases of
mystical experiences, soul-consciousness can be experienced
directly by spiritually open persons through the supercon-
scious. But these play a very small part, if any, in our experience as incarnate persons. So what happens to us *as
Persons* is our major question.

The death of its body changes the person from the incarnate
(which means "in-the-body") to the excarnate (which means
"out-of-the-body") plane of personal beingness, but some
fail to make it successfully. The person who on earth was
convinced that personal life was all there is, and that the
death of the body was the end of its personal existence, can
carry over that consciousness either into a conviction of its
own personal death, or into a peculiar conviction that since
it clearly is not dead therefore it is still on earth. But any
kind of teaching, usually from religion, that there is an
afterlife, will keep the person's consciousness open so that its

attention can be caught and the transition made to the new environment.

This story is told in detail in the Religious Research book *Diary After Death* (by Dr. Franklin Loehr), which traces Henry Clements through his own sudden death to his reunion with Gertrude, his wife, who had predeceased him and who at his death came for him. She took him to their new home in "Post-Mortemia," actually the lower astral plane, in which Henry learned what life is like in the non-physical realm and from which they both progressed to higher spiritual realms.

So for us as people, the greatest effect of death is upon us as persons. We are changed, quickly or slowly, from an earth-oriented existence to a spirit-oriented existence – "spirit" meaning non-physical, non-material. Some never awaken to the fact that there is this other place and that they have come to it. These earthbound personalities run down the energies of their beingness rather quickly and fade out of existence. Others are not potentialed, in intelligence or spirituality, to go very far; these end their existence in their own appropriate "Post Mortemia," living out their understandings and desires and energies there on the lower astral plane. Others can go "from glory to glory," as St. Paul says – into ascending realms of spirit, usually known as the middle and higher astral, then the etheric, and on.

In time the person, all it is and all it has experienced, is absorbed back into what the Hindus call "the seed atom," which Christians call the soul. Here, if it is a limited personality, in time it loses its sense of personal identity. But if it is a spiritually awakened person it grows into the experience of its own soul identity – thus trading the little for the larger. And through what each person experiences and expresses and becomes it adds to the soul, and the soul grows.

Because we have three levels of beingness – soul, person, and body – death (the death of the physical body) affects us in three ways. For the body, death is the end. For the soul, death is the freeing from a major responsibility, and in time it has a new incarnation. (The death of the final incarnation frees the soul to go on into further, higher levels of God-child beingness and development.) For the person, our major concern, death is the transition from the incarnate to the excarnate stage of personal life and new experience, and we go on. It is as simple, as natural, as sensible as that.

To die with even this much understanding gets us off to a much better start than to die with no understanding of death.

CHAPTER FIVE

THE SCIENTIFIC STUDY OF DEATH

Science now substantiates life after death with an ever-
growing body of facts. Breakthroughs and major developments are coming in all areas, and now scientists have begun
to probe the non-material, non-physical (spiritual) areas
formerly left to religion and psychism. Six significant areas
have emerged:

A) Psychic Communication with the dead
B) Dream Research
C) Out-of-Body Experiences (OOBE)
D) Near-Death Experiences (NDE)
E) Pastlife Recall
F) A Larger View of life including death and the after-
life (See Chapter Six)

(A) PSYCHIC COMMUNICATION WITH THE DEAD

Throughout history psychics and mediums have kept alive
the realization of a continuing life after death. Their evidentials that those who died still lived, and could be con-
tacted, brought comforting assurance to many, comfort and
assurance based on convincing evidence of reality. Spiritualist churches and teachers have made a major contribution

through their persistent efforts to instill the knowledge that
persons we knew and loved on *this* side of death are the same
loved ones and still live on the *other* side. The spiritualist
religions and teachers, together with other psychics and
mediums, kept this light of truth steady, especially during
the early years of science when the spiritual pendulum
swung, for awhile, to the extremes of skepticism and materialism.

Dr. John pays tribute to these pioneers of the spirit:

> We who use mediums have been somewhat the
> trail-blazers. Now in the past-life recalls, roads are being
> built along the trails we blazed. But let us pay tribute
> to the psychics of all centuries. They have helped to
> assert that there is a life after death. They have helped to
> keep for human consciousness the reality of a non-
> material portion of human nature. They have brought
> much of good.
>
> So let us pay tribute to them as pioneers, even as
> we are glad that the study of death now comes into a
> more careful understanding and an enlargement, so
> there is a road, and not just a trail blazed through a
> forest. (A8037:20)

In the present Age of Science psychic experiences and
phenomena are given better research authentication than
ever before. At this point, psychic communication with the
dead is well-established in public consciousness. There is
extensive media coverage of the psychic theme in television
programming and popular movies, and it is common to pick
up a magazine or newspaper today and find something of
the psychic. Even the daytime "soap operas" cover communication with the dead in a matter-of-fact way.

We base our belief in psychic communication with the dead
not only on our personal philosophy and experience, but on
trained observation – objective, systematic, non-biased,

honest, skillful, competent, repeated, carefully-recorded observations – of actual happenings and experiments. In this we find scientific substantiation of communication with those who have made the transition called death.

The British Society for Psychical Research (BSPR) was founded in 1882. Its purpose is: "To examine without prejudice or prepossession and in a scientific spirit those faculties of man, real or supposed, which appear to be inexplicable on any generally recognized hypothesis." Many distinguished scholars can be found among its founders and early members – Sir William Barrett, Professor of Physics at University College, Dublin; Henry Sidgwick, Professor of Moral Philosophy at Cambridge; Eleanor Sidgwick (his wife), Principal of Newnham College, Cambridge; Sir Oliver Lodge, the physicist. The Society's presidents have included William James, Andrew Lang, Henri Bergson, Lord Raleigh, Sir Alister Hardy, and many other illustrious intellectuals.

The American Society for Psychical Research (ASPR) was established in 1906 with James H. Hyslop, formerly Professor of Logic and Ethics at Columbia University, as its first leader. Professor Hyslop established a vigorous program of psychical research and initiated publication of the *Journal* and *Proceedings* which have continued uninterrupted to the present. A tremendous amount of carefully documented scientific proof of life after death has been recorded there over the years.

Both the British and American Societies have been in excellent position to investigate some of the most outstanding cases of psychic phenomena ever published. The older cases are just as relevant and fascinating today as they were when first published, as the examples throughout this section attest. Our first case was sent in by a Dr. Burgers to Dr. Hodgson of the BSPR, and published in the *Journal* in 1902. Dr. Burgers gives an eye-witness account of what happened at the death of his friend's wife. The friend is referred to as

'Mr. G.' to protect anonymity. He had been hostile to anything of a psychic nature prior to this experience. Mr. Burgess writes:

At 6:30 I urged our friends, the physician and nurses, to go to dinner. Fifteen minutes later, I happened to look toward the door, and saw floating through the doorway three separate and distinct clouds. My first thought was that some of our friends were smoking outside the bedroom door, and the smoke was coming into the room. I went out into the hall and no one was there. Astonished, I watched the clouds approach the bed and completely envelop it. Through the mist, I saw a figure, transparent, sheen of the brightest gold, a figure so glorious no words could describe it. The figure remained motionless with hands uplifted over Mr. G.'s wife, seeming to express a welcome, quiet and happy, with a dignity of calmness and peace. Two figures in white knelt by his wife's bed. Then, connected with a cord proceeding from her forehead, there floated in a horizontal position a nude white figure, apparently her astral body. At times the suspended figure would lie perfectly quiet, at other times the astral body diminished in size and struggled violently, threw out her arms and legs in an apparent effort to escape. But always the figure was perfect and distinct.

It would struggle until it seemed to exhaust itself, then become calm, increase in size, only to repeat the same performance again and again. The process continued for approximately five hours. At last the final moment arrived. With a deep gasp, the astral figure struggling, his wife ceased to breathe. She apparently was dead. With that last gasp, the person left the body, the cord was severed suddenly, and the astral figure vanished. The clouds and the spirit forms disappeared instantly. With that, all the oppression that had weighted upon us during those five hours was lifted.

Another fascinating BSPR case taken from *Proceedings* (Vol. VIII, p. 180-93) is the narrative of a Dr. Wiltse. He was in a state he perceived as death, and related this experience in his own words:

> I came into a state of conscious existence, and discovered that I was still in the body, and I had no longer any interest in it. I looked with astonishment and joy for the first time upon myself, the me, the real person me, which the not-me enclosed upon all sides like a sepulchre of clay. With the interest of a physician I beheld the wonders of my bodily anatomy, intimately interwoven with which, even tissue for tissue, was I, the living soul of that dead body. I realized my condition and calmly reasoned thus: I have died, as man terms death, and yet I am as much a man as ever. I am about to get out of the body. I watched the interesting process of the separation of person from the body. By some power, apparently not my own, I was rocked to and fro, literally, as the cradle is rocked, by which process the spirit's connection with the tissues of the body was broken up.
>
> After a little while the lateral motion ceased, and along the soles of the feet, beginning at the toes, passing rapidly to the heels, I felt and heard, as it seemed, the snapping of innumerable small cords. When this was accomplished, I began slowly to retreat from the feet toward the head, as a rubber cord shortens. I remember reaching the hips and saying to myself: 'Now there is no life below the hips'. I can recall no memory of passing through the abdomen and chest, but recalled distinctly when my whole self was collected in the head, when I reflected thus, 'I am all head now, and I shall soon be free.'
>
> I passed around the brain as if it were hollow, compressing it and its membranes slightly on all sides towards the center, and peeped out between the sutures of the skull, emerging like the flattened edges of a bag of

membranes. I recollect distinctly how I appeared to my-self something like a jelly fish as regards color and form. As I emerged I saw two ladies sitting at my head. I measured the distance between the head of my cot and the knees of the lady opposite the head, and concluding there was room for me to stand, but felt considerable embarrassment as I reflected that I was about to emerge naked before her, but comforted myself with the thought that in all probability she would not see me with her bodily eyes as I was in spirit.

As I emerged from the head, I floated up laterally like a soap bubble attached to the bowl of a pipe, until I at last broke loose from the body and fell lightly to the floor, where I slowly rose and expanded to the full stature of a man. I seemed to be translucent, of a bluish cast, and perfectly naked. With a painful sense of em-barrassment, I fled toward the partially open door to escape the eyes of the two ladies whom I was facing, as well as the others who I knew were about me. But upon reaching the door I found myself clothed, and satisfied upon that point, I turned and faced the company.

As I turned, my left elbow came in contact with the arm of one of two gentlemen standing in the door. To my surprise his arm passed through mine without appar-ent resistance, the several parts closing again without pain, as air reunites. I looked quickly up at his face to see if he had noticed the contact, but he gave me no sign, only stood and gazed toward the couch I had just left. I directed my gaze in the direction of his and saw my dead body, and suddenly discovered that I was looking at the straight seam down the back of my coat. 'How is this' I thought, 'How do I see my back?' I looked again to reassure myself, putting my hand to my face and feeling for my eyes. They were where they were supposed to be, and I thought, 'Am I like an owl that can turn my head half way around?' I tried the experiment and failed. No! Then it must be that having been out of the body for a few minutes I have yet the power to use the eyes of the body, and I turned about and looked back in at the open door where I could see the head of my body in line with me.

I discovered then a small cord, like a spider's web, running from my shoulders back to my body and attaching to the base of my neck, in front. I was satisfied with the conclusion that by means of that cord I was using the eyes of my body, and turning, walked down the street. A small, densely black cloud appeared in front of me and advanced toward my face. I knew that I was to be stopped. I felt the power to move or to think leaving me. My hands fell powerless at my sides, my shoulders and my head dropped forward, and I knew no more. Without previous thought, and without effort on my part, my eyes opened. I looked at my hands, and then at the little white cot upon which I was lying, and realizing that I was in the body. In astonishment and disappointment I exclaimed: 'What in the world has happened to me? Must I die again?'

Mrs. Leonore E. Piper (1859-1950) of Boston, a trance medium prominent in the history of psychical research, was told by her spirit-control, Pelham, of his own death which resulted from a horse-riding accident. This type of death-and-awakening experience is common.

All was dark to me. Then consciousness returned, but in a dim, twilight way as when one wakens before dawn. When I comprehended that I was not dead at all, I was very happy.

Another BSPR case, related by a Mr. Tudor-Pole, is that of Private Dowing, a soldier killed in WWI by a shell explosion:

Something struck, hard, hard, hard against my neck. I shall never forget the memory of that hardness. It is the only unpleasant incident I can remember of my death. I fell, and as I did so, without passing through any apparent interval of unconsciousness, I found myself outside myself. I am telling my story simply for you to understand what a small incident dying is.

The expanded dimensions of the after-death state can leave even those who believe in it before they died, amazed and deeply gratified. This message is from the excarnate William Stead (English journalist, politically influential, and psychic researcher, who died on the Titanic in 1912) as quoted by his daughter Estelle Stead in *My Father*.

When I think of the ideas I had of the life I am now living, when I was in the world as you are, I marvel at the hopeless inadequacy of my understanding. The reality is so much, so very much, greater than even I could imagine. It is a new life, the nature of which you cannot understand.

Literally thousands of books have been published of psychic communication with the dead. One read widely in the mid-1900s is *The Other Side* by the Rev. James Albert Pike (1913-1969), Episcopal Bishop of California. This book is a powerful account of communication with the dead, as Rev. Pike narrates in detail the tragic death of his own son Jim, who suicided after involvement with the drug culture and LSD. Startling poltergeist occurrences after Jim's death (strange movements of objects, noises, etc.) led the bishop into psychic consultation with various mediums in America and England. Every interview was carefully documented by eye-witnesses and word-by-word recording. What emerges is a straight-forward, lucid exploration of his son's life after death.

In 1967 a Canadian television program was put together by Allen Spragett, the religious editor of the Toronto Star newspaper, wherein a responsible medium would appear with Bishop Pike and Spragett and go into trance right on the program, seeking to contact young Jim. The internationally

accredited American medium Arthur Ford (author of
Nothing So Strange) accepted the challenge, and during
the several-hours long trance session, not only did Jim
come through, but also messages from others on the Other
Side of death, who had known Bishop Pike. These messages,
given in the full glare of television, were highly evidential.
Here are several of them:

> Jim said that his father's friend Marvin Halverson
> was there with him. Bishop Pike had not seen this friend
> for several years and had no idea if he was living or dead,
> but after the program made a phone call to someone who
> would know and discovered Halverson had died about the
> same time as Jim.
>
> Then an elderly gentleman with Jim in spirit com-
> municated that his son was Professor Donald MacKinnon,
> well known to Bishop Pike, and then gave evidential
> material on two cats Donald had had when a child, and
> further such details. Another phone call to England, this
> one to Professor MacKinnon in person, who confirmed
> all the details brought through by his father.
>
> Throughout the trance session, Jim disclosed many
> otherwise insignificant details, significant now because
> they were known only between Bishop Pike and his son.

After Bishop Pike had completed the last chapter of his
book, he had one more sitting, this time with Mrs. Ena
Twigg, a well-known British medium, in trance. Jim came
through again in a beautiful and clear communication, and
Bishop Pike decided to add this as an appendix to his book.
The following is an extract:

> I'm going to do my best to use this opportunity to
> tell you the pattern as I see it. You know I came over
> here in a state of mental confusion and great — not
> antagonism toward the world — but in a state of not
> understanding, and being almost afraid to trust many
> people. You know that. And I had to come to terms

with the situation. And when I came over here they said,
'Now, come along. Academic qualifications won't help
you here. Let's get down to the basics,' and they helped
me to find out what are the things that really matter —
to have compassion and understanding and be kind —
yes, they are wonderful things, but not as things. You
have to put them into operation. You have to relearn
how to think, how to really understand, and be able to
put yourself into the other guy's place to see how you
would work out in the same circumstances.

And gradually I began to get a sense of pattern, you
know. I began to feel that this was one way of release.
This was religion, without somebody forcing God and
Jesus down my throat. And I find that by working this
way I could find a philosophy that religion hadn't been
able to give me.

Dr. Ralph Harlow, for fifty years a Professor at famous
Smith College in New England (largest all-woman's college
in the world), was for thirty-five years an investigator for the
ASPR. He had many psychic experiences himself, especially
centering around his highly psychic sister Anna. His best-
selling book *A Life After Death* (Doubleday) is one fascinating account after another of psychic communication with
the dead, and is particularly notable for its understatement
and its clarity.

His sister Anna was 'sensitive' from an early age and carried
that psychic openness all her life. Dr. Harlow tells about a
time when his wife, Marion, and Anna were walking in down-
town Boston, chatting and window-shopping, when:

Suddenly Anna stopped and clutched my wife's
arm. 'Marion,' she said excitedly, 'do you see that woman
walking ahead of us? The one dressed in black?' Marion
nodded. 'Do you see the man walking beside her?...No?''
Anna said with some disappointment. Then quietly she
said, 'But he is there. He is a man from the spirit world.

It is probably her husband who has just passed over.' She turned to Marion again. 'You can't see him?' Marion shook her head, and Anna said, 'He has just turned to look at me, and he seems to know that I am able to see him.'

Anna had the following experience shortly after her sister-in-law died:

Anna's husband, Kingsley, was out of town attending a church conference. During the night Anna was awakened by a touch on her hand. Sleepily she reached out, thinking it was one of her children who had padded from their room to be with their mother, but she felt nothing. She immediately became wide awake. Looking up she saw her sister-in-law, Marguerite, standing beside her bed. Then the vision vanished and she was alone in the room. The next morning Anna received a telegram from her husband stating: 'Marguerite passed on last night. Going to Maine for the funeral.' It was then Anna remembered the pact her siblings and their spouses made years ago. All were interested in survival after death, and it was agreed then when one of them died, Anna would be the logical one to contact because of her psychic sensitivity. It was also agreed their evidence of survival must be *clear-cut*. This contact with Anna, shortly after Marguerite's transition – and before either Anna or her husband knew of their loss – certainly passed the test of clear-cut evidence.

Later in the day Marguerite gave further evidence of her survival. Anna was walking in her garden and felt a sudden urge to look up to her bedroom window. There, holding back the white curtain, was Marguerite silently waving to Anna. Marguerite left the window, and then reappeared, waving, three different times.

Anna died suddenly in 1925. After her funeral, Dr. Harlow

returned to his office at Smith College where he had a
scheduled appointment with one of his honor students. As
he was sitting at his desk talking with the student – his
thinking filled with Anna – he toyed with a thick glass inkwell, an empty article kept many years on his desk because
of its beauty and used upon occasion as a paperweight. He
slid the inkwell aside, turned to his student and started talking about Anna's psychic ability.

> And then suddenly the inkwell split with a report
> like a revolver shot. It happened at the precise moment
> I spoke my sister's name. (At this, the very frightened
> student fled the room.) I carried the inkwell to the men's
> room and carefully washed it. There were no slivers, and
> the newly opened sides were as smooth as its polished
> exterior.
> Back in the office I sat again at my desk, staring at
> the inkwell halves, attempting to reconstruct the last
> few minutes in exact detail. And then I heard a voice,
> sharply and distinctly. It said, 'Is this clear-cut evidence?'

Two weeks after Anna's death Dr. Harlow visited his parent's
home in Canton, Mass. where his father was a Congregational
minister. While there, his mother showed him a note she had
found on her bedside table upon awakening. She asked her
son if he recognized the handwriting. Dr. Harlow instantly
identified it, as his mother had, as Anna's writing. The note
read:

> I cannot find words to express the joy and satis-
> faction of this work. We are busy every minute of the
> day, and sometimes of the night too, but happy – oh,
> so happy! You (and this word was underlined) must
> come and see for yourselves if you would be convinced.
> So come, ALL (this word was triple underlined) of you.

This note was in Anna's writing, her words, her phrases, and
even her habit of underlining. Dr. Harlow's mother searched

but was unable to find any such note paper in the house. There was nothing on the bedside table when his parents retired, yet the note was in plain sight when they awakened in the morning. Dr. Harlow later showed it to his wife, asking her who had written it. "Why Anna, of coure," she said very matter-of-factly.

A rich source of evidence for survival can be found within the pages of *Fate Magazine*. A hundred thousand faithful readers of *Fate* each month find a dozen or so intriguing, personal accounts of encounters with those who have died. In the "My Proof of Survival" section are reports sent in by readers who live typical, conventional, everyday lives. Their experiences with departed loved ones hold endless interest. For example, this in the June 1982 issue, from Dennis Porter of Lake Charles, Louisiana.

When I was five years old we lived next door to my beloved Uncle Lee. My entire world revolved around him. All the children liked him, and he returned their affection, but I felt I held a very special place in his heart.

Every day after breakfast, I would run next door to his house, and he was always happy to see me. But one day he didn't come to the door. I didn't understand because he was always there. And if he was going out, he usually let me know – or more likely he would take me with him. I went home, dragging my feet, very disappointed.

When I told my mother Uncle Lee was not home, she told me he was on a little trip and would soon be home. She didn't tell me he was in the hospital, and very ill. I supposed I wouldn't have understood it anyway.

Everyday I went over to his house to see if he was back. Finding him gone, I would sit on the doorstep and cry. He hadn't even told me goodbye.

A few days later I was alseep in my bedroom when I was awakened by voices in the living room. I got up to see what was going on. I found my mother and grandmother crying, but they told me not to worry and to go back to bed.

As I lay wondering why they were crying, I saw someone standing near my bed. I thought at first it was Grandma, and I called out to her. Then the person came closer, and I saw that it was my dear Uncle Lee. He was smiling at me and he began to tell me a story – just like old times. And just like old times, I fell asleep as he talked.

The next morning I told my mother Uncle Lee had come to see me. Only then did she tell me that Uncle Lee had gone to heaven and we would not see him again. I did not understand about death and not seeing him again, but I did know I had seen him the night before.

In the same issue Rosalee B. Tipton of Imperial Beach, Calif., shared the experience she had with her beloved, deceased grandfather:

I loved my grandfather. He was the best grandfather a little girl ever had. He was my idol. My grandfather was a stubborn, hardheaded man who believed that when you died your body was a dead thing to be put into the ground. And then your soul either went to heaven or hell – period! There were no exceptions.

He was totally unbending on the subject. Ghosts or spirits did not exist, so such things, if they did exist, were tools of the devil, he thought. So such things were never discussed in his presence.

Grandfather died in June 1977, at the age of 91, of cancer. The dread disease, with its lingering, painful illness, left him hardly recognizable as the healthy, sun-tanned, blue-eyed farmer I had known and loved all my life.

My grandfather's nickname for me was 'Bosum', and he had called me by that name since I was a baby. The night after grandfather's death I was weeping softly into my pillow when I heard someone say clearly and distinctly, yet softly, as grandfather always spoke, 'Bosum?' I lay for a moment not believing what I had heard. Then I whirled around.

My grandfather stood at the foot of my bed smiling, his bright blue eyes twinkling. It was quite dark in the bedroom, yet I could see him clearly. He looked as he had years before, sun-browned and glowing with health. I stared at him, speechless.

'Bosum?' he spoke softly, yet strongly, and it was definitely my grandfather's voice. 'I came to tell you that I'm all right – and to say goodbye.' My heart filled with joy. I put my hand out to him, but he was gone. He just faded from view.

That was the end of my grief. I went to the funeral with the knowledge that the grandfather I loved still existed somewhere, happy and full of health.

What a wonderful surprise it must have been for him to discover that death, as he believed it to be, did not exist!

The world respected, admired, and loved Anwar Sadat, the President of Egypt who made peace with Israel, gained back for Egypt the great Sinai peninsula and its oil wells, and who was later assassinated by a small extremist group in his own army. His beautiful wife Jehan was his companion, and likewise won our affection. She has this to say: "Our religion says that when the body dies, the soul continues to live. But I was surprised by Anwar after he died. I was in bed and found him beside me as if he were still alive. It was so real I asked, 'Anwar, are you here?' I stretched out my hand to touch him and ensure it was really he, in the flesh. And he lay there and smiled at me."

Dr. John had an instructive comment in answer to a question in a group teaching session in Evansville, Indiana, October 28, 1979. The question was asked, "Is it possible to contact our loved ones on the Other Side?"

The answer is largely yes. . . Now the loved ones may have gone on to where they do not really have much connection. Let me ask you, after you had entered high school, how often did you go back to visit eighth grade?

When one enters the next world, so to speak, one enters the lower astral and then learns the higher planes available. There isn't too much point of returning to earth. Now when there are still loved ones, or for those who are selected to serve in some way or other, yes a contact is maintained. Or when the consciousness of an excarnate entity is so low and so bound to earth that he is, as we say, earthbound, yes. But in general, we go on to high school, leave eighth grade, and sixth and fourth and kindergarten, behind.

Question: Will I see my loved ones when I make my transition? What happens when I go over?

They may have gone onto the higher astral and to the ethereal, more spiritual planes, and still have come back to meet you, to greet you, to catch your consciousness with someone whom you recognize and help you make the transition in consciousness that you have already made out of the physical body into the next plane of personality expression.

Question: Would they have to keep an eye on me to know when I'm coming over?

The council of guides and teachers keep an eye on you and there is an interlocking information center, as it were, so the word can be gotten. Even in an accident some one can be summoned very quickly. Of course, most things called accidents are known ahead. But those who die are met, even if they went out in an accident. (A8006:13, 14)

Belief in personal immortality, our own life after death, in the past has been often a leap of faith. But today that leap of faith is undergirded by science, modern man's new tool for getting facts, for learning what is true. The ages-old, history-long human experiences of psychic communication with the dead are now abundantly authenticated, and today additional evidence comes from new lines of research.

(B) DREAM-RESEARCH

Sleep gives us a more frequent, but less clear, window into the death experience. It does, however, give insight into what may be the first stage in the disengagement of the spirit-self from the physical body, a first stage withdrawal, with death being the second and final stage. Scientific research into the phenomenon of sleep seems to indicate this two-stage dissociation.

Out-of-Body experiences apparently occur rather frequently during sleep, usually without the conscious mind accompanying the out-of-body self. What may seem to us an occasional dream of flying or springing along with steps that float, or dream visits with deceased friends and loved ones, appear likely to be fringe-remembrances brought back into consciousness from these occasional out-of-body events during sleep.

There is customarily a sleep-displacement of the astral self from its usual alignment with the physical body, and this may play an important role in the physical rejuvenation during sleep.

Often in dreams, the personality has astrally traveled. At the beginning of the waking consciousness there may be some perception of some aspects of the more immediate portions of the astral realm. This is usually the

cause of the phenomenon happening at times upon going
to sleep, the personality coming into some of the less
pleasant areas of this lower astral realm, and it learns
then to avoid them.

. . . It appears that the sleep process involves quite
regularly, maybe not all the time but quite regularly, a
certain dissociation of the astral person from the physical body, a certain projection which may be measured
in space almost an eighth-of-an-inch. It may be more
of a consciousness thing, but it appears to be an actual
projection in space, a very small bit. And that the release of the astral body, the personality, the spiritual
personality, is what allows the physical body to sleep.
For the mind can continue its activities, although it also
has – and must have – its times of rest.

As you go to sleep, give your mind, your consciousness, your self, instructions that when you awaken, you
will before you awaken, put more and more of the
knowledge of where you have been and what you have
been doing into the basket of remembrance and carry it
back through the opening door of awakening. Try this
patiently over a period of time, and I believe you will
remember more; and if you do, it can be quite rewarding.
(A8006:9)

The spiritual significance of dreams was a matter of great
importance among the wise at an early period in the history
of civilization. Ancient Hebrew literature abounds with
accounts of dreams in which their God Yahweh communicated His will and purpose. The Old Testament tells how
Joseph was able to forecast seven years of plenty for Egypt
followed by seven years of famine. By interpreting the
Pharoah's dreams and coming up with a clear-cut plan of
action based upon them, Joseph earned a top place in court
as the Pharoah's vizier. Joseph had been a slave there for
thirteen years, albeit building a reputation for his psychism.

Dreams figured prominently in the records of early Christianity. Indeed, in the New Testament they were a very usual means by which God communicated His will – e.g., Joseph was instructed in a dream to marry the pregnant Mary, who was to bear the Savior; the Wise Men and Joseph were advised in dreams of Herod's evil plans.

The wise men of Babylonia, Mesopotamia and Assyria divined the future from visions seen in sleep. In ancient Greek and Roman societies, dreams were regarded as one of the chief means whereby the gods communicated with men and men learned of their future. The ancients regarded sleep as a second life in which the soul was freed from the body, and therefore more active than during the waking state.

Dream research is a fascinating study in itself, but our concern now is with our survival of death. Here dreams have two elements of significance. First, they indicate we can and do have an active life of our consciousness and our very beingness aside from the active life of our body. Secondly, dreams occasionally bring solid evidence that the dead still live.

Edgar Cayce, famous American psychic of the mid-1900s, interpreted some 1600 dreams, in many of which he reported valid communications from deceased ones. The most common message given the dreamer by the departed is for the bereaved to stop grieving, that the deceased is just fine and there is no need for the earthly survivors to be so unhappy. Elsie Sechrist quotes one of Cayce's dream cases in which a woman dreamed of her dead mother drowning in a pool, saying, "Daughter, these are the tears you have shed for me. Let me go, for I am drowning in them."

Dr. Robert Crookall, former Principal Geologist for H. M. Geological Survey (England), Demonstrator of Botany at the University of Aberdeen, and a psychic researcher, majorly using BSPR data, reports various cases of communication with the dead via dreams in his book *The Supreme Ad-*

venture. He states the first wish of the newly-dead is to assure the still-embodied family and friends of their (the deceased) survival and well-being. The second wish is usually to entreat the bereaved not to indulge in excessive grief, as it may hold back the deceased from progression in the excarnate stage. Negative expressions such as grief, depression, self-pity, etc., represent "low or slow vibratory rates" and are unpleasant, even painful, to the deceased. A discarnate soldier communicated to this mother:

> I can tell when you are fretting about me, and I was glad when you got a bit better; your grief made me miserable.

A month after Raymond Hodge died, he contacted his mother in a dream:

> You used to sigh, it had an awful effect on me, but I am getting lighter with you.

Raymond promised to attend the family Christmas party, but appealed to her:

> No sadness: keep it jolly, or it hurts so horribly.

Late in her life when her fame had dimmed and she was sick, actress Mrs. Patrick Campbell was tenderly nursed by actress Sara Allgood. In gratitude she gave Miss Allgood a framed watercolor of a heron. She then went to France, and Miss Allgood returned to Hollywood. There, her first dream in a new house was of Mrs. Campbell, who asked her, "Have you found my gift from the grave? Look behind the picture." Behind the heron she found a Max Beerbolm caricature of Mrs. Campbell, worth $2,000. She was puzzled because she thought Mrs. Campbell was still alive. Miss Allgood later found her benefactress had died the day of this evidential dream.

The following case has been legally documented. It was first reported in ASPR's publication *Proceedings* (Vol. 36, pp. 517 ff):

A farmer, James L. Chaffin, who lived in North Carolina, made a will on November 16, 1905, in which he gave the farm to his third son Marshall, leaving his widow and other three sons unprovided for. On January 10, 1919, he apparently repented of this and made a second will, which was unwitnessed, but which would, according to the state law, have been valid provided there was proof that it was in the testator's own handwriting. The new will read as follows: 'After reading the 27th chapter of Genesis, I, James L. Chaffin, do make my last will and testament and here it is. I want, after giving my body a decent burial, my little property to be equally divided between my four children, if they are living at my death, but personal and real estate divided equal. If not living, give share to their children', etc.

He placed this second will between two pages of an old family Bible which had belonged to his father, folding the pages over so as to mark the place. No one knew of the existence of the second will, and the eccentric farmer took no steps to indicate its existence except that of stitching up the inner pocket of his overcoat with a roll of paper inside it bearing the words: 'Read the 27th chapter of Genesis in my Daddy's old Bible.'

The old farmer died suddenly on September 7, 1921. The third son, Marshall, obtained probate of the only known will (the first one) in September of that year and was given the farm.

In June 1925 the second son, James, started to have vivid dreams of his father. In one of these the old man appeared to stand at the son's bedside wearing his black overcoat, and said to him, 'You will find my will in my overcoat pocket.'

Being convinced by this, James visited his brother John, who lived twenty miles away and had possession of the coat. On discovering the roll of paper with its message, James went with his daughter and two other witnesses to his mother's home. After considerable search, they found the old Bible, and located the second will at the indicated place. In December 1925, a lawsuit took place and the second will was admitted for probate.

From this intriguing research into dreams, two facets stand out as pertinent to our special study of death: First, sleep gives us a nightly window into what may be the first stage withdrawal of the spirit-self from its connection with the physical body. This gives us insight that death is simply a further and final step in this withdrawal.

Second, we have a large body of reported cases of communication with the dead in dreams, many substantiated by convincing evidentials. Here in these vivid dreams, and at times in lucid dreams where we know we are dreaming, we visit with friends and family members who have made the transition into the excarnate realm of expression, and who may make their own significant communication with us.

(C) THE OUT-OF-BODY EXPERIENCE (OOBE)

Out-Of-Body Experiences (sometimes called "Ecsomatic Experiences") are cases when people have the experience of leaving the physical body, observing it and their surroundings from some vantage-point outside. This phenomenon seems particularly likely to happen in situations of stress such as an auto accident, being hit by a bullet, undergoing surgery, etc. However, it also can happen under very commonplace situations. There is an ever-growing body of OOBE among ordinary people in normal circumstances who suddenly find themselves outside their physical body. When the

Institute of Psychophysical Research in Oxford, England appealed to the public by means of press and radio for first-hand accounts of OOBEs, 400 cases were reported, and it was clear that with further publicity more cases would have been forthcoming. These experiences are now being carefully documented and analyzed.

The significance of Out-Of-Body Experiences in the study of death is obvious. If you are able to leave your body even before it dies and still be completely yourself, alive and with a conscious knowledge of yourself and your surroundings, it follows that the 'you' part of you is not the body at all. Thus the survival of you is not dependent upon the survival of the body.

Secondly, since it is possible to separate the conscious thinking-feeling nature of you from the body while the body still lives, it seems reasonable to assume that the death experience is simply a further and permanent stage in this separation.

Researchers of OOBEs believe the Biblical reference to "the silver cord" (Book of Ecclesiastes) is direct reference to this connection of the spirit-you with the body, while the body still lives. At death, the cord is severed and the person is freed permanently much as the severed umbilical cord frees the infant from the mother's body.

Research indicates that under normal-waking circumstances, the astral and physical bodies are in register (are in alignment) but under certain conditions the two bodies move out of alignment. It has been found that infants, the elderly, the very weak and ill, and those under the influence of alcohol or drugs, are more likely to get out of register, get out of alignment. Visual-Motor-Dissociation experiences are definitely of this "out-of-register" type.

It is only in recent years that OOBEs have been seriously

studied by competent scientific researchers. One such, who
has made a substantial contribution to these particular
studies, is Celia Green of the Institute of Psychophysical
Research at prestigious Oxford University, England. Many of
her carefully researched cases are published in the *Out-Of-
Body Experiences* (1968). She states from her research:

> One also wants to know what is the electrical activity
> of the brain (as measured by the electroencephalogram or
> EEG) during an OOBE. In many cases the subject appears
> to be deeply unconscious. Now if the electrical records
> of the brain in such cases show the patterns appropriate
> to the subject's physiological state (for example the slow
> delta rhythms observed during sleep as opposed to the
> faster waves which are dominant in waking states) we
> have to reconcile this with the fact that the subject is
> apparently having a conscious experience at the time.
> Alternatively, if the subject's EEG shows the rhythms
> appropriate to conscious experience, we have to recon-
> cile this with the fact that his physical body is apparently
> inert and unresponsive to physical stimuli. At all events,
> OOBEs present science with a challenging phenomenon.

Several of Green's subjects had their OOBEs while doing
something quite routine, dull or monotonous, suggesting
this might lull a person into a state of mind conducive to an
out-of-body experience. The following is a case in point:

> During the morning hours, while driving fast along a
> road, the drone of the engine and the vibration seemed to
> lull me into a stupor and I remembered I seemed to leave
> my motorbike like a zoom lens in reverse and was hover-
> ing over a hill watching myself and friend tearing along
> on the road below and I seemed to think, 'I shouldn't
> be here, get back on that bike!' and the next instant I
> was in the saddle again.

Many of her cases suggested fatigue might also be a contributing factor in activating an OOBE. The next subject was a waitress who had been working non-stop for twelve hours. Exhausted, she left the restaurant to go home and found she had missed the last bus. She decided to walk home.

> I started walking, as in those days I lived in Jericho, a 15 minute walk at most. I remembered feeling so fatigued that I wondered if I'd make it, and resolved to myself that I'd keep going. . . The next I registered was of hearing the sound of my heels very hollowly and I looked down and watched myself walk round the bend of Beaumont onto Walton Street. I was up on a level with Worcester chapel (a hill). A saw myself clearly. It was a summer evening and I was wearing a sleeveless shantung dress. I remembered thinking, 'So this is how I look to other people.'

British novelist and playwright William Gerhardie gives a vivid description of his own OOBE published in his semi-autobiographical novel *Resurrection* (1934). When he came back into his body after this experience, he found his earlier ideas of life after death had been shattered:

> In this experience, I went to bed exhausted and as I was drifting off I became conscious of being suspended in mid-air, light as a feather. Once on my feet, I felt as if I was defying gravity. In appearance I seemed to be identical to my physical body on the bed — to which I was attached by a luminous cable.
> When I tried to open the door, I found I could not turn the handle. Then I discovered I could pass right through the door. I moved around the apartment, making observations, lit by my own cord.
> My new body responded to my thoughts and floated this way and that according to my whims. Part of me wished to fly to distant places, but another part was afraid this might sever the link with the sleeping body.

Biologist and author Lyall Watson tells about his extra-ordinarily vivid OOBE while on safari in Africa, published in his book *The Romeo Error* (1974). Below is a condensation of this experience:

> I was driving with a safari party through the bush of Kenya when suddenly the small bus skidded in the dust and overturned. It rolled over twice and then balanced precariously on the edge of a gully.
>
> A moment later I found myself standing outside the bus looking at it. And yet I could see my own physical body slumped unconscious in the front seat. A more alarming sight was the head and shoulders of a young boy who had been pushed through the canvas top of the vehicle when it had come to a stop. If the bus fell into the gully, the boy would be crushed.
>
> The thought scarcely crossed my mind when I found myself regaining consciousness inside the bus. I rubbed the red dust from my eyes, and at once climbed through the window and freed the boy, just moments before the vehicle rolled into the gully.

Dr. Fowler Jones, a psychologist at the University of Kansas Medical School, with her two colleagues, psychiatrists Dr. Stewart Twemlow and Dr. Glen Gabbard, conducted a research project on OOBEs. This was a large study involving over 500 people from the United States and Europe reporting out-of-body experiences. Here are four abridged cases taken from their carefully documented files:

> One night a woman found herself out of her body, and was much surprised to find others in her home. The others were completely oblivious to her presence and were chatting among themselves. She also reported encountering a Being whom she perceived as emanating love.
>
> * * * * *
>
> A man had an OOBE while attempting to take a nap

one afternoon on his sofa. He finally decided he couldn't sleep and got up to go to another room. At the doorway, he looked back and was startled to see himself still on the sofa. He was so surprised, it zapped him right back into his body.

* * * * *

There are several reported cases of people getting up at night to go to the bathroom, looking back and seeing their bodies still in bed. (This can lead to nocturnal enuresis.)

* * * * *

A young man living in the country with his parents decided one winter day to walk to the country store a mile or so away. On the way back, he was caught in a severe snow storm. He lost his way and fell into a ditch. He almost froze before his father found him and carried him home. While all of this was going on, he found himself floating about ten feet above his body like a kite, and observing with keen interest all that was going on. He reported seeing his parents crying after they got him home, while they tried to revive him.

Writer Ernest Hemingway had an OOBE in 1918 while fighting in World War I. He was hit in the leg by shrapnel. As he lay in the trench, he suddenly felt as if "my soul or something was coming right out of my body, like you'd pull a silk handkerchief out of a pocket by one corner. . . it flew around and then came back and went in again." Hemingway used this experience in his *A Farewell to Arms*, a novel based on his war experiences.

The case of Dr. "X" was reported in the *Journal* of the British Society for Psychical Research, 1957. Dr. X wrote his account forty years after the event, which occurred in 1916, but he stated his memory of this experience was as clear as if he had experienced it but yesterday.

I was a medical officer in World War I and was

stationed at a small country airfield in England. One day word came through that a pilot had been shot down at another airfield and could I help release him from the wreckage? It was to be an event unique in the history of aviation, the first time that medical help had been taken by air to a casualty. All the top personnel turned up at the runway. Seconds after takeoff, my plane crashed. I was thrown out of the plane, into a dip where the airfield was obscured from view. Suddenly I found myself hovering about 200 feet above my unconscious body, in a state of pleasant awareness. I could see the frenzied activity at the airfield. The ambulance started, the medical orderly jumped in, others were running to the crash.

Then I began to move in what seemed like a delightful journey over the countryside and sea, until I felt a kind of retraction and was pulled back again — finding myself hovering over the body. Then with a pop I was aware of an orderly pouring something down my throat. Later, all the incidents I had seen at the airfield while out-of-the-body were confirmed by others. I found this experience so pleasant that it completely removed my fear of death.

There have been many reported OOBEs while under the influence of anesthesia or drugs. In their published work *The Phenomena of Astral Projection*, Sylvan Muldoon and Hereward Carrington report: "Anesthesia, producing deep unconsciousness, is ideal for producing astral projection. . . . Although anesthesia is a state of total blankness for most people, there are many cases on record in which more or less complete consciousness is retained by the patient, and afterwards he is able to describe all that went on in the operating room, e.g., the conversations of the physicians and nurses, and any unusual details which may have developed."

A British surgeon Dr. George Save published a volume of reminiscences and reflections in 1953, *A Surgeon Remembers.* In it he brings out some of his anesthesia-induced OOBE cases. In his book he states, "It is indeed a disquieting thought that every time one operates one's activities are under observation from the patient's astral body hovering overhead, a fascinating yet frightening possibility." The experience that gave rise to these disquieting thoughts was in connection with an operation he performed on an elderly woman, Mrs. Frances Gail:

> Mrs. Gail was in a post-operative coma and seemed to be sinking fast. An urgent call from the hospital brought me from my home, and I worked hard to bring the patient back to consciousness. I was successful, and when Mrs. Gail was able to speak she told me of being out of her body and would have preferred to remain out of it, but she had to come back because her friends had called her back. I was sympathetic but not particularly impressed, considering it just an old woman's fantasy. But what she said next astounded me:
>
> 'You didn't carry out the operation you first intended, did you. You kept my body lying there under the anesthetic while you and the others discussed whether I was strong enough to withstand what you proposed to do. You took away some pieces of bone. You were chiefly troubled about the anesthetic and asked the anesthetist if she thought I could stand three more hours of it, and if my heart was all right. The anesthetist just nodded and said, "She's okay, especially considering she's no spring chicken." Am I right?'

She was absolutely right, every detail of the patient's account corresponded exactly with what actually went on in the operating room.

Dr. Robert Crookall held professional doctorates in both general science and in geology. He built an eminent career in science as a faculty professor of the University of Aberdeen, Scotland, and a member of His Majesty's Geological Survey of England, and of the National Coal Board in London. In midlife his attention was caught by facts he felt indisputable and important, in the field of parapsychology. He collected reports of OOBEs and was struck by the similarities he found in them. He expressed his belief that the study of out-of-body experiences validated the religious concepts of the soul and an afterlife, and wrote several books in this general field – *The Study and Practice of Astral Projection* (1966), *Out-of-Body-Experiences* (1970), and *Casebook of Astral Projection* (1972).

Among Dr. Crookall's voluminous reports are many cases reporting OOBEs while under anesthesia. It was found generally the patients were too interested in watching the operation, seeing what was being done to their body, to leave the operating room. But in one case:

> After the patient took a casual look at her body on the operating room table, she left the surgeon to go on with his job while she went off to see what the members of her family were doing. She saw her husband waiting in the corridor of the hospital for news of her. She then wondered what her daughter was doing, and at once found herself in the hospital gift shop where her daughter was picking out a card for her. Over the unsuspecting girl's shoulder she read the text of the two cards under consideration. The daughter finally rejected the one with the flippant text in favor of the more dignified one. The patient then returned to her body. When the operation was over and she was able to receive visitors, her daughter came in bringing the card in the envelope. Her daughter was astonished when her mother recited the exact text word-for-word of the rejected flippant card.

The similarities and patterns Dr. Crookall found as he analyzed the OOBE data – he collected over 1,000 cases –

ensured to him that this was a genuine phenomenon and worthy of scientific attention. Six primary features in particular stood out:

1. The percipient often (not always, but often) felt that he left the body by being drawn out through the head;
2. Often a blackout occurred at the precise moment of separation;
3. The "phantom double" (astral body) initially hovered directly over the physical body;
4. The "phantom body" resumed this same position before re-entering the physical body;
5. A blackout again occurred, characteristically, on re-entry;
6. A rapid return to the body would cause the physical repercussion of a distinct jolt.

Dr. Crookall, who got his initial impetus to study OOBEs from Dr. Charles Tart, a psychologist at the University of California, further observed that:

OOBEs can be broken down into two large groups. In the first were placed those OOBEs which had occurred naturally – or spontaneously – when the percipient was near sleep, ill, or exhausted. The other category consisted of those cases that were forced by the use of anesthetics, shock, suffocation, hypnosis, willful attempts at projection or other artificial means. After analyzing the two groups, Crookall found the natural OOBEs are much more vivid and have different overall characteristics than those which are forced. Such experiences as leaving through the head, seeing the silver cord, and demonstrating ESP were consistently more common in the natural group than in the forced cases.

A comparatively rare but highly significant phenomenon is the out-of-body manifestations where the OOBE is seen by others. A Chicago physician, Dr. Hout, who had himself experienced projections, reported in the American monthly magazine *Prediction*, the following:

> I was privileged to see the spirit counterparts of three patients who had operations under anesthetic. Soon after the first patient, an elderly woman, was brought into surgery, I saw a form rise up and float free in the space above the operating table. As the anesthetic deepened and the physical body became more relaxed, the freedom of the astral body became greater, and the spirit form floated more freely away from the physical counterpart. During the height of the anesthesia, the astral form was quiet as though it was also in a deep, peaceful sleep. I knew the direct process of surgical activity was not affecting it at all. At the finish of the operation, while the wound was being closed, the astral form came closer to the body, but had not yet reentered its vehicle when the patient was wheeled out of the operating room.

An amusing account of an OOBE was given by the French Roman Catholic journalist and occultist Mille. Anne Osmond, who died in 1953. She reported that on her first out-of-body attempt she succeeded in leaving behind physical evidence of what she had done:

> I was friendly with a husband and wife, both sculptors. The wife, who was called Annie, had one evening expressed a strong disbelief in the possibility of astral projection. I resolved to prove her wrong that very night.
> It took a full quarter of an hour's effort to project myself out of the body. I then passed through the wall and went to my friend's flat. They both were in bed, asleep. I took note of the color and style of their nightclothes, but thought that was poor evidence and looked around for some object to topple. On the mantlepiece was a gilt liqueur glass, and I tried to move it. It seemed

as difficult to move as a piano, but presently I noticed it had moved a litttle. With continued effort I finally got the glass to the edge – and over. It smashed to the floor. The couple sat up in bed with a start, and I heard Anne say grumpily, 'I bet it's that imbecile Osmond!' On my next ordinary visit, I first saw the husband and repeated Annie's words to him. He recognized the reference and told me his wife was very angry as the goblet had been a family heirloom. . . . After this strenuous OOBE of moving the goblet to the edge and over, I was desperately exhausted for several days from the effort.

Fate Magazine brings fascinating accounts of OOBE's to their many readers each month in their "True Mystic Experiences" section. These reports are not sent in by professional researchers, but by everyday folks like you and me who found themselves outside of their physical bodies. The following was reported by Todd Fenner, and was published in the January 1983 issue:

Although interested in psychic phenomenon for several years, I could not be sure I had had a genuine out-of-body experience until April 1971. At the time I was an undergraduate visiting my home on Kenton Avenue in Chicago during spring break. Stirring from sleep late one Saturday morning I remembered thinking that my body felt heavy, and I didn't want to move. However, feeling duty-bound to get up, I arose. My body seemed charged with electricity and the room was strangely bright. Then I saw my body on the bed, still under the covers, although now it seemed foreign.

Anxious to confirm a true out-of-body experience, I went downstairs to the kitchen to look at the clock. Walking was difficult because I kept floating upward. The kitchen clock showed the time was nearly 10:30. Still anxious for solid proof, I thought I would go to the house of my friend who lived on another street. She had been influential in interesting me in the occult and perhaps she might sense my presence.

Not a second after forming the desire to leave I felt myself lifted up and pass through the walls of my parent's home into the air. I looked down and saw the north side of Chicago, and then found myself right above my friend's house. Distance didn't seem to matter; the journey was almost instantaneous.

I passed through the walls of her place into an empty living room. I then floated up the stairs into an area I had never seen before. Sounds came from the end of the hallway and I moved in that direction. There was my friend sitting in a chair watching TV. Next, I felt pulled away as if I had to concentrate to remain there, and my concentration was slipping. I soon found myself back in my own room, floating near the ceiling above my body.

The thought to go back in arose, and just as quickly I felt pulled in. There I was back inside. It was a heavy, clammy feeling – like being encased in moist clay, and it took a little time to orient myself. Then I went downstairs to look at the kitchen clock again. It was now exactly 10:30. Next I phoned my friend. She said she had been thinking of me. Anxiously, I asked her what she had been doing before answering the phone. She said she had been upstairs watching TV. There was confirmation! I also described to her the upstairs hall and TV room; they were exactly as I had seen them. Since that time I have never doubted the reality of out-of-body travel.

The two decades of the '60s and '70s, and continuing now into the '80s, have seen a very large increase both in publication of personal out-of-body experiences like the above, and in scientific OOBE research studies and publications. These, added to the scrupulous corroboration and reporting of uncounted psychic evidentials of life after death, and the probing work of dream researchers in several countries, add solidly to our new scientific enlightenment into the nature of death and the new greater life after death. No longer is there reason or excuse for a human being to face death without understanding. A long, long darkness is lifting.

(D) NEAR-DEATH EXPERIENCES (NDE)

During an otherwise routine tonsillectomy Erma Russell's heart stopped. Hospital records show that for three minutes doctors performed open-heart surgery, cutting open her chest to massage her heart. Erma relates her Near-Death Experience during those three minutes:

> All of a sudden I was aware, and I was rising through a white mist. Then it was all dark. I wasn't afraid, just a little curious. I did not think it strange at all that nothing was underneath me and that I didn't have a body. I felt quite at home. This was not the world I was used to, but it didn't bother me. I then felt this sense of absolute love and peace embracing me. I could see it was coming from this glowing circle of light.
>
> Then somehow the thought came into my mind that I ought to go back, that I have two children. But I said, 'No, I don't want to go back,' even though I loved my life and I loved my children. This presence of love was so powerful – a pure love without all the earthly attachments of guilt and anxiety – it was all I wanted. But then out of pure logic I decided I had a job to do and I had to return.
>
> The next thing I knew a nurse was standing over my bed, saying, 'I thought we had lost you!'

Accounts like the above are moving and inspirational, but they are not new. We've heard many similar accounts written up in numerous books and magazine articles. We find Near-Death Experiences in newspaper human-interest stories and on television talk shows. But what *is* new is the readiness in the past few years of physicians, researchers and scholars to take these experiences seriously, and to study them as legitimate data worthy of professional research. Today, many scientists who formerly regarded NDE stories with skepticism are becoming convinced of their authenticity and value.

With improvement in medical techniques, more and more people are being brought back from clinical death and are revealing what they saw and heard. Pollster George Gallup, Jr. recently found that an estimated eight million Americans have experienced some sort of mystical encounter in conjunction with a near-death experience.

Dr. Elisabeth Kubler-Ross, Assistant Professor of Psychiatry and Assistant Director of Psychiatric Consultation and Liaison Service at the University of Chicago, proposed "A series of conversations with the terminally ill which would make it possible for them to talk out their feelings and thoughts in their crisis situation of dying. . . And by these conversations others could learn how better to work with the dying". Of this she writes, "It is a gratifying experience to listen to these patients who can teach us so much."

Kubler-Ross, through her pioneering work in counseling terminally ill patients, was able to accumulate an amazing amount of research data which she has used in her seminars, workshops, and later publications. Her 1969 best seller *Death And Dying* became an essential reference work for the counseling profession. Her primary emphasis was to train people in the art of helping other people die. As part of this she reported that some of her near-death patients had "heavenly" experiences of peace and happiness and visits with departed loved ones. Their NDE released them from their previous fear of death and gave them instead a positive anticipation.

Raymond A. Moody, Jr. holds a Doctor of Philosophy degree from the University of Virginia, and has taught philosophy for three years at a North Carolina University. During this time he decided to go to medical school to become a psychiatrist, and then teach the philosophy of medicine in medical school. He became interested in near-death studies while a medical student. Quite by chance he overheard his clinical professor of psychiatry relate his own near-death experience to a small group of interested students. It immediately sparked Moody's interest in this phenomenon. Since that start he has studied in detail 150 NDE cases, and reports over 100 of them in his 1976 book *Life After Life:*

> I was in the hospital, but they didn't know what was wrong with me. So Dr. James, my doctor, sent me downstairs to the radiologist for a liver scan so they could find out. First they tested this drug they were going to use, on my arm, since I had a lot of drug allergies. But there was no reaction, so they went ahead and used it on me. But this time there was a reaction and I arrested on them. My heart and breathing stopped. I heard the radiologist who was working on me go over to the phone, and I heard very clearly as he dialed it. I heard him say, 'Dr. James, I've killed your patient, Mrs. Martin.'
>
> And I knew I wasn't dead. I tried to move or let them know, but I couldn't. When they were trying to resuscitate me I could hear them telling how many cc's of something to give me, but I didn't feel the needles going in. I felt nothing at all when they touched me.

The most common element in these near-death accounts is the encounter with a Being of Light, a Being of luminous, radiant white (sometimes golden) light. At first it appears dim, then it rapidly becomes brighter until it reaches a brilliance. The light is not glaring but soft, and seems omnipresent. Its outstanding property is the feeling of total love and total acceptance emanating from it to the dying person. The communication with this Being of Light, in a direct transmission of meaning, is purposeful and personal. The person is either told he must return, and why, or he is allowered to make a free-will decision to either return or go on. In some cases the Being asks questions, such as, "Are you ready to die?" or "What have you done with your life that is important?"

I knew I was dying and there was nothing I could do about it because no one could hear me. I was out of my body; there was no doubt about it because I could see my own body there on the operating table. This made me feel very bad at first. But then this really bright light came. It was a little dim at first, but then it was this huge beam. It was just a tremendous amount of light, nothing like a big bright flashlite, it was just too much light, and it gave off heat to me. I felt a warm sensation. I just can't describe it. It seemed to cover everything. I could see clearly, and it wasn't blinding. At first when the light came I wasn't sure what was happening, and then it asked if I was ready to die. It was like talking to a person, but a person wasn't there. The light was talking to me in a voice.

I think the voice that was talking to me actually knew I wasn't ready to die, you know, kind of testing me more than anything else. Yet from the moment the light spoke to me, I felt really good, secure and loved. The love which came from it is just unimaginable, indescribable. It was a fun person to be with, and it had a sense of humor too – definitely!

I got up and walked into the hall to go get a drink, and it was at that point, as they found out later, my appendix ruptured. I became very weak and fell down. I felt sort of a drifting, a movement, of my real self in and out of my body, and I heard beautiful music. I floated on down the hall, and out the door onto the screened-in porch. There it almost seemed that clouds, a pink mist really, began to gather around me, and then I floated right through the screen, just as if it weren't there, and up into this pure crystal-clear light, an illuminating white light. It was beautiful and so bright, so radiant, but it didn't hurt my eyes. It's not any kind of light you can describe on earth. I didn't actually see a person in this light, and yet it had a special identity. It definitely did. It was a light of perfect understanding and perfect love.

*   *   *   *   *

I heard the doctors say that I was dead, and that's when I began to feel as though I was tumbling, actually kind of floating, through this blackness which was some kind of enclosure. There are not really words to describe this. Everything was very black, except that way off from me I could see this light. It was a very, very brilliant light, but not too large at first. It grew larger as I came nearer and nearer to it.

I was trying to get to that light at the end because I felt it was Christ, and I was trying to reach that point. It was not a frightening experience. It was more or less a pleasant thing. Immediately, being a Christian, I had connected the light with Christ who said, 'I am the light of the world.' I said to myself, 'If this is it, if I am to die, then I know Who waits for me at the end, there at that light.'

From Dr. Moody's research, as well as from studies conducted by other researchers, many cases report approaching what seems like a border, a limit of some kind, beyond which they cannot go and return. This boundary is depicted in various ways, sometimes as a body of water, a gray mist, a door, a fence, a line, etc.

I died from cardiac arrest, and as I did, I suddenly found myself in a rolling field. It was beautiful and everything was an intense green, a color unlike anything on earth. There was light — a beautiful, uplifting light — all around me. I looked ahead of me across the field and saw a fence. I started moving toward that fence, and I saw a man on the other side of it moving toward it to meet me. I wanted to reach him, but felt myself drawn back irresistibly. As I did, I saw him too, turn around and go back in the other direction — away from the fence.

* * * * *

I had a heart attack, and I found myself in a black void, and I knew I had left my physical body. I knew I was dying, and I thought, 'God, I did the best I knew how at the time I did it. Please help me.'

Immediately, I was moved out of that blackness, through a pale gray, and I just went on, gliding and moving swiftly, and in front of me, in the distance, I could see a gray mist, and I was rushing toward it. It seemed that I just couldn't get to it fast enough to satisfy me. As I got closer to it I could see through it. Beyond the mist, I could see people, and their forms were just like they are on earth, and I could also see something which one could take to be buildings. The whole thing was permeated with the most gorgeous light, a living, golden-yellow glow, a pale colour, not like the harsh gold color we know on earth.

As I approached more closely, I felt certain that I was going through the mist. It was such a wonderful, joyous feeling; there are just no words in human language to describe it. Yet, it wasn't my time to go through the mist, because instantly from the other side appeared my uncle Carl, who had died several years earlier. He blocked my path, saying, 'Go back! Your work on earth has not been completed. Go back now!' I didn't want to go back, but I had no choice, and immediately I was back in my body. I felt that horrible pain in my chest, and I heard my little boy crying, 'God, bring my mommy back to me.'

Dr. Kubler-Ross' and Dr. Moody's professional standing has helped to focus public and scientific attention on this previously cultural-taboo area of death and dying. These pioneers have added knowledge and techniques to this coming new science of thanatology (the study of death), and became the leading advocates of the Death Awareness Movement. Their work also spread credence to similar studies conducted by independent death researchers elsewhere.

Dr. Michael Sabom, author of *Recollections of Death: A Medical Investigation*, is a cardiologist at Atlanta V.A. Medical Center and assistant professor of medicine at Emory University. Upon reading Dr. Moody's book *Life After Life*, his first impression was, "This is utterly ridiculous!" To confirm his skepticism he began talking with patients who had been "brought back." Much to his surprise, some told him of near-death experiences which they had not shared before for fear of ridicule. He then began systematically studying NDEs. Over the next five years he talked with 116 patients who had suffered near-fatal medical crises.

What he found astonished him. Almost half — 43 percent — of patients resuscitated from near-death crisis reported an NDE. Moreover, the group reporting the NDEs was no different in age, sex, race, area of residence, education, occupation, religion, or frequency of church attendance than the group that could recall nothing from the period of unconsciousness.

Here are some cases taken from Sabom's research:

> The patient, a 43-year-old man, suffered a heart attack following open-heart surgery. A medical team revived him, but for a few brief moments he was clinically dead. Later he relates a vivid remembrance of those moments:
>
> 'I came to some place and there were all my (deceased) relatives; my grandmother, my grandfather, my father, my uncle. They all came toward me and greeted me. All of a sudden they turned their backs on me and walked away, and my grandmother looked over her shoulder and said, 'We'll see you later, but not this time.'

* * * * *

A 37-year old housewife describes her NDE:

> I was looking down and could see myself going into convulsions. I was starting to fall out of bed and the girl in the next bed screamed for the nurses. It was like being up in a balcony looking down and watching all this. Everything was clearly seen like watching television.

Over 80 percent of these cases after the experience feared death far less than they had before. Many sick and dying patients said the experience had made them feel more peaceful about living out their remaining days. For many, human love and compassion became paramount after the NDE, along with a deepened religious conviction. Said one man who had suffered a massive heart attack shortly after his 33rd birthday:

> It (NDE) just changed my whole life like a flip-flop. I used to worry about trying to get ahead and working harder to make more money. Now I just live from day to day. I know where I'm headed to, so that I don't worry about dying anymore.

University of Connecticut psychology professor Dr. Kenneth Ring has researched another group of people who have come close to death. In his thoughtful and lucid book, *Life At Death: A Scientific Investigation Of Near-Death Experiences,* he recounts over one hundred cases researched in detail. Ring is co-founder of the International Association for Near-Death Studies headquartered at the University, and he edits the association's journal *Anabiosis.* The primary purpose of IANDS is to promote the study of near-death experiences. This association has no partyline on the interpretation of this phenomenon, other than that NDEs and other related experiences deserve thoughtful professional study and public discussion.

In Ring's continuing research since his book was published, he has uncovered evidence that a small number of near-death survivors saw the future events of their present life during the life-review phase of their NDE. This rare phenomenon has been dubbed the "flashforward" experience. Presently Dr. Ring is conducting a special search for such cases. In a lengthy paper entitled "Precognitive and Prophetic Vision in Near-Death Experiences." Ring published several of these experiences in the June 1982 issue of *Anabiosis.* Here are two cases taken from that study:

A woman living in the midwest had a near-death crisis when her cervix was torn as she was giving birth to her youngest child in 1959. During her NDE she met various beings who conveyed knowledge of the future to her. The beings told that it was not yet time for her to die. They showed her where she would be living and what she would be doing at a time in the future of this life:

I saw myself in a kitchen tossing salad, dressed in a striped seersucker outfit. My hair had streaks of silver in it; my waist had thickened some, but I was still in good shape for an older woman. There was a strong feeling of peace of mind about my bearing and I was in a joyful mood, laughing with my older daughter as we prepared dinner.

The younger daughter (the newborn) had gone somewhere with some children. This daughter was grown up too, but still there were two small children involved who were not in the picture at the moment (i.e., time of the NDE in 1959). My husband had just come out of the shower and was walking down a hallway wrapping a robe around himself. He had put on more weight than I had and his hair was quite silver. Our son was mowing our lawn. The offspring were only visiting, they didn't live with us. I could see, hear and smell just as if I was physically living the scene.

Today, I look exactly as I did during the 1959 flashforward, and I correctly saw what my children and husband would look like. My elder daughter eventually divorced, and I took over the responsibility of helping raise her two children. My daughter's two children, therefore, fulfilled the prophecy of the two small children in the flashforward. The description of the town I would live in was also accurately foretold.

An example of a global-prophecy type vision is reported by a woman who had her NDE in 1967 when she was only sixteen years old:

> The vision of the future I received during my NDE was one of tremendous upheaval in the world as a result of our general ignorance of the 'true' reality. I was informed that mankind was breaking the laws of the universe and as a result of this would suffer. This suffering was not due to the vengeance of an indignant God, but rather like the pain one might suffer as a result of arrogantly defying the law of gravity. It was to be an inevitable educational cleansing of the earth that would creep up upon its inhabitants who would try to hide blindly in the institutions of law, science and religion. Mankind, I was told, was being consumed by the cancers of arrogance, materialism, racism, chauvinism, and separatist thinking. I saw sense turning to nonsense, and calamity, in the end, turning to providence.
>
> At the end of this general period of transition, Mankind was to be born anew, with a new sense of his place in the universe. The birth process, however, as in all the kingdoms, would be painful. Mankind would emerge humbled yet educated, peaceful, and at last unified.

This example is typical of prophetic-vision cases. One specific theme crops up time and time again in these NDE prophetic visions, and that is the geological upheavals and the breakdown of the world's economic system. What about the possibility of a nuclear war? The accounts indicate that the chaos in the world's economic and geophysical conditions will bring us to the brink of war, but *none saw an actual war take place.* Many of these near-death visionaries saw a new era of peace and brotherhood which will emerge from the upheavals. They feel these disasters are a necessary purging process which will prepare Mankind for the New Age.

Dr. Ring, and other researchers, found during the course of their studies, subjects spoke of what has come to be termed the "core experience" when they were close to death or clinically-dead. They told of floating up and away from their bodies; of communicating with loved ones who were already dead; of gliding down a dark tunnel toward a lustrous light; of reaching a place they sensed was a limit, a threshhold, but from which they were drawn back, sometimes by a sense of responsibility toward others. Although there are variations in the accounts – not everyone told of the happenings in the same sequence, or experienced all of them – the *feelings* during the NDE were always the same: there was a sense of peace and great happiness in which the person longed to remain. Often, for the ones told to return, there was almost a feeling of horror that they would have to leave this place of absolute beauty, love and happiness and return to the pain and suffering in the physical world.

Perhaps the greatest number of medically detailed cases have been quietly collected over the past twenty years by a prominent cardiologist, Dr. Fred Schoonmaker, Chief of Cardiovascular Services at St. Luke's Hospital in Denver, Colorado. Since 1963 Schoonmaker has amassed medical records and case histories of over 2,000 patients who came close to death. Of that number over 1,400 – some 70 percent – reported having near-death experiences similar to those reported by Kubler-Ross, Moody and Ring.

The cases Schoonmaker investigated represent a wide range of people, and because of the complex and sophisticated equipment used at his hospital in monitoring patient's vital signs, detailed physiological information is recorded. This is the reason other NDE researchers are so eager for Schoonmaker to compile and publish his studies, adding new and important knowledge to the interesting phenomenon of Near-Death Experiences.

Sociologist John Audette of the University of Connecticut, co-founder with Dr. Ring of the International Association for Near-Death Studies (IANDS), and now its executive director, has directed his own near-death studies at two major medical centers in Illinois. He approaches his research with a cold eye but states, "It is simply impossible to account for the large number and wide range of these near-death stories by using the traditional areas of knowledge." He is convinced much of the scientific scoffing is because it's easier for those people to scoff than to deal with new and unacceptable information.

Dr. Greyson, Assistant Professor of Psychiatry at the University of Michigan Medical Center in Ann Arbor, has studied more than 150 NDEs resulting from attempted suicides. From his studies he has found for the most part these NDEs are, as he relates, "suicide-inhibiting rather than suicide-promoting. People who live through these experiences come out of them with a real sense of purpose in their lives." One woman who had attempted suicide and had a NDE expressed, "Taking one's own life is a devastating thing. It is like killing a plant or flower before it's full grown, or before its purpose has been served."

Dr. Greyson conducted his particular suicde-NDE studies partly in response to a fear among researchers that the public might, in view of the widely publicized accounts of beautiful, inspiring, blissful NDEs, romanticize death or even seek it out.

Dr. Michael B. Sabom, for one, stated, "Yes, no matter how inviting the great beyond, some people don't give in.

There is much to suggest that one's will to live may be an important psychological component in sustaining physical life. I can do everything medically possible in certain situations and the patient will die, even though I would have expected the opposite outcome. Conversely, some patients who I thought would never have had a chance are revived. The more I practice medicine, the less I feel we really do control the final results."

Tommy Clack lost both of his legs above the knee, and all of his right arm, as a result of stepping on a land mine during the war in Vietnam. In a matter-of-fact manner he gave this account of his NDE:

> I didn't know how badly I was hurt but suddenly I felt death coming on, and all of a sudden I was looking down at my body on the ground below me. All those people were running around. I watched them put my body on the helicopter to take back to the hospital. They had covered my face with a poncho, so I knew they thought I was dead, but I felt very nonchalant about it all. All the time I was watching, I knew something unique was happening to me. It wasn't like being in shock though; it was all very real.
>
> Back at the hospital I watched them put my body down with the others. Then a doctor came near and looked under the poncho and started to shout. I remembered very clearly trying to stop him, trying to say, 'Just leave me alone, I'm okay.'
>
> Then somehow, I was back on the battlefield, floating above the ground. And my men were there with me, the ones who had died before me. No, I don't mean in some sort of heavenly chorus, but as individuals. They were there! I felt each one of them, and we communicated with each other. There was a very bright light all around us.
>
> Then I was back at the hospital again. The doctors were still trying to save me and I was still trying to stop

them, because I was very happy just where I was.

The next thing I knew it was ten days later, and I was back in my body and in a hospital bed. No one wanted to tell me I had lost my legs and an arm, but they didn't have to. What they didn't know was that I had seen for myself exactly what had happened.

Clack is now a staff assistant to the director of a Veterans Administration Hospital in Georgia. He has had opportunity to talk with many servicemen who suffered serious injuries in Vietnam, and Clack states that about 80 percent of them had experiences similar to his own.

There are many cases reported that during a NDE the whole panorama of one's life may flash before him. Our first case was published in the British *Psychic Research Quarterly*, issued in 1920 (title changed to *Psyche* in 1921):

> Professor Heiron of Zurich slipped in the Alps on a snow-covered crag, slid head-first about a mile and then shot sixty feet through the air, landing on his head and shoulders. He was not killed. Returning to consciousness he not only testified to having seen the panoramic view of his life, but also hearing the most delightful music. He interviewed many people who had gone through similar NDEs, and the great rapidity of mental action and the absence of terror and pain was narrated by all.

This second case was taken from *Proceedings*, the official publication of the British Society for Psychical Research. Professor A. Pastore of the Royal Lyceum of Genoa, Italy, reports his NDE:

> I had been through a very severe illness. At the crisis, when I had entirely lost consciousness of physical pain, the power of my mind was increased by an extraordinary degree, and I saw clearly in a most distinct confusion (two words which do not accord, but which in this case

are the only ones which will express the idea) myself as a little boy, as a youth, as a man. I saw myself at various periods in my life; a dream, but a most powerful, intense, living dream. In that immense blue luminous space my mother met me – my mother who had died four years previously. It was an indescribable sensation.

The next case is taken from *Psychic Research,* Journal of the American Society for Psychic Research, published under that title between 1928-1932. Leslie Grant Scott reports:

Dying is really not such a terrifying experience. I speak as one who has died and come back and who found death one of the easiest things in life to do, but returning to the body was a different matter. That was difficult and full of fear. The will to live had left me and so I died. I had been ill for some time but not seriously so. I was in a run-down condition, aggravated by the tropical climate in which I was then living. I was in bed, a large old-fashioned bed, in which I seemed lost. I lay there quietly thinking and feeling more at peace than I had felt for a long time. Suddenly my whole life began to unroll before me and I saw the purpose of it all. All bitterness was wiped out for I knew the meaning of every event, and I saw its place in the pattern. I seemed to view it all im-personally, but yet with intense interest, although much that was crystal-clear to me then has again become some-what veiled in shadow. But I have never forgotten or lost the sense of the essential justice and rightness of things.

My consciousness was growing more and more acute. It seemed to have expanded beyond the limits of my physical brain. I was aware of things I had never con-tacted. My vision was also extended so that I could see what was going on behind my back, in the next room, even in distant places. I wondered if I should close my eyes or leave them open. I thought that it would be less gruesome for those around me if they were closed, so I tried to shut them, but found I could not.

I no longer had any control over my body. I was dead, yet I could think, hear, and see more widely than ever before. From the next room came great engulfing waves of emotion, the sadness of a childhood companion. My increased sensitiveness made me feel and understand these things with an intensity hitherto unknown to me.

The effort to return to my body was accompanied by an almost unimaginable sensation of horror and terror. I had left without the slightest struggle. I returned by an almost superhuman effort of will.

One of the most famous BSPR cases is that of the Reverend Bertrand, a Huguenot clergyman. Both Richard Hodgson and William James (two serious 19th-century psychical researchers) heard his narrative first hand, checked it out and were convinced of its authenticity. It was first published in BSPR's *Proceedings* in 1892:

While climbing in the Alps with a party of students and an old guide, I felt weary. I decided to rest while the others went up to the summit, which I had in any case visited several times before. I instructed the guide to take the party up by a path to the left and to come down by the right. When they had gone I sat down to rest with my legs dangling over the precipice. After a time I put a cigar in my mouth and struck a match to light it, but suddenly a curious feeling came over me. I watched the match burn my fingers, but I couldn't throw it down, nor could I move my limbs. Realizing that I was freezing to death, I began to pray; then, giving up hope of survival, I decided to study the process of dying.

I remained conscious while the icy paralysis progressively gripped all my bodily functions, then I felt my head become unbearably cold and suddenly had the sensation of separating from my physical body. I could see it below me, deadly pale with a yellowish-blue color, holding a cigar in my mouth and a match in its two burned fingers. I felt I was a captive balloon still attached to earth by a kind of elastic string and going up, always up. I felt exultant and alive and only wished that I could cut the thread that still connected me with the body.

I could see the party continuing their climb, and noted that the guide had disregarded my instructions and gone by the right instead of the left. I also watched the guide steal a leg of chicken and some drinks from my bottle of wine, and I thought, 'Go on, old fellow, eat the whole chicken if you choose, for I hope my miserable corpse will never eat or drink again.'

Traveling further in my astral body, I saw my wife who was due to join me in Lucerne the following day, descend from a carriage with four other people and go into a hotel at Lungren. But my only emotion was regrret that the thread, though thinner than ever, was never cut.

Suddenly I had a sensation of being irresistibly pulled downward. The party had returned to where they had left me, and the guide was rubbing my body to restore circulation. I felt like a balloon being hauled down to earth. My re-entry into the physical body emphasized the unpleasantness of the experience which numerous other projectors had noted. When I reached my body again, I had a last hope I would not be able to re-enter. But suddenly I found Bertrand was Bertrand again.

The examination of Near-Death Experiences is particularly pertinent to our study of death. This particular branch of knowledge carries our understanding through the transition experience, and at times gives us a brief glimpse into the astral expression as well. We then return to our physical life from this experience with a new and expanded perspective of our spiritual nature, enabling us to live out our remaining years more productively, and without fear.

(E) PAST-LIFE RECALL

At a time when medical models of psychological treatments

are coming into question and ambiguity pervades assessment of the effectiveness of psychotherapy, researchers are searching for new and more effective methods of treatment. Past-Life Recall is one of the latest disciplines on the therapy scene. Qualified psychologists, psychographists, hypnotists, counselors, ministers and other therapists are working with clients whose present-life problems are discovered to have their roots in past lifetimes. In regression therapy various simple techniques are used to sideline conscious thoughts, quiet the body, and relax the client into a state of consciousness conducive to past-life recall. Reverie, tapes, music, hypnosis and meditation are some of the methods used to achieve this altered state of consciousness (ASC).

The increasing number of psychotherapists admitting their own discoveries of past-life phenomena and its effectiveness as a therapeutic technique, attests to its authenticity and value. Many psychiatrists working in the field are now saying, "There is no doubt about it, this is the coming therapy." The Holistic Movement in medicine and psychology finds that Past-Life Recall fits right in. The transpersonal nature of past-life recall shows our individual oneness with something bigger than ourselves. We discover that many relationships, problems, abilities, and other characteristics of our present personal self have deep forces from former incarnations – with the concurrent realization that what we do now will affect subsequent, future incarnations of our own soul-self.

We have only begun to recognize and utilize the great versatility of this therapeutic tool in the resolution of painful, difficult relationships and in relieving other emotional and physical afflictions and ailments. But already many therapists maintain that a two or three-hour session of past-life therapy at times does more good than six months of conventional psychotherapy, and that the changes are more permanent.

Past-life recall in itself alone may prove the case for life after death. If there is something which was you, the essence of you, in a previous incarnation, and which carried over without a body from that person's death to your birth, and is the essential part of you now – that is *de facto* the soul, the immortal part of you surviving the death of your body. Reincarnation proves that claim of religion to be true.

In addition, three bonuses, three valuable plus factors, come with past-life recall: First, there is a cleansing emotional impact and validity for the experiencer. Past-life recall is a practical, realistic, emotionally alive actual living again the events of that life. *You are that person.* You feel within your mind and body the emotions and physical sensations of that past-life person. The client is not simply an observer with an overview. For those coming to the therapist with emotional or other problems, reliving that problem lifetime can bring release. The release can come immediately or gradually. In the gradual release, each time the past-life trauma is relived there is less charge to it, until finally the carried-over sensations or emotional attachments associated with that event are mastered, released, put into a different perspective, integrated positively into the present life personality. Present-life personality forces are then reconstellated, with the skillful counsellor helping the client to build new, more peaceful and productive patterns. Past-life recall adds new dimensions to re-experiencing therapy, that well-proved workhorse of psychotherapy.

Second, in past-life recall the client often can be taken through the death experience of that past incarnation and on into the beginnings of its excarnate life as well. Here on the astral plane the person can objectively and with detachment review the incarnate life just lived, discern its purposes, evaluate its achievements and its failures, surmount its pulls.

Third, when we thus re-experience several past deaths and find them liberating and pleasant, we lose the "doomed" attitude toward death in general. Losing this fear, we feel freed, and we are able to give better attention to living the present life well.

Stanford-trained Barbara Findeisen, co-founder of Matrix Center, Palo Alto, California, specializes in prenatal and past-life factors in personality problems. She says, "Life is a continuum. . . We do not begin at conception and we don't end at death. There is a continuum as a conscious being." When asked, "Is it more painful to be born than to die? Is that the experience of your patients?" She answered, "Yes, of course. The painful part about dying is the fear that goes up until death. Death itself is a release. People have the most incredible experiences. Birth is usually an experience of being squeezed, sometimes of tremendous pressure. So maybe we have everything backwards. Death is not to be feared."

From where come these past-life persons into our conscious-ness? This question was put to Dr. John when a life reading client asked, "If I understand the outline given in the 'The Soul in Earthliving,' the personality is only a tool of the soul. What is the mechanism by which the present personality is affected by the experience of its past-life persons — since it was brought out that the past-life person itself does not reincarnate, but the new person is a new incarnation from the soul?"

> The soul-forces from past-lives, the soul's learnings, the soul's successes and its failures, are carried by a part of the subconscious mind. The subconscious mind of the individual does not begin with the birth of the physical body. It is the subconscious which carries memories of past lives, and memories of the in-between life experiences. It is into the subconscious area that the soul forces flow. And then it is the subconscious which affects the 'I' of the present personality conscious experience. (A4046:11)

Not everyone has past-life recall ability, perhaps for the same reason not everyone has psychic development ability, as Dr. John points out:

> The development of clairvoyance, telepathy, etc., is not entirely in the hands of earthbeings. It is guided and directed from the Other Side of life as well. When that development is not a part of the pattern for a particular life and has no place, or where there is a very real reason feeding out of the past why the individual should not have that development, the individual could work for a long time and get nowhere. This is evidenced every day in earthliving. There are many, many beings who are honestly and sincerely working for extrasensory perception and not attaining it, although they follow all that is known on how to do it. They are completely sincere in their efforts, but it cannot be done completely on the personality side. (A2599:13)

Past-Life Recall is by no means a new concept. It has been in use by therapists since the early 1950s, with Dr. Loehr one of the early pioneers, but because of its link with reincarnation it was not at first readily acceptable to some of the more orthodox psychotherapists.

The increasing public interest in experiencing past-life recall has created a growing demand for counselors and therapists skilled in regression techniques. Many professionals have responded to this need, and the American Psychographical Association, Inc. (APA) is a professional organization founded to train and credential counselors, therapists, ministers and teachers in using past-life recall along with other psychological procedures.

In general English terminology, the suffix "-ology" in a word usually means the general knowledge or usage of, or the general science of, the subject designated by the prefix. "-Ology" comes from the Greek word *logos*, meaning word, plural *logoi.* Hence we have Geology, the general science of Geos, planet earth; Psychology, the general science of the psyche, the person; etc.

The suffix "–ography" in general changes the meaning to the graphing, contouring, mapping of whatever is designated by the prefix. Hence Geology, the general knowledge of earth – and Geography, the graphing, contouring, mapping of it. Psychology, the general science of the psyche – and Psychography, the mapping of the forces within the person.

So Psychography is much more than pastlife recall. It recognizes five general causative areas of forces within the personality – heredity; conditioning (environment, etc.); karma (pastlife influences); purpose (the pull toward a better future, which emerges as inherent in humanity); and the individual's own decisions, which are the decisive edge throughout. The push from the past (# 3 above) and the purposeful pull of the future (# 4) are both spiritual, meaning non-material, forces. Psychography recognizes that all the above are influences at work upon us, but its particular contribution at this time – the new step it represents – is concentrated on the influence of past lives upon the present life (personality, life-framework, relationships, problems, decisions).

The forces from pastlives are carried over in what is called the subconscious mind – a large and composite area of the human personality in which, among other things, past events which have an unresolved emotional impact are stored or "repressed." Psychographical counselling is a form of re-experiencing therapy, that most-used form of psychological counselling. An event with which the then person did not adequately cope, leaves an emotional residue, still with force in it. In pastlife recall that former experience is brought from the subconscious, where it may have lain for hundreds even several thousand years, into the present consciousness, in which the present person (1) is more able to cope with it, and (2) has the help of a trusted, skilled counsellor. Thus inner forces which had been "constellated" – arranged – in such a way that the person was able to live with the unresolved experience will now be re-arranged ("re-constellated"), which accounts for the cleansing and freeing usually experienced. Unfinished business is now finished, and the feeling is good. It also means that there is quite a shuffling of forces within the subconscious, which at times is tiring – not always, but at times. A skilled psychographist watches his client and may advise a recess of several weeks before another pastlife recall session. Along with the actual recall must be integration into the present life of what is discovered – new understandings, release from fear and guilt, forgiveness of wrongs perhaps a thousand years held, growth as a person and as a soul.

The seed for the research and development of APA was planted in 1952 with the founding of the Religious Research Foundation by Dr. Franklin Loehr. Past-life Recall was developed simultaneously with the Loehr-Daniels Life Reading program.* These two methods of examining past lives worked together for many years to corroborate and balance each other. Finally the time came when the two were given separate emphasis, with the Life Reading program becoming the major project of the two. Now with the forming of APA, new emphasis has been placed on past-life recall.

The following, a 1952 case taken from Dr. Loehr's files,

---

* The Loehr-Daniels Life Readings, from their higher vantage point, add these additional spiritual factors: (1) The placement and purpose(s) of your present life in your soul's progression. (2) Your spirit guides and teachers, your "Council." (3) The pull of the future upon your present life, the ongoing purposes of God for you. See Chapter VI, following.

shows love not only conquering death, but also blending the physical and the astral planes of our human expression:

> She was a young woman – hardly more than a grown girl – and she was very much beloved by the son of a Raj, meaning ruler of a small area or province in India. The two were happily planning marriage.
>
> But one day as she was being borne by her bearers along a rather steep hillside, one of the bearers slipped and she was thrown out of the carriage, fell down the hillside, and was crippled. The prince could not then have her as his wife. They both recognized and accepted this, although it was a blow to each of them. They were young, and later the prince married another, and in time became himself the ruler, the Raj, of that little province. The girl never married, and she did not live a long time thereafter, although it was some years before she did make her transition.
>
> But the two of them often met at night in their projected states. This was not as a clandestine earth affair carried on by the two on the physical plane. They had accepted what had happened with the stoicism more prevalent in that country and in that age when pain was simply to be endured. Also their religious teachings which were in the pre-Buddhist early Hindu strain, had taught them a certain acceptance of the events of life. So although there was a very real sorrow that their very real love could not be consummated in marriage and in a life together, they accepted it. This is part of the 'anaesthetization' in that instance which allowed them to bear the situation more easily and positively.
>
> But at night in their astral projections during sleep, they often came together, particularly for a period of some years. . . . They were astrally conscious of it, but the earth consciousness would not have to be there. The Indian prince and girl were not aware in their earth consciousness of their astral meetings, but there was a certain surcease that came to both which was of the nature of

having married, of having been joined and united and made one in love.

Agatha Richards, a counsellor who took Psychography training with our Religious Research School of Spiritual Studies, has shared with me the transcript of a past-life recall of one of her clients as an Eskimo woman. It is a firsthand insight into Eskima family life, which turns out to have so many points of similarity with human life elsewhere that we can relate warmly with this lovely recall. (P is for psychographist, in this case, Agatha Richards, C is for client.)

P. Let's go now to your destination.

C. We are on a floe at the edge of open water. My husband is trying to harpoon with a long rope. I'm not too confident that we are safe. I have never been fishing before.

He finds a fish! It is a young seal or sea lion. It means lots of food and a nice bit of fur. We give thanks to the Great Father for the seal and apologize to the seal for taking his life, reminding him of how he takes the life of fish when he is hungry. We eat first the fat. It's very tasty not cooked. I carefully cut the fat off, then scrape the rest off and chew for the last residue. He gives the intestines and lungs, etc., to the dogs. The baby chews a little fat. I cut the meat into strips before it freezes and pack it in moss and put it on the sled. I was so busy I forgot to worry.

I hear voices coming over the water. A canoe comes in and they hail my husband. They are not from our village. They laugh and say, 'We are mighty hunters with plenty to spare.' They give us the hindquarter of a bear. Only mighty hunters give such an amount of food, especially to strangers.

P. Do you take this meat back to the village?

C. First we must observe the courtesies. We brag on them. We ask blessings for them from the Great Father. Then the baby cries and I take her out and they hold her and play and laugh. All of us do. The baby is wrapped in furs with moss around her bottom.

The leader of the men is named Norshol. They get back in their canoe and leave. As soon as they are out of sight we go back to the village. We could not go until then.

On the way back I sing a song to my husband about how he is a good hunter and a good man. And this is why the Great Father sent him the little seal and the strangers who were mighty hunters and gave us food. My husband's name is Lamine. I praise him much and make him feel good. Then he sings to me that it was not just his goodness but also the goodness of 'the one who walks beside me.' (This is what he calls her, his wife. No other name for her.)

P. Let us go back to the village, and let me know if anything else happens on the way.

C. As we get to the village the dogs announce us. The children come running. The women walk toward us. The men stand and watch us. There are only old men because the young men are out hunting. The women watch our faces and say, 'You return. You must have food.' We tell them that we do, and everyone is happy.

We stop in the center of the village. To the old men my husband says, 'Would you do me the favor of accepting this food? Just as you nourished me when I was young, I am honored now to nourish you.' To the women he says, 'Just as your men would share their hunt with me, I am honored now to share with you.' They accept the food and sing a song of the mighty hunter, then leave to prepare it. To the children my husband says, 'When all have eaten I will tell the story of the hunt and the kind strangers.' The children race off happily because they have news now for the others.

P. How nice this is! You have respect for all ages and make sure that each one feels good. Is everyone like this?

C. How else could we live so closely if we were unkind? When one is continually unkind he is asked to leave. This doesn't happen too often because we need each other to survive.

P. At the beginning you said you were changing camp.

C. That's what I thought at first because when you go on a hunt you take so much with you. You need it for survival. We were apparently just on a hunt.

P. I noticed the other women did not go with their husbands on the hunt. Is it unusual to go?

C. Women don't usually go. When the wife is young sometimes she will go. This was my first time to go. When there is food in the village the women need to stay. (The psychographist moves her up to a later time in that life.)

I am older but not old. It is summertime and we are in tents made of skin. I am very busy. We move inland for summer and put up tents. The women are hunting berries and birds' eggs.

P. In what kind of home do you live in the winter?

C. In the winter we cut blocks of frozen earth – not snow or ice. There are roots of small plants in it. These blocks are piled up one on the other. There are poles in the ground at the corners – not poles across – and blocks of ice and earth on top. We can have very small fires. We are burning oil. There is a vessel with a wick in it for light. We do not cook inside, and I believe the fires are mostly for light, perhaps a little for heat, but not cooking. We cook outside. We enter our home on hands and knees. But this does not look at all like the usual pictures of igloos. (Later, she said she had tried to make it look like what she thought it should, but just could not.) We use the same poles for summer and for winter. Part of a man's preparation for marriage is to gather the poles. He must go a long way to do this, but they are essential for us. I think it is ash wood. It is very strong wood.

P. We will go back to summertime. Thank you for

that good description of your home. Now we are back in summer and I'll bet you like that quite a bit better.

C. No! There are all kinds of insects: mosquitoes, flies. We burn much oil to try to keep them away. The hunting of the big animals is not good in the summer. This is the time when the woman is very important because she provides much of the food. This is the play time for the men. They are running, jumping, wrestling.

P. Do the women play in the winter?

C. They work some, but not as much as in summer. I see the women gathering to dance. We visit together a lot, especially when the men go hunting. Our dance is a dance of protection for the men. We sing that the Great Father will protect them, how they will be able to out-think the bear and outswim the walrus, etc.

P. You are older now. Do you have any more children?

C. Yes, I have two sons now. My daughter still lives. She is learning to chew the skins and handle the needle. Our sons have small spears and knives that their father teaches them how to use. Gifo and Guno (two in the village) tell them of the Great Father.

P. Let's look now to see if you recognize anyone in the village, particularly among your own family, whom you know this lifetime.

C. Because of courtesy I will look first to the old ones. (She looks but does not see anyone she knows this lifetime. The psychographist now takes the client to some important event in her life, letting her 'inner know-er' decide which one.)

It is winter. There are great lights in the sky. My husband takes me out of the home and says, 'Great Father is lighting your way with all the colors. He is welcoming you because you've been such a wonderful one beside me. You have nurtured our children and many others. Now he calls you home.'

He takes me out of the village but he doesn't leave me. He stays singing to me for awhile. The Great Father has not called him yet but will soon. The call has come for me. It is the custom to leave the one who receives the call. I ask him to go. Cold is now taking my body. He sings one last song reminding me of the day when we went on the hunt and strangers gave us food.

P. How did you know the Great Father was calling you home?

C. I just know. Each of us knows when it is time.

P. Now let us ask your inner knower if she has anything to bring us about why she brought this life to you at this time, and what you have learned from it.

C. (Inner knower:) My soul has always longed for growth into God. This is not the first I have lived with a seeking after knowledge of God. This was a life nourished in a simple culture, kindness one to the other and openness to the spiritual. This is why I seek others. In a sense I am seeking the nourishing society of that life. But just as I lived that life in a nourishing society, I am now to be one of the nourishers.

Another Senior Psychographist has stated: "Integrating the past-life forces into the present life is the major purpose of psychography. Once the negative portions of a difficult life have been brought from the subconscious, where they have been stored perhaps for centuries, into consciousness, where they can be re-lived, reviewed, and handled properly, with the aid of a skilled counselor, it is possible to experience the strengths gained by that past life." He shares these cases with us:

Wrongful deaths can leave a cancerous fear and anger in the soul beingness.

A past personality was attacked, raped and killed in a barn. The first fear to surface in the personality handling this situation was a fear of entering barns. As she grew older, she was frigid. After the past-life recall, the client was more receptive to sexual counseling, while the fear of barns disappeared almost immediately.

*   *   *   *   *

Another young woman had very sensitive skin, and recalled a lifetime as a young woman who ran into a burning church to rescue her children. She rescued the children, but her long dress caught fire and enveloped her in flames. Shortly after the pastlife recall, the skin sensitivity began to subside.

*   *   *   *   *

A gentleman recalled a pastlife as a Roman gladiator, slave to a powerful Roman senator. He was first trained as a soldier and later became a gladiator. He lived a relatively long life. Since the games were rigged, the gladiator's survival or death depended on the power of his owner. The gladiator was well taken care of, provided with women, excellent food and wine, but the killing began to penetrate his life until he imagined blood streaming from his hands. Finally the gladiator arranged his own death. Defying the plans of his owner, he was killed by a friend and fellow gladiator in the arena. The after-death experience was very short. The gladiator personality saw his hands form streams of blood, his arms, finally his legs. Then, at last, the entire personality melted into a pool of blood. The client recalling that past life reported he could actually taste and smell blood for several days. After the immediate impact of that life integrated into his thinking, the strengths of the personality could be felt. The gladiator had been a very strong man, in many ways a good man. The client reported he knew how football players felt when they entered the playing field – the cheering crowds and the sensation of the adrenalin running. It added excitement to the game.

*   *   *   *   *

As spiritual forces develop, the soul will dedicate

several lives toward a spiritual commitment. The first life to surface for a client may be a former spiritual life.

One such client was a young student of psychology who wanted to incorporate a more spiritual aspect to her studies.

The first recall she had was as a nun in France. As she described the daily prayers she experienced again a glowing feeling, although there were certain spiritual practices and dogmas that bothered the nun. The present study of psychology addressed the lacks in that life, and explained why she was seeking a spiritual input in her studies now. This knowledge helped her to add another component to her life and her work.

* * * * *

Another person relived a life as an Indian man who was taught to respect all living things. As a young boy playing with his bow and arrow, he shot a turtle for no reason. His bow and arrows were taken from him until he understood that life was not taken needlessly. The Indian man lived to be quite old, and developed a feeling of oneness with nature.

By recalling this pastlife as an Indian, the client experienced the spiritual seeking he had reached for in this life, the feeling of oneness with nature.

* * * * *

By developing psychography and the Religious Research Life Readings simultaneously, patterns of soul evolvement have emerged. Some of these patterns are rather obvious once we think about them. For instance, getting the opposite view of a situation.

One man presently living in Tennessee, couldn't believe he was a 'damned Yankee' who fought against the South in the Civil War. The recall was strained at times, since the client had difficulty admitting he actually lived in New York instead of somewhere in the South, and that the President was Lincoln. The recall became easier once he accepted the idea he actually fought for the North. We explored the issues, the position of the North. Once he saw it was to keep the states united into one nation, he was willing to fight for that principle — and die for it — which he did.

*   *   *   *   *

As the client progresses, the after-death experience can be explored beyond the first realization that the body is dead. The next realization is usually the joyful reuniting with loved ones. Sometimes a very special loved one is waiting, as in this case a client who did not marry in this life, but searched for that special love all her life.

In the immediate prior life she had that special love, living as a housewife with two children and a devoted husband. The husband died when he was about fifty years old, a young man even for that time. Within six months the wife died, too.

Since that 1800s wife person had been healthy, I asked why she was dying. 'Heartbreak,' she replied, 'I don't want to keep living without my husband.' The re-union of the husband and wife on the Other Side was so joyful that tears ran down the client's cheeks, and for a moment she couldn't talk. They progressed in the astral plane together, experiencing its wonders along with the joy of being together.

*   *   *   *   *

Until the excarnate personality rejoins the soul, it is necessary to work with the client for some time before he/she is ready to explore the higher realms of the pastlife personality, and experience the wonder of unit-ing the excarnate person with the soul. It is amazing to fcel the expansion of the personality as it integrates itself with the much larger forces and consciousness of the soul. The 'I-Am-ness' of the personality remains intact, yet the sensation of completeness can be felt – a completeness the personality seeks throughout its existence – the returning home.

The Association for Past-Life Research and Therapy (APRT) was organized on the West Coast in 1980 to promote research and education in the field, with four primary purposes in mind: (1) The progressive application of Past-Life Therapy, (2) promotion of research in the field, (3) establishment of clinical standards for training regression therapists, and (4) provision of a communication network for exchange of information and experience. A major part of their objective in establishing clinical standards, is the beginning work on a text book setting up professional guidelines for regression therapy. Another APRT goal is to educate the membership, and the public, on the various criteria that may be applied in choosing a past-life practitioner. The APRT further states that another objective is to promote a program of education to integrate the dynamics of Past-Life Therapy with psychosomatic medicine, integrative therapeutic approaches, and the traditional forms of healing and psychotherapy.

The following are two cases taken from APRT's rapidly growing body of research material:

This woman is 48, a mother of four grown sons, and late in life had a daughter. Her marriage is happier than most, and she and her husband engage in many activities together. She is an excellent typist and worked as a secretary for many years. Recently she took part-time employment as a secretary, but before long her hands began to give her trouble, and she would make errors in her typing. Her fingers felt numb. She wondered if it could be arthritis and was considerably distressed by this. The therapist suggested doing a regression to see if the symptoms could be relieved.

The client was a good subject, and found herself the captain of a ship in a severe storm. He was very much disliked by the crew. He expressed a feeling of heaviness in his arms and hands, like a great weight pulling down on him, but insisted he was not in pain. After some prodding he explained that the wind had blown out one of the masts, which had fallen across his body, pinning him down and crushing the abdominal area. This apparently caused a paralysis, and so there was no pain.

The crew did not know what to do with him, and did not know any way to help. So they tied weights onto his hands and threw him overboard. The person connected the experience of being tied down and thrown overboard in that life to being 'tied down' to raising an unexpected small child at her age in this life, with the resentment and anger of that past-life sea captain at being incapacitated, weighted and thrown overboard, and drowned. The counselor spent enough time on this experience to explore all the parallels, and how she could best handle them. Her hands immediately released the pain and numbness. Six months later she is still completely free of any discomfort, and no longer makes errors in typing.

*   *   *   *   *

Case: Female, late 40s, divorced, four children — three grown sons, one daughter in college. Housewife most of her life, then went into real estate. Her presenting problem was pain in her legs, particularly in the knees; at times she was in considerable pain when she walked.

In regression she saw the details of her life in which she was a military officer. He had knowledge that was valuable to the enemy, and was captured and tortured. When he did not give the enemy the information they wanted, they pulled his legs apart, literally, at the knees, threw him into a ditch and left him to die. This insight completely eliminated the pain in the present personality's knees.

Hazel Denning, Ph.D., specializes in humanistic and transpersonal psychology, and is founder and executive director of Parapsychology Association of Riverside, California, Inc. She is an early president of APRT. Denning has been a researcher in past-life regression for over 30 years. It would be difficult indeed for anyone to improve upon her excellent summation of this very important work:

Despite the score of years and more that past-life therapy has been practiced, it is still one of the latest modalities on the therapy scene. One reason for its slow acceptance is its connection with reincarnation. While the belief in reincarnation is not essential to the success of regression therapy, the evidence for its validity continues to mount.

Few Past-Life Therapists would deny the evidence emerging from the case histories for a Universal System of Values, which, when violated, creates varying degrees of havoc in the lives of individuals.

Nothing clients hear from us, or read in books, can transform their lives as dramatically as an exploration in the altered state of their own destiny and purpose. The answers are all there. Our responsibility is to develop the skills to ask the right questions.

We are privileged to be living in an exciting era, an era of dramatic change in the entire spectrum of all cultures. A New Age is being born both in technology and in man's understanding of himself. In the past, only a gifted few were able to contact their own spiritual reality. Today, I believe we can say that even as science has leaped into the electronic age, regression therapy has immeasurably reduced the time it takes human beings to discover who they really are. Let us always keep in mind that we are individually a spark of the Divine Creative

Intelligence, and cooperatively we generate great power for good.

The list of books published on Past-Life Recall is growing, and articles are increasingly appearing in numerous periodicals. Among the authors and leaders in this relatively new field of past-life therapy is Dr. Helen Wambach. She has been a practicing clinical psychologist since 1958 and her work with emotionally disturbed children has made psychological history. Dr. Wambach authored two best-selling books, *Reliving Past Lives* and *Life Before Life.* In both publications she draws upon material from her many years of practice. She has been instrumental in introducing new concepts and therapeutic approaches to illuminate new horizons in past-life therapy.

Wambach describes her own first spontaneous experience in reliving a past life:

> I went to a memorial and felt that I had been in that place before. I picked up a book from the bookshelf and found myself riding across a stubble field on a mule with this book propped on the saddle. For the next three years I regressed to that lifetime, not looking any further since I knew who the memorial was for. I know there were records regarding this John Wolman, that he was well-known among the Quakers. Quakers keep excellent records. So of all the people who had a pastlife that could be checked out in detail, it turned out to be me.
>
> John Wolman wrote a journal of his experiences, and there were several biographies of him known only to the Quakers. These were available after 210 years.
>
> After three years of regressing to that lifetime, and making notes, I checked it out with the Quaker records, finding everything checked out.
>
> I read a little Quaker book by a woman who had known John Wolman, and she said at the age of seven he had first gone into trance. The Quakers believe in going

into the trance state. John Wolman's trance symbol was a tree. When I read that, I felt a sense of awe because the very first time I went into a regression as John Wolman I saw a tree. At the time I had no idea what it meant, so there was this kind of evidence I couldn't disprove. To me, it was a shocker!

This was followed by a second shocker: The details of Wolman's death were clear to me after three years of regression, but he had died in England, and I had to go there for verification. I checked this out, when I got there, with the Brighton Quakers, but checking it out wasn't shocking. What was shocking was that before leaving for England I drove my family crazy saying, 'I'm going to stop wearing these moccasins. I have to get proper-looking shoes.' So I bought black pumps with heels, and I remember my daughter saying, 'Mom, you're crazy! Just wear what you always wear.'

When my agent and I arrived at the Quaker library in England, we found two books on Wolman. We both read the first paragraph of one and stared at each other. When John Wolman arrived in England he wanted to address a Quaker meeting, but they wouldn't let him speak because of his crude American leather shoes – moccasins!

Dr. Edith Fiore completed her doctorate in psychology at the University of Miami, and has been a clinical psychologist since the early 1970s, first in Miami and now in California. The early years of her practice were devoted only to the use of classical psychoanalysis, being convinced of the value of bringing subconscious material to the conscious level where it can be dealt with. She found classical psychoanalysis a helpful method, but an extremely slow and expensive one.

On the spur of the moment one weekend Fiore decided to attend a seminar on the techniques of hypnosis, and this introduction to hypnosis started her on a whole new approach to the treatment of emotional problems. She found

that by the use of hypnosis, what had formerly taken years
to help was often cleared up in a matter of months or weeks.
But in those early years of her work with hypnotic therapy,
she only regressed patients back through this lifetime – and
gradually further back, discovering the emotional problems
arising from the nine months in the womb.

Up to that time she was totally uninterested in the idea of
reincarnation. Then, quite unexpectedly she regressed a
patient to a former lifetime. This radically changed her professional life and her personal beliefs. She reports this first
case:

> He came to me because of crippling sexual inhibi-
> tions. When I asked him, while under hypnosis, to go
> back to the origin of this problem, he said, 'Two or
> three lifetimes ago, I was a Catholic priest.' We traced
> through this 17th century lifetime, looking at his sexual
> attitudes as an Italian priest, and found the source of
> his present sexual difficulties.
> I was aware the patient believed in reincarnation.
> Therefore, I felt his vivid description of his past life,
> colored by a great deal of emotionality, was a fantasy.
> However, the next time I saw him, he told me he was
> not only free of his sexual problems, but felt better about
> himself in general. I then began to take note of this new
> therapeutic tool.

Following through from this first experience, Fiore became
convinced that many problems of her patients had their
roots earlier than conception, in former lives, and that
previous lifetimes have a profound impact on the current
life in myriad ways. In a recent interview with Hazel Denning
of APRT, Fiore stated her work now is 100 percent past-
life therapy because that is where the answers can be found.
Further, she states, this new therapeutic method is changing
the public's belief in reincarnation, life after death, and immortality, with definite past-life evidence that many present-

day problems have their beginnings in previous lives.

Fiore has authored *You Have Been Here Before.* In it she shares many of the human dramas which have unfolded in her office during her years of helping patients face once again the traumas of a previous life. She then watched with fascination their growth and new freedom, developing as a result.

The following is a sampling from this remarkable book:

> The patient worked as a social director on a cruise ship. She was very eager to solve two problems she'd had for many years. The first was her dangerously strong impulse to jump overboard, and the second, paradoxically, an irrational fear of getting lost at sea.
>
> Under hypnosis she found herself as a small Norwegian boy, Sven, on his father's boat, being urged to jump as the boat crashed onto the rocks. He disobeyed his father and was drowned.
>
> During this same session she found herself in two other lifetimes, one as a fisherman, the other as a sailor — both lost at sea, both eventually drowning.
>
> When she came out of hypnosis, she exclaimed that she understood both her fascination with the sea and the origin of her fears.
>
> Six weeks later, back from a trip across the Pacific, she was exuberant when she told me she no longer had either of the two problems. She had felt comfortable and free of anxiety during the entire trip.

*   *   *   *   *

> A patient came in with a phobia of snakes. After combing back through her life under hypnosis and finding nothing, I tried a hunch. I asked her if she had an encounter with snakes before she was born.
>
> She saw herself as a fifteen-year-old Aztec girl in

front of a pyramid, watching priests dancing with poison-ous snakes in their mouths. She trembled with emotion and reported the bizarre rites in vivid detail. Returned to the present, but still deeply hypnotized, she puzzled about what she had just experienced. She asked who she had been. She was quite distressed and vehemently stated, 'I don't believe all that stuff!'

Here was a person who definitely rejected reincarna-tion, but who had just relived a lifetime that took place four hundred years ago.

*   *   *   *   *

It was found that almost all patients with chronic weight excess have had a lifetime in which they either starved to death or suffered food deprivation for long periods.

One woman patient who had a persistent fluid re-tention problem found herself, several lifetimes ago, dying from dehydration and starvation, as well as small-pox.

*   *   *   *   *

Craving for particular foods has also been traced back to past lives.

One patient referred to me by her physician had severe hypertension and was approximately a hundred pounds overweight. Time after time — against her will — she devoured bags of potato chips and other salty junk food. This compulsion played havoc with her futile at-tempts to lose weight and to lower her dangerously high blood pressure.

During one of her hypnotic regressions she went back to a lifetime as a young American Indian boy who was desperately hungry because his tribe no longer had the salt to cure their dwindling game supply.

Since that regression, she has not had the slightest

compulsion to eat salty foods and is losing weight at a healthy rate.

* * * * *

Many of my patients have discovered that the cause of their phobias, fears and even aversions were rooted in some traumatic event of a previous lifetime. Fear of the dark, especially, seems to originate in some terrifying incident that happened in the dark in a former life.

One woman found that the origins of her phobia of staying alone at night — and her conviction that she would be murdered if she did so — came from an earlier experience in which exactly that had happened.

Another female was amazed to find her lifelong avoidance of train travel had its beginning when, in her last lifetime, she saw her sister crushed beneath the wheels of a train.

A young woman who couldn't bear to look at anything red (and consequently grew very anxious every Christmas) relived discovering her mother bleeding to death after having been brutally stabbed, in a former life.

Insomnia and other sleep disorders also stemmed, in many cases, from horrifying things that happened during sleep in past lives.

One teenage boy who could only sleep if alone and in total silence traced his problem back to being bayoneted to death by a Japanese soldier while asleep on the sand of a Pacific Island during World War II.

Dr. Denys Kelsey, a British analytically-oriented psychiatrist, with the extrasensory abilities of his wife, Joan Grant, used past-life regression in treating patients back in the early 1950s. At that time, they were among the early pioneers in this fresh, new approach to psychology and medicine.

Joan Grant developed a remarkable ability early in life enabling her to recall previous lives in fine detail. She termed

this "far memory." Many of her books published as histori-
cal novels, and praised for their extraordinary vividness and
detail, were in fact the author's memories of former epochs.
Some of her better-known publications are *Eyes Of Horus,
Lord Of The Horizon, Scarlet Feather, Life as Carola*, and
Return To Elysium.

In their joint book *Many Lifetimes*, Kelsey states he found
empirical evidence, when recalling his first past life, in
the intensity of the experience. Prior to that time he had
been skeptical of his ability to recall anything. This is that
first regression:

> The transition of a skepitcal psychiatrist lying on
> his own couch to a man racing a chariot was instantane-
> ous. On my left there was a barrier surrounding an island
> of spectators in the center of the arena. On my right, a
> chariot was overtaking me. I knew I should give way as
> the chariot was overtaking me. I knew I should give way
> to it, but instead I forced my pair into the narrowing
> gap. There was a shuddering impact as our wheels inter-
> locked. I was catapulted forward and felt a wheel run
> over my chest. As the chariot overturned, it swung the
> horses against the barrier. The last thing I remembered
> was their screaming. I realized, through a desire to show-
> off, I had caused the destruction of a pair of beloved
> horses, and this brought a degree of shame which in my
> current life I had never experienced. That the event had
> occurred two thousand years ago was entirely irrelevent.
> It was I who had done it, and it was happening now.
>
> Some months later, the thread of my debt to horses
> reappeared in a life centered around horses. I bred them
> and schooled them, and sometimes gave one to a trusted
> friend, but I never sold any.

Morris Netherton, Ph.D., whose work is presented in the
paperback *Past Lives Therapy* (1978), seems to specialize in
some of the more violent and horrendous personality prob-

blems — suicidal tendencies, wracking irrational fears of many sorts, sexual compulsions and frigidities, vicious wishes to wreck vengeance upon others, etc. It is fine that a strong man such as Dr. Netherton draws these cases, and his success with them of course has caused more of such cases to come to him for help. Not unexpectedly, his clients find the more traumatic experiences in their pastlife recalls, such as earthquake death, death in a jousting tryout, a slaveship death in a hotbox, murder when caught in illicit sex, poisoning, being burned alive, incest, extreme female circumcision, necrophilia (an erotic attraction to corpses), gross sadism in sex, being thrown from a cliff, and a 1940 death in an early electric chair, etc. One example:

> A woman of twenty-four came, on the eve of marriage, with many fears, and the discovery of incipient uterine cancer. Dr. Netherton, who views cancer as often a result of emotional stresses — usually with past-life origin and/or reinforcement — took her through several recalls which had built that relationship of fear and the womb.
>
> In one of these she was a pregnant young pioneer woman in Montana. Her husband, returning home in the late afternoon, is set upon by some Indians who strip him to the waist and carve his chest in the familiar herringbone pattern of torture, then released him to run to her. But an arrow thuds into his back, and he falls dead in her arms. Then the young Indian who had killed him rides up and in a skillful, gentle sexual arousal brings her to a shattering climax, then slits her throat and her abdomen in one skillful sweep, and her baby, and she, are dead.

Such cases are not common, but of course such cruelities have happened and have made their deep impressions of fear, physical afflictions and ailments, guilt and insufficiency, to be worked out in subsequent incarnations. Dr. Netherton, who correctly avows that he is no researcher in reincarnation, simply knows these past-life recalls work. He has found that finding the cause opens the way to the cure of many of his clients' troubles.

Dick Sutphen is an author, hypnotist, seminar trainer, and skilled psychic researcher. His hypnosis-regression work started in 1972, and he set about almost at once to develop a technique whereby he could hypnotically regress a whole roomful of people at one time.

Here is a case taken from his May 1977 Atlanta, Georgia, seminar:

> Barbara was one of the participants, and she had traveled all the way from Houston, Texas, to attend. I asked her why she had come that far just for a two-day seminar. 'I missed you when you were in Houston, and something or someone up there told me it was really important to experience this. I have several problems. Some you can see, and some you can't.'
>
> She was obviously referring to her excessive weight, 225 pounds being carried by an otherwise attractive twenty-nine year-old woman. I'd observed her earlier in the day during the first two group regressions, trying to be comfortable in two chairs, because her weight made lying down on the floor impossible. As a deep-level somnambulistic subject, she practically fell off the chairs the moment I began the induction.
>
> As part of the demonstration session, I do some individual regression work so everyone understands how the verbal questions and answers work. On this particular night I asked Barbara if she'd like to participate. She agreed, along with eleven others. I gave them all the following instructions:
>
> 'I want you to think about something in your life that you want changed. In a moment I'm going to hypno-tize you, and when I touch each of you on the hand I'll be talking directly to you and only you. I will count

backwards from three to one; and on the count of one, you are going to move back in time to the cause of your present problem. You will see and relive this situation before your own inner eyes, and thus you will understand and begin to release it.'

Group hypnosis was now completed, and I began to move down the line, touching each subject on the hand. When I came to Barbara, she cried out screaming and began to shake. Her voice was that of a young girl, 'Oh, no, no, please! Please! Why are you doing this to us?' Her reaction was too extreme to allow her to continue under the present circumstances. I brought her out of the hypnotic sleep.

After all the subjects had been awakened, I asked Barbara if she'd like to explore in more detail the prior life she'd touched on. This time, I told her, it would be on a one-to-one basis so that I could devote all my time to her. Once again she anxiously agreed.

The hypnotic trance was induced again, and she was instructed to return to the same lifetime, but a month earlier. She was soon speaking in the voice of a twelve-year-old French girl describing her luxurious home and life in eighteenth-century France at the time of the Revolution.

When we moved forward in time, she experienced the arrival of soldiers to take her family to prison. Numerous humiliations followed, and she was eventually killed by the revolutionaries.

From her Higher-Self, when asked how this French life related to today, Barbara cried, 'Pretty people get hurt! I was so pretty and they killed me. The only way to be safe is to remain ugly to the world. Then you are safe, then you will be safe!'

Sutphen authored two books exploring cause and effect in man-woman relationships, *Past Lives, Future Loves,* and *You Were Born Again to be Together.* Both books abound in true love stories of lovers reunited across the barriers of time and locale. One example:

Jonathan Wells slid his gold pan into the creek bed in search of placer deposits. He spun away when he heard the unmistakable sound of a rattlesnake in the bush beside him. The snake struck, sinking its fangs into his wrist. Jonathan reeled backward, grabbed a rock and quickly killed the large diamond-back rattler. He then sat down and cut open the wound and began to extract the poison.

A short time later a young Yavapai Apache woman found him lying unconscious, his wrist swollen and bleeding from his own incisions. She immediately took the blanket from his bedroll, made him comfortable, and began to treat the wound. Repeatedly during the night she changed the poultice used to draw out the poison, and maintained the fire to keep him warm.

The time was in the 1800s near Wickenburg, Arizona. It was summer and the hills were filled with prospectors and mine workers.

Jonathan recovered, and the Indian woman remained with him. Together, for several years, they worked the rivers and creeks of central Arizona, making a living but not much more. A daughter was born, and they settled down in the desert foothills in an adobe house they built. They had a small herd of cows.

Then in late summer, seven years after they first met, they were panning in a creek near their home. A flash flood from the mountains to the north rose as a wall of water, and almost instantly engulfed them. Jonathan was able to swim to the high ground, but he never saw his wife again. Not until 1971, nearly one hundred years later, when they met at a party in Los Angeles, California. They fell in love at first sight and were soon married.

*   *   *   *   *

As Dr. John has stated:

> "We who use mediums have been somewhat the
> trail-blazers. Now with past-life recall, roads are being
> built along the trails we blazed. Let us pay tribute to
> them (the psychics) as pioneers, even as we are glad
> that the study of death now comes into a more careful
> understanding and enlargement." (A8037:20)

Pioneers all, and we honor them, those early ones in the then
scientifically unpopular but now authenticated and growing
fields of: Psychic Communication with the Dead; Dream
Research; Out-of-Body Experiences (OOBE); Near-Death
Experiences (NDE); Reincarnation; Life Readings. They
built step-by-step this firm foundation of scientific facts
upon which we are privileged to stand, and from which new
progress is being made almost daily. And now with Past-
Life Recall becoming accepted and used at an accelerating
rate, we have a new, clearer, and a very personal understanding of death and life after death.

We see again there is no longer any reason, any excuse, for
ignorance and fear of death.

CHAPTER SIX

THE DEATH EXPERIENCE FROM A HIGHER
PERSPECTIVE

The vague, limited, frequently incomprehensible teachings of the many churches about death and the after-death experience are no longer acceptable to many, as new knowledge of death and the life after death is pouring out from many sources. As with all religion in this transition day – before religion becomes a seeking, vital science on its own – the imagery conjured up by the ancient teachings are either repellent or inconsequential to our living today. The attitudes of many who turn from the churches are aptly summed up in the saying, "If hell offends – heaven bores." As mankind enters the new age, traditional Christianity must now grow into its own new age of teaching, if it is to keep up with those whom it would serve.

Death is a common denominator for us all. Everything that has ever lived either is dead or will die. In this keen awareness of our mortality we demand true knowledge of what death itself is like and of what comes after death. We want facts, and we want the facts within the larger framework of God's purposes, God's value–system of life.

In chapter five we looked at documented, substantial facts from the scientific study of death going on increasingly today. These facts, this knowledge, is fast becoming acceptable to the public in general. These facts are based on true scientific research, critical intelligence, and a wholehearted respect for the rules of evidence. But now we press on in this field which religion has not yet accepted, and ask what these newly ascertained facts about death really mean to us. Scientific facts of themselves are never enough for human living – the facts must be woven into the fabric of everyday life, the way we see and understand life and live it.

Sir Oliver Lodge, outstanding English physicist of the early twentieth century, caught this vision in his statement, "What does 'proof' mean? Proof means destroying the isolation of an observed fact – the bringing it into its place in the system of knowledge." Knowledge of scientific facts must be balanced with a readiness to grasp a wide range of converging evidence. It must be balanced with God's values, the purposes of the Creator which lie behind the established facts of His creation. Dr. John, chief guide of Religious Research, brings this out:

> The *facts* ascertained by science must also be balanced by an understanding of the *purposes* of the Creator. . . . The tremendous advance in the understanding of truth by science, which truly is 'the spirit of truth which will lead you into all truth' and is sent by the Master and by God, is only the preliminary to the even greater changes in understanding and in wisdom as man gets more understanding, and then gets more wisdom. (A3620:2, 3)

Science has searched for answers, found many, but has not been able to touch the holy purpose of human life. To learn the values of God behind the facts of science was the next logical step in our development.

Since 1952 a man and his organization have been the liaison in filling that missing link, testing and establishing the spiritual within a scientific framework, The man is Dr. Franklin

Loehr. The organization is the Religious Research Foundation of America, Inc. The idea: If science can discover the facts of the material world, why not use the same scientific research and evaluating system to discover the facts of the spiritual realm.

A major project was undertaken by Religious Research to actively research the soul, which is temporarily in a body during incarnation. In the soul lies our immortality, our survival after death. This has become a major Religious Research project. Reincarnation, researched by both past-life recall and the Loehr-Daniels Life Readings of Religious Research, is the story of the soul — its nature, its experiences, its growth and its setbacks, its progression or its ultimate failure and recyclement.

Dr. Loehr has taken hundreds of people into thousands of past-life recalls, helping them to discover the who, what, and why of their present incarnational personality, relationships, and experiences. Gradually the work grew into organized psychography, as brought out in chapter five.

The second part of this research of the soul, supplementing and independently corroborating the first, is an ever-growing body of advanced spiritual teachings from the 5,500-plus Loehr-Daniels Life Readings and Teaching Readings given to date for clients world-wide, with another approximately one hundred fifty given each year.

The guiding wisdom behind them is the spirit guide who reads the akashic records, called in the Bible "God's Book of Judgment." He calls himself Dr. John Christopher Daniels, but this meaningful name has been shortened to simply Dr. John, which fits his loving, compassionate nature. His channel, Dr. Loehr, is put into deep trance for the readings. It is Dr. John who reads the akashic records and reports his findings through his channel.

What are Dr. John's qualifications? Let him speak for himself:

> As an individual soul I come from the realm of the Light Bearers, which identifies me as one committed to the message and service of the Christed soul known best for His incarnate expression as Jesus of Nazareth.
>
> My unearthy existence has come about by the merging of many personalities of my soul with my total soul beingness, to produce an individualized expression we call a solity. As a solity I enter into and out of many cosmic realms. In the astral realm I have a personality name by which I am identified, Dr. John Christopher Daniels. This is not a name representative of a past earthlife experience, but rather a requested future earthlife experience.

Dr. John expects the future life he speaks of to be in England in the twenty-first century as a medical doctor. He has requested this assignment and feels it will be granted.

> I have not incarnated since the twenty-fourth century B.C. The earth-time interval since then has been used in learning to read the akashic records in preparation for the life readings being brought to earth consciousness in this century, and in other work on the Other Side — for even the life readings are essentially part of a larger project.
>
> There are different ways to read the akashic records. They can be viewed from many realms, including the earth realm as they are reflected there. I found the particular realm from which I felt I had the best overall view and made that my celestial monastery. I go out from my monastery to render other services as called upon by my teammates, returning to it in preparation for that which I am called upon to give in a life reading.
>
> The verification of whether my choice for a celestial monastery was wise and my training thorough, lies in

the readings themselves, and in what happens in the earthlives of those who have secured these readings. (AB548:21,22)

What was the reason for this extensive training? As Dr. John comments, the twentieth century – this scientific century – would be ready for a new spiritual knowledge breaking through to earth, balancing and working with the physical-world scientific discoveries. As these life readings are presented on an individual approach (each reading is for a specific person), Dr. John is able to bring out the purpose of that person's present life, and as it fits within the framework of the reading, additional life-centered spiritual knowledge. In this way a new philosophy has been built, slowly, over these more than thirty-five years:

> While the reading of the akashic records is geared to be of practical helpfulness to each person, there is another important reason for these life readings. Through them our team has been building in earth consciousness, a particular philosphy or theology which we feel is a basic contribution to the efforts of all cosmic teams to bring the earth realm into its true stature as a cosmic school of learning.
>
> As the teachings from the readings given to date are disseminated, it will be recognized, we believe, that they touch upon all major areas of earthliving presenting problems to earthbeings. From these teachings we believe many individuals in the framework of personal study and prayer can find their particular need met by what has been brought through. Of course, there are many other earth frameworks of cosmic thought providing needed answers, for God does not put all His eggs in one basket. (ibid, p. 22, 23)

What we are shown in the akashic records are the lifetimes important for the contributions they make to the present life. We are shown the records of the lifetimes that hook up with the present lifetime. (AB930:5)

It was decided that the 4300 years of study Dr. John put into learning to read the akashic records demanded as clear a channel as possible from his high spirit realm to the earth realm. Therefore Dr. John's soulmate incarnated to act as channel. That soulmate is Dr. Franklin Loehr, who provides the necessary link as well as the firm earth base for Religious Research. In fact, this project did not begin in 1952 with the organization and founding of Religious Research, but has been a soul project from the beginning – Dr. John in his celestial monastery taking the "high road," and Dr. Loehr taking the "low road" through many incarnations, many earthlives.

To complete the organization, teams were formed on both sides of the veil. We call them the "upstairs team" and the "downstairs team." During a teaching session with Dr. John a member of our group asked why she felt an almost instant friendship with a certain other, wondering if their souls had had a past life or lives together. Dr. John said no, but that a group of approximately two hundred souls had been selected and gathered to view and study the Religious Research project prior to incarnating with this spiritual purpose in this century. And in the case of these two people, their souls had been introduced as two who would work with this project. So the downstairs team really had its first introduction upstairs, long before the dawning of the twentieth century.

Upon the foundation of this introduction to Dr. John Christopher Daniels (Dr. John), Dr. Franklin Loehr, and the organization of Religious Research, we take the death experience to a higher perspective. Dr. John brings in the values of God behind the facts of death, bringing us to the larger dimension of God's plan and purpose for that particular soul, and that specific person of the soul, in the framework of many lives.

Each case brings helpfulness to the life reading client, plus new spiritual knowledge for us all, but also each case is a fascinating human interest story in itself. We will bring you a dozen cases – actually, seventeen – because each one has firsthand information on death as seen from this higher perspective. Death, like life, is such an individual thing.

The first teaching we now bring points out that the soul and the excarnate person do not always accept the death of the physical body with calmness. Often it is important to both that the body receive the proper respect and care. Thus the funeral service can be helpful not only for the loved ones left behind in accepting the death, but many times it is helpful to the continuing person, and the soul itself as well.

DAVID

David had a great fear of death. He states, "The thought of my own ultimate death chills me. It is a fear. The thought of my body being 'put in a box' disturbs me very much." This is a case in point where Dr. John brings helpfulness to the client in alleviating his fear, and at the same time brings through an important teaching on the significance of showing respect for the dead body:

> This personality with these particular strengths feeding into it, is not going into oblivion when death comes to the body. The personality continues, and not in a wishy-washy dream-like state, but with vigor and vitality – with the same quality of expression that it has now. Now that's not quite a true statement. Rather we should say: with the quality of expression it has now, expanded. Nothing will be lost from the personality as it is now in its post-life framework upon the death of the body. True, the body dies. The body returns to dust. It is a physical substance. It is not reused. The body does not resurrect, it does not come together again – it disintegrates.
> This is a difficult thing for a strong personality, and

often for a strong soul, to accept. There is a beingness of the physical which to some degree wins the allegiance and support of the personality and of the soul. So it can be quite difficult for the soul and the personality to simply slough off that degree of allegiance it has to the physical beingness. This is one reason why, upon the death of the body, the body is not simply discarded. It is treated with respect, it is handled with a sense of the fitness of things. It is put into a resting place. On the whole it has a certain amount of beauty, of good-lookingness, to it when it is prepared for burial. It isn't simply chucked in a sack somewhere.

Now there is reason, a very definite reason, for this. It is not simply an earth custom that has grown up over the centuries. It is for the sake of the continuing personality, and that portion of the soul which was connected with that physical body. Although they continue in individual expression following the death of the body, it is very difficult for many of them to move on and progress until that degree of allegiance which they gave the physical beingness is honored by proper disposal of the physical body that is no longer usable.

When that is done, then the personality and the soul are ready to proceed in their learning. So funerals often are very important. Oh, they are important from every aspect, but we particularly wanted to bring out this aspect.

We relate this to this present personality because of his concern over this matter of death. . . . It is a legitimate pattern, and that is why we show that this is a legitimate concern. But fear is not legitimate. Fear is due to ignorance. Ignorance can be corrected. There is enough knowledge, actual, factual, knowledge of what goes on following death of the body, so that no earth personality can any longer legitimately fear death. (A3208:5, 6)

ARLENE

Our second teaching on death as seen from Dr. John's perspective deals with cremation. This question was asked in a
public psychic session, which often is given by Dr. John
(through Dr. Loehr, in deep trance) as the concluding session
of a Religious Research conference or seminar. These public
sessions are always fascinating, as Dr. John, for an hour or
two, or even more, fields all manner of questions asked
spontaneously from the floor except personal questions. (He
is not in touch with the akashic records in these sessions.)
Here an amazing variety of information has been recorded
in these readings over the years. This particular question was,
"Would you talk about cremation and its effect on the soul?
I got a message from the Other Side telling me cremation
causes much suffering and is damaging to the soul."

Dr. John: Oh, cremation. This is an individual thing.
If the person, before death, has chosen cremation in his
consciousness, he is ready. The separation of the person
from the body does not always take place completely
at the moment of death. There are some who feel it takes
a period of about three days, and with some perhaps it
does. The fact of cremation, however, is no more appall-
ing than the fact of burial. The person who has inhabited
that body, when he comes to the realization that he no
longer is a tenant of that body, and that that body is
no longer a living organism, can be separated from the
consciousness of what happens to that body and can
accept whatever disposal is made of it.

So there is no one word about cremation, for or
against. If it is chosen, so let it be. If it has not been
chosen but still is used, then the excarnate person, if he
or she continues to be disturbed by it, is in an earthbound situation, and one might say should be disturbed
by it until he shakes loose from the limitations of thinking of himself in earth terms. The discomfort or dismay
at cremation may be the prod used to shake him into the

realization that he is now free, he is separated from the body whether he wished to be or not. The body is no longer his responsibility, let alone his habitation, and is no longer a living organism.

At death there is a slight carry-over of the body. It is a brief carry-over. It is sometimes picked up psychically. There is a great carry-over, of course, of the person, the self-conscious person.

Conductor: Arlene says that Madame Blavatsky sent a message after her death that if somebody gets cremated, it should be after the third day, because if it's before the third day it's very painful. I do not know how this message is supposed to have been sent, maybe through some psychic?

Dr. John: Some persons leave their bodies so quickly that their body could be cremated ten minutes later. It would not only not be painful, but it would not even be known to them. The person of whom you spoke may have had an experience of someone who had stayed close to the body for three days. Fine. That was an experience of that person.

As the knowledge of two things becomes more prevalent: the knowledge of the nature of death, and the knowledge of the spirit nature of the excarnate person (and really, the spiritual nature of the incarnate person) — as these become more prevalent, then the manner of the disposal of the dead body becomes inconsequential. It is more consequential to the earth-beings who are left behind, as here is an object which becomes now somewhat of a symbol of the person who formerly inhabited it. So that treatment given to the symbol may be symbolically the treatment given to the person.

But cremation can be just as reverential, just as respectful, as putting the body under the ground forever. Some people much prefer the concept, prefer to think of the body being disposed of in that way. It is a matter of individual consciousness and individual preference.

You're not quite convinced?

Conductor: Arlene states that Madame Blavatsky was a very highly evolved soul, and she said the third day it can be, but not before.

Dr. John: I would imagine then that all who read her posthumous instructions will wait until the fourth day before cremation. Perhaps a tag should be put on the body, 'Do not cremate until the fourth day.' and for them that certainly would be right.

This sparked some further questions from others in that session including: "In making a decision between embalming or cremating the dead body, which of these two methods is better for the ongoing person? Does embalming have an adverse affect on the spirit?"

Sometimes yes. It can contribute toward keeping the soul earthbound. Sometimes that is very good, and sometimes it is purposeful that the soul remain earthbound, particularly when the soul is on the service path. At other times it is not desirable, and for that reason should hardly be made a tenet for earthbeings.

Question: For those who are on the service path, and where there is a psychical carryover of the person to remain in close contact with earth, is cremation a detriment?

Dr. John: No, it is not a detriment. Cremation can be a positive contribution made to the soul by earthbeings for it can bring a rapid releasing. If that releasing is to go on to other realms, that's fine. But oftentimes the release is to give the soul the freedom to serve. In these cases cremation is a positive experience. Embalming may be positive or negative. We would not say that there is a negative aspect to cremation or to embalming in themselves.

Question: How long after the body is pronounced dead, after the breathing is no longer detectible or heart beat, should one wait before embalming?

Dr. John: The time the spirit is truly freed from the body varies of course with each one. Three hours is a safe time.

Question: How soon does the soul leave the body at death?

Dr. John: Well, here again there is a certain individual pattern. Some souls are very much involved with the life of the body, and will stay close to that body until it is laid to rest after the funeral, to make sure the body is taken care of. Then there are those souls who just as soon as the body is dead and the 'silver cord' is cut, go on without a backward look.

Question: Then, I suppose, all variations in between?

Dr. John: Some deceased persons will attend their own funeral service, some will not. (A8034: 5-7)

HARRY'S MOTHER

Harry asked, "Was it time for my mother to die?" The "time of death" aspect of incarnate life is Biblically substantiated in Ecclesiastes 3:1,2, "To everything there is a season and for everything under the sun. . . a time to be born and a time to die." Dr. John reported it was time for his mother to die.

The individual feature in this death was that the mother made the transition in full consciousness. This is not always the case. The particular type of death experience a person has depends upon the ongoing purpose, and the use of that aspect by the other side.

The time had come for his mother to go over, so a method was used which was conveniently available, let us say. The death experience was simply another experience. The mother was aware she was going to die, or was in the death process, or something. I do not see the details, but she was aware that death was coming. As it were, she died in full consciousness. This has many advantages, although it can have certain disadvantages too, such as shock to the incarnate person; but the mother was a resilient, strong personality. She had an element of strength about her, of toughness, in a good sense, and so she was not, as a personality, thrown into a mental swoon or an emotional tizzy by the death experience. And before she realized she actually had failed to maintain her life, had died, she was in consciousness on the other side. Some of her own loved ones who had gone before, I believe her own father and mother were there. Also, along with her parents were three or four or five or six there waiting for her, waiting somewhat anxiously, waiting with a great openness to her, and she recognized these. So she went over in full consciousness of their presence.

The dying in full consciousness can be used most constructively to make a rather quick transition. The requisite, of course, is that the consciousness of the person who died be caught and enlarged to the understanding of what has happened, to a realization and an acceptance that the person has crossed over the invisible line and is now in the excarnate plane. In other words, has died.

Then the training can come, and when things are right it can come very, very quickly. There can be simply the question, 'Is this what death is like?' and the answer, 'Yes, this is what death is like, and come with us and we'll show you more.'

Now the transition of death can be very involved, a very esoteric process, but it does not need to be. It's a simple thing. This twentieth century is the period in human history when the hidden, the esoteric, the exotic, the items which have been shrouded in mystery and wrapped in cloudiness and fogginess, are being made clear, are being simplified. Including the process of death.

The mother's death was what would be called a 'good death.' She is on the other side, is free from much that was on this side. She is a larger intellect now and has larger interests. She reaches back to her son occasionally, but not often. The son is doing a good job in a different pattern, and the mother is rather kept from reaching back very much. The mother goes on in her way and the son is being carefully guided by his own council of guides and teachers in the son's way.

Conductor: Harry read in the Cayce material that some people who die suddenly find it difficult to realize they are dead, and he asks about this.

Dr. John: Well, some who die suddenly do find it difficult to realize they are dead. If they are not caught in consciousness, and if they are not acceptive of their new estate, if they rather egotistically insist on being in their old estate or on limiting their knowledge in the new estate to their own knowledge, then they can cause more concern and be in the borderline state, the borderland of just coming over, for a longer time.

But not the mother. His mother made it quickly, adjusted within a period of what might be called a day or two, then was rested and now is being led into a new stage of beingness through new understandings, new experiences, new teachings, and new feelings as well. (A4130:5-7)

DALE

Dale asked about his father who was born and died in the same month, and on the same day of the year, although the death of course came many years later. Dale wondered if there was significance, or symbolism, in this coincidence.

Dr. John: You mean he died on his birthday? He was born and deceased in the same month, the same day? Well, there are 365 days in a year, so about three persons in each 1000 might expect to die on their birthdays. Yes, it could be considered appropriate, because death is really a birth into another plane of experience. But death on the birthday usually is more of a coincidence than a planned event. However, since it so seldom happens let us take advantage of the opportunity to say that death is truly a birth. It is intended to be, and was for him. (A281:3)

THE FLOATING SAILOR

Donald had attended a lecture where the speaker was involved in psychic rescue work, working with entities who were earthbound, the dead who do not know they were dead. The speaker reported a "psychically-rescued" case where a sailor, who had died in a shipwreck over a hundred years ago, was still hanging onto a log in the icy-cold waters of the North Sea. Donald asked Dr. John to comment on this report:

All right, number one: The time on the other side, on our side, is not the same as on your side. We work by events, not by clocks, so this one hundred years would be simply an event in the life of the sailor who had drowned, and it would not mean that he had been suffering there in the icy seas for one hundred years.

Those who die are reached fairly quickly, within a matter of hours, days, weeks, months – months at most I would say – in rare cases, a few years. For if they are not reached in that time, the life in the astral personality ebbs away. It is expended without being replenished. The earthbound person does not exist very long.

Number two: Even though the sailor was probably reached and taken quite quickly, the thoughtform of holding onto that piece of wreckage and floating in the cold and angry sea had not been destroyed. So that thoughtform was picked up by someone quite possibly of a random psychic nature, making a psychic contact, and if that thoughtform was laid to rest, that's fine. But it was not of major significance even in the life of the sailor, you see. The earthbound entities are of relatively short duration, for the reasons I have given. (A8036:26, 27)

HARRIET'S EARTHY GRANDFATHER

The following case should help lay to rest an erroneous earthbound-entity teaching which caused much concern for Harriet. Her grandfather had recently died, and she was told by a psychic the grandfather was still earthbound because of his earthy lifestyle while incarnate.

> Dr. John: He has gone beyond the lower astral plane. I do not know just how far he has gone, but he was quite a person, and I would think that he would be able to participate in many experiences in ascending planes of the excarnate person. Please send her a copy of our book *Diary After Death*. This will help Miss Harriet understand what happens at death, and the progression beyond, and it will help her parents as well. I recall they were concerned about a rather silly misunderstanding of earthbound. Perhaps I should not call it silly that they had accepted really such spiritual foolishness, it may have been in honest ignorance. (A4554:11)

DEATH WILL PART THESE TWO

This woman was locked into a difficult, painful marriage relationship, and she was concerned that she might be required to have another incarnation with her husband, which she did not want. Dr. John brought out a past life where these two had built up karmic forces to be worked out in this life, within the marriage framework.

> As to the future, no, it is not patterned that they come together again. If there should be anything go greatly wrong with their relationship in this life, they might be brought back together again. It will be wise to let the pattern of this life's relationship complete itself, and then in friendliness, these two souls will go their separate ways.
>
> Now they will know each other on the other side,

that is, after the physical death of this life. They will come together briefly to say hello. But they will not come together in a future incarnation to remain together as husband and wife on this earth.

Incidentally, she will find the next stage of life, when she comes to the astral and the higher spiritual realms, more' fulfilling, and truly more enjoyable, and she will have more invigorating companionship there than she has at present. (A1349:4)

DORIS

Doris asked about her brother who had recently died, and an interesting past life she shared with him was reported. This life gives us a glimpse into a significant event in earth history, the French Revolution.

Doris and her brother were then cousins, in the same gender as this life. This was a life in Paris during the drastic and traumatic events of the French Revolution, and the children were often disturbed, viewing the unwholesome scenes along the street. They did not participate in the conflict, they were too young, but they did observe it.

The French Revolution was followed by the Napoleonic Era, and here the masculine cousin was old enough to participate actively, and because of the close relationship between the two, the feminine personality could participate vicariously:

> Dr. John: This life of course really gave them quite an experience in earthliving because Napoleon followed the uproar and tumult, the excesses of idealism and pseudo-idealism and stupidity, of the French Revolution there in Paris. Napoleon brought a lot more common sense into the picture even though he likewise brought much suffering. But one must remember that Napoleon brought excitement and a sense of meaningfulness into

the lives of many people for whom there would be only mediocre beingness and mediocre living without him. This does not justify the bloodbaths that Napoleon brought upon Europe, but it in its way was a spiritual contribution because a life without meaning is a life that is rather low in spiritual content, and for many people, particularly in the uneducated, illiterate classes, life then did not hold much meaning in itself. It was only great events from outside that gave excitement and meaningfulness to them.

So the young man was caught up in the Napoleonic Era, become a soldier. Well he was not too young a man at that time. He was twenty, and into his twenties. He survived up to the ill-fated adventure in Russia. He was one who was lost there. I do not see precisely how.

Well, these two were quite close and there was a telepathic closeness which developed when their physical closeness was interrupted. They were close enough so that on inner levels she followed him when he was on the campaign and knew rather well what was happening with him, and with the particular aspect of the campaign in which he was involved.

So this was quite an experience for her as well. Indeed, it allowed her, a girl, to participate more directly in the experience than any woman was allowed to do physically.

Here in a sense the caution of the soul paid off in that she did not face the bullets in battle, but the curiosity, the outreach of the soul brought it much of the good of the experience, much learning, as though it had been there.

And that certainly helped to give the soul experience in earthliving. This was the last life before the present life.

And the girl went on. She knew when the boy died. She was pretty sure of it in the actual event because he suffered, he was wounded and died about eighteen hours after the wound. He was reaching out to her, and she was there with him all through one night in spirit, and in sort of an astral projection. Then she accompanied him somewhat as he went into the excarnate realm. Even before he realized he was dead.

His outreach to her carried him to her when he did die. He was confused, confused from the pain and the suffering, and the cold had come along with the pain of the wound, and the bleeding, and so he was reaching out, and death was rather gradual, and the outreach to her when at last he was free from the body simply brought him to her. He quieted down when he came to her. He was there with her for a period of about five days. For five earth days he really was there in his astral personality. Then he was taken up by others. His consciousness had quieted to where he could be reached, and he was taken into the astral realm where he was put into quite a healing sleep.

At this point she had the good sense to relinquish her concern for him. She no longer had to care for him, for now he was in good hands. She could not have told you what was happening to her, but on inner levels she simply knew this.

So this was a life that really brought a wealth of experience to both of them, in both the incarnate and the excarnate phases of it. It also brought a good relationship between them. She can reach out to her brother. He is on the other side, and he knows more now than he did then. Both of them are more advanced persons, you see. So she can reach out to him quietly, and he will be happy to be with her quite often. He is not a source of great wisdom because he is still himself, even as Doris after she makes her transition will be herself, not magically someone else. However, the magic is there, in that new possibilities are opening as one comes into this larger-potentialed spiritual realm into which the excarnate entities go — at least for those who are potentialed for this progression. (A1570:5-9)

CLOY

As we study what death is like from the higher perspective of the Other Side, our next case gives us another interesting glance into a different culture and level of life, at a distant time and place. This was a hard life in a cold climate, but a successful life in that particular framework.

Dr. John brings this interesting death experience, and then follows the person into the reawakening on the other side. In a sense this is a love story, one appropriate for that time and place:

> Let me go back quite a ways, because they have had quite a number of lifetimes together. I will not sketch them all in but let me go back and pick out – well, here is one that was not at all easy but was really quite meaningful. This was in the 700s in China. They were husband and wife, she in the feminine, and life was pretty hard.
>
> They were not in the rice bowl area. They were more in the northern area. The climate was something to contend with. They had some animals, which were brought right into the house in the wintertime. The animals had one room or rather one part of the house. The house was especially built for them. The humans had the other part. That way they all helped to keep each other warm, the animals particularly helping to keep the humans warm.
>
> The house had very thick walls. It may have been made of mud. It may have been in the southern Mongolia area, somewhere in that area. Not all the animals came in. Some were very hardy. But the animals they depended on primarily for their food were brought in out of the extreme cold.
>
> It was a difficult life. Only two of their children lived to maturity, maturity being probably puberty. The husband and wife died in their latter twenties or early thirties. I think one was twenty-nine. I do not see yet

the death of the other. But is was a successful life in that framework.

I think I will follow the then incarnation of Cloy through the death and into the after-death stage. I do not know yet if she died first or not. I intend to find out. But the first thing after her death was that she came into a warm place. There was a lot of sunshine and, as it were, she gradually took off the heavy blanket of wool and skin which had covered her on her sickbed.

She did not realize she had died. She seemed to awaken out of sleep and just lie there a bit, still in somewhat the slightly confused mental state she had been in in her sick fever. But as it were she awoke and lay there – the death was the awakening – and she began feeling warm and strong.

She threw off in her own consciousness that heavy robe. Of course, actually her body just lay there and the husband was watching. He did not know the moment of death. It was only in her own consciousness that she threw off the thoughtform of the heavy robe, and that felt better. She still was dressed very warmly. There was an inner blanket which was fleecier and had the wool side down around her body. Pretty soon she threw that off too.

Then she stood up. She saw the sun shining. She was out in a field in her consciousness, and actually was in the astral setup for her there. She stood up, watched the sun, turned her brown face to the sun, closed her eyes and drank it in through her face. She got very warm and took off the – we might call it a parka I suppose, a jacket with the hood attached that came up over the head.

She had more on than that, but she found it was warm enough there and the grass was green, so she took off this heavy winter parka and laid it aside. Then she sees someone coming. She doesn't make out that someone very well, because it is a being that is somewhat shimmering, somewhat encased in light as it comes. But as it gets closer she recognizes her own mother, and with her, her own father.

Her father and mother had been close, and the two of them came along with a sister of the mother to get this one. Let's see if I maybe can pick up the name. I think it would translate into English with five letters with a 'n' and a 'k,' N-k-m-g-o. Don't hold me precisely to that, but her name was something like that, Nkmgo.

She recognized them as they came, and they were smiling and they were dressed really differently, in sort of shifts. Is that sort of a shapeless robe? These were sort of shapeless robes. One was yellow, one had an orange cast to it, and one was very light pastel blue. She thought these were just beautiful and they shimmered. They called her name several times and she recognized them.

Of course, as she had known them, their faces usually were — well, not dour, but rather sober in life. But now they were smiling. Their movements were more graceful. One of them took a very simple little dance step, several steps quickly together, and not necessarily forward. This interested her. She had seen one of her children do something like that when young.

So her attention was caught, and she went with them and was held in that consciousness for several days, not being allowed to think of her husband and children and home. During this time, of course, the husband discovered that the wife was dead, and the body was taken out of the home. The death was accepted. He missed her, but there was a stoicism, and he also was sick. So his sensitivities were dulled. All right! So she was the one who died first.

He carried on the best he could, but he was running a fever. As he carried on his strength ebbed, and within a matter of several weeks it was apparent that he was quite ill. At this point the two children — well the elder was married and in his own home. The younger was a daughter who had recently been married. But the two children recognized that their father was sick probably unto death.

They brought him broth. They took over the care of the animals. They watched him die.

Inevitably his wife's consciousness could not be held from thoughts of her home, her husband, and her children. I think there was one grandchild by then or a grandchild on the way. The son's wife was expecting a baby. She asked about him. With suitable buffering supplied by beings higher in nature and knowledge on the astral realm and serving those who just came over, she was allowed to know that she had died and that her husband soon would join her.

She was not allowed to look back. She was simply told that he soon would join her and she could meet him, which she did.

A story like this should end 'and they both lived happily ever after.' But the equivalent of that for them was 'and they both went into a nice warm land and resumed their life and their love' in the excarnate phase of their personhoods.

So there was that experience, which in both the incarnate and the excarnate phases of it had drawn them closely together. (A3189:9-11)

JAMES

The next case brings out an interesting sight-seeing trip after the death of the incarnate person. James, in his excarnate body, decided to visit several places in the United States, and his trip played a part in his soul's choice of locale for its next incarnation.

This life reading excerpt covers the lives and deaths of the two immediate prior incarnations of the James soul, both in the masculine, both in the United States, and both building foundation for the present lifetime.

James asked if there had been a past-life experience with his brother:

> Yes, they were together in the latter part of the 1700s A.D., in England. They were brothers. The present brother was then an older brother. He came to the new country, America, into the central southern part, probably Virginia or one of the Carolinas, as a businessman and established a successful business. He was, I believe, engaged in the buying and marketing of tobacco and expanded a bit to add some tobacco fields of his own. This of course gave him reason to hire people and he brought over several of his own family from England, including this younger brother. The younger brother then was put in charge of a small tobacco farm. It was a small enough operation that the younger brother had to work and the younger brother enjoyed it. He rather exulted in physical labor. He had a good body. He enjoyed the use of the faculties and the abilities that he possessed and which he developed. He liked to use his muscles. He also was in charge of other workers, including some slaves. I see three slaves here. With the slaves he did not have a close relationship. He was not cruel to them, but he did not really understand them. However, he treated them as he would have treated a good dog, a good horse, with respect and with care for them. But he didn't think that they had the capacity for being really human. Which was the prevailing way of thinking at that time and place.
>
> The young man did not marry until he was twenty-four. By this time he had accumulated a grubstake of his own, and had established a close friendship with a suitable girl quite similar to his own station and nature. So the two of them married. The older brother helped provide them with a house and they lived there and worked for the older brother for five years, had two children who lived. By this time the younger brother was twenty-nine, and here his story ends rather abruptly.
>
> It was some illness that produced a fever and took

him off within three days, within seventy-two hours. This, well let me first look at what happened to the wife and children: The older brother helped take care of them and within several years the wife, the widow, who was still a young woman, and these two children, two boys, were very attractive, married again someone in the employ of her older brother, although not a family member, and she continued her life.

Now let us look at the excarnate life of the young man who was so abruptly taken from the incarnate: He stayed rather close to the earth plane, the physical plane, for a while. He did not really realize he was dead. He was surprised that he could put his hand right through things and that his wife did not hear when he spoke to her, that his boys did not respond when he held out his arms and spoke with them to come to him.

Gradually he then did realize that he was out of the body, did not possess a physical body such as he had before. Of course he thought of himself in identical terms as before. But there was a companion, another young man, a little older but still close to his age, maybe he would be about in the early thirties, who came along and became friendly and gained his attention and then conversed and gradually this other one – who of course was excarnate and had been sent to help bring this one into the knowledge of his own excarnate life – gradually was able to tell him that he had died and he was very much alive and just what it was all about.

Then a very interesting thing happened. The young man who died, the then incarnation of the James soul, wanted to see more of this new country America. He had been right there at the farm and not very far away from it for five years of good industrious work, and that was good. That was a real achievement. But now he and his companion took off and visited around there. This was in the North Carolina area. They expanded their visitation. He was not very interested in the new lands to the West, but first he went down into the South Carolina area and Georgia and Florida, and really was quite interested and wished he could have continued that life.

So it was arranged or evolved that the next life was in that same general area – well, I believe this probably was northern Georgia but it may have been west of there into Tennessee or – oh, that general area.

He was born about, oh, in the 1840s, and this time for a change, because the soul did have an interest in animals, he was born as a worker on a horse-breeding ranch. The young man took very naturally to the horses, and the horses, although at first they were shy of him, came to learn they could trust him. He loved the horses that could really as it were 'let loose and tear.' He loved to ride them fast and there were several horses or more there who loved to run fast. Of course he was not allowed to take the prize horses out for these rough-and-ready rides, but he had some good horses that he could ride in this way.

An interesting thing happened. The boy joined the Confederate forces – well, shortly after the war broke out, not immediately. I think he may have had to wait for his sixteenth birthday for some reason, or just about. Anyway, about that time he joined, within the first year of the war. And since he could ride, and since the horse ranch he worked for had an owner who was a patriotic southerner, the ranch owner provided him with a good horse and he became a member then of the Confederate cavalry. He loved this life. He loved the camaraderie of it and such. This too ended rather abruptly in a charge – in some skirmish, not a major battle. He took a ball directly in the forehead which of course killed him instantly. Not knowing he was dead he continued the charge but this time it was a little easier for his attention to be caught after he was dead – and carried to the other side.

Now he was given more training – that is, the soul was given more training. Well, also the excarnate person was given a larger understanding of what the soul is and of the person's relationship to the soul, and the ongoing nature of the soul's evolvement which involves of course quite a number of incarnations.

This was a good training, and the young man having in a way somewhat satiated his young manhood – well, let's not say satiated, but fulfilled – the forces of his young manhood in this and the previous life, was now ready to look at some of the larger dimensions of life very consciously.

The training actually was given to the soul and the person somewhat together, not entirely. The person was taken to schools in the 'Post Mortemia' area and given training on different types of lives and what is accomplished in each, and particularly the androgynous nature of the soul which needs to be expressed and experienced and developed in incarnate living as well. The soul attended these classes along with the person. Then the soul was given additional training so that when the person was taken 'Over the Mountain into the Land of Lights' (which you recognize as a phrase we use meaning out of the astral realm – into higher spiritual realms) the soul was given further preparation for coming in this incarnation. Many of the forces, some of the nature of the past several lives, were woven into the formula, the recipe, for the present person, and so James was born. (A119:4-6)

ETTAMAE

Ettamae asked Dr. John a three-part question in reference to a book she recently read, in which the author had a continuing communication with an excarnate entity. The entity was bringing through a body of teachings, and Ettamae wanted to know if these teachings were accurate, and if the medium-author were a qualified transmitter.

Ettamae commented that after she had read the book, she was now looking forward with anticipation to her own excarnate experience. But that she had a certain antipathy toward reincarnation. She wondered if coming back into another earthlife was mandatory, or if one could use his free will and refuse:

> Dr. John: There are three questions here. First, concerning this psychic. I do not believe she is one of the finest of the transmitters of this information, but certainly she has transmitted much and has been of great helpfulness to many people. She has been able to disseminate that which she does transmit rather widely.
>
> No one is freed at any time from the necessity of using one's own judgment, one's own discrimination. As Ettamae and others learn — well, let's say, look through the windows onto the larger aspects of life, opened by this and that and the other medium or whatever — they will see many things, and they will see many different things. Learn to judge and to choose and to discriminate among that which you see.
>
> Yes, the excarnate phase of life can be a very exciting and rewarding part of any personhood's total experience. Some persons are simply not potentialed or energized to go very far at all. Some, in fact, do not in consciousness make the transition to the excarnate realm. They die in actuality, but not in consciousness, and they still think they are upon earth, and they dwindle out the remaining energies of their being in that rather sad state.
>
> Thirdly, persons who wish not to come back to another incarnation usually must. The soul that has reached its final stages is saying to its guides and teachers, and to the great purposes of God, that let it be placed wherever it can learn and wherever it can serve, that it wants to complete both the learning and the serving on the earth plane as fully as possible, that it accepts in the same spirit as the apostle Paul expressed when he said, 'In whatsoever state I am, therein I have learned to be content.' So the Ettamae soul will have further incarnations, yes.
>
> They will not be the Ettamae person coming back.

The Ettamae person is absolutely unique in all history, including the history of its own soul. The previous incarnations of the Ettamae soul have been as other persons. The future incarnations will be as other persons. The Ettamae soul has only once the Ettamae person's experience and expression. This experience and expression of the Ettamae person goes at death from the incarnate to the excarnate stage of its personhood.

I believe I have answered the three aspects of her question. (A1101:18, 19)

HOWARD

After the death of the physical body, it is necessary for the attention of that person to be caught by the other side in order to make a transition in consciousness from the incarnate to the excarnate stage of its personhood.

As we study death from this higher perspective available to us, we see that this process is customized to the requirements of the individual person. In this instance, the fever and resulting delirium was used to catch the attention and simplify the shifting of consciousness.

Howard asked about his step-father:

Dr. John: The then incarnation of the Howard soul was born between 1850 and 1855. It was in the masculine. This was in essence a preparatory life for the present incarnation. It was deliberately designed to continue only to a certain stage and then to be cut off, so that certain forces there would not be fully expended, would not be completed, but could be fed into the present incarnation.

I think the boy was about fifteen when he died. He had come through puberty and had selected the girl he wished to be his mate, and she was agreeable. They had not announced their wedding plans officially, but they were planning. This was in Italy. They had not yet spoken to the priest, and the marriage announcement had to be made several times in church; consecutively, I believe, or possibly once a month for several consecutive months. I do not see that completely, clearly. It had not reached that stage yet, but it was getting close.

Then he was taken rather quickly. He was struck down. It was not an accident. It was some kind of a disease. I do not see the nature of it, but he was stricken suddenly and died within thirty-six hours, which was rather merciful. At the end he went into a delirium. His girl was really quite devastated but kept close with him during the illness. She was recognized by the boy's family as being his intended bride and they quite approved.

The delirium frightened her. She loved him much, but she was frightened, and this fright was used not to alienate her from him but psychologically it was used in some oblique fashion, mainly by her own council, to make her more amenable to marriage to someone else. This, however, did not happen right away. She was almost fifteen when he died, but she was sixteen before she did get married. It was more than a year. It took quite awhile to get over him.

The delirium was used in a very interesting way to help him make the transition in consciousness. In the delirium there was a certain breaking away of consciousness from reality as experienced on earth. There was a seeing of strange forms, of strange animals, new people, and such, and it was a fairly easy transition in consciousness from these strange forms and people to those who came for him in the afterdeath stage, on the lower astral plane.

I do not see who these were. They were some loved ones. A grandmother, I believe, was one, and a grandfather, and the patron saint, and also a priest and a nun teacher, a convent teacher. Of course, there wasn't very much schooling for them then, but there had been a little bit. The one who had helped him to learn to write his own name had made her transition, and she came and was recognized. So the delirium actually was used for a rather quick transition in consciousness. Well, that's one way. Not necessarily a widely used way, nor even a highly recommended way.

The present step-father was the father then. He mourned his boy. He had planned on this boy succeeding him in the family business, whatever that was. He had to make other plans now. The next son was not really of the capability of this son, although he proved to have capacities when the father paid more attention to him. But the father missed the boy. (A2175:14, 15)

LUCY

Some may wonder if there is indeed validity to the religious teaching of hell as a place of confinement, a confinement for those who have allowed themselves, while incarnate, to become infused with darkness. The next teaching, in part, answers that question.

The life reading client asked, "Since I have a child of my own, I have become concerned over the plight of abused children. I will never understand how anyone could hurt a child or an animal. When persons who have abused children or animals die, what happens to them? How are they punished?"

Dr. John: Well, it is an individual matter, because the forces leading to this are so diverse. Sometimes there is a crying grief, a hurt within the person or within the soul which strikes out. This of course is one of the horrible ways in which the striking out can take place. Sometimes there is a personal karma between the abuser and the abused child, or the victim and victimizer in other relationships, which would seem to have a certain justification, but it is not a justification of love, and in a sense it creates more karma, at least for the one perpetrating the abuse.

Now there are areas in the afterworld, the lower astral, which are populated by this type of person. Sometimes it is just a very gray and dismal area from which some of them are redeemed. Sometimes it is a darker area akin unto hell where these spirits range in evil and in their own torment, their own not knowing themselves, you might say. And this area is pretty tightly fenced in. Sometimes a person dies who has much evil, who is not caught and fenced in right away. And of course there are other realms of evil too.

So there is no one answer, unless we would say this: It does not commend the individual who perpetrates the abuse, when he comes over into the realm of greater justice and further progression.

Conductor: But they do have a chance to work it out, don't they?

Dr. John: Some of them are judged to be hopeless, and at that point the excarnate person and personality of the soul may be given one last chance as it were. Then if it doesn't make it, that person and that soul are taken apart. The elements are plunged into the redeeming fires and then such as remain returned to the reservoir, cleansed, for use in some other individual soul, yes.

Well, I would say one additional thing here. I might say one additional thing about the former question too. This matter of child abuse cannot be separated from the general evil that feeds upon humans and encourages evil conduct. I cannot single this out as the great evil or such. It is part of the great pattern of evil, for which of course the soul is bringing redemption to earth, and must know redemption itself. (A119:17, 18)

MABEL

Mabel asked if she and her father have had a previous life experience. Dr. John brought out a life where they were

father and daughter, with the father the then father also.
This was in England, and they were of a low social status.
The Mabel-soul person of that lifetime died of an infection
following childbirth. Here again, hallucinations, caused by a
high fever, were used by the Other Side to facilitate a quick
and easy transition.

Dr. John follows the person into an interesting excarnate
experience. The astral experience of the person, as with the
earth experiences, is tailored to accommodate the purposes,
the state of consciousness, and the potential of that individual person:

> Dr. John: In that life the then incarnation of the
> Mabel soul died in the third childbirth, of an infection.
> She died fairly shortly after the childbirth, within three
> weeks or so. She stoically endured the pain which came,
> not really realizing at first that this would be fatal. The
> consciousness was dimmed somewhat by a fever before
> the realization did come that there would be the transi-
> tion made.
>
> The transition itself was accomplished fairly easily.
> In the hallucination of the fever for two days before the
> actual transition, she was in the company of others she
> had known – the mother, who had preceded her, and a
> brother who had preceded her. He had been nearly nine
> when he died. That friendly relationship of siblings was
> reestablished. And there were others. So the transition
> was fairly easily made.
>
> It was more than two weeks after the transition
> before the consciousness was allowed to dawn that it had
> made the transition, and the restoral to awareness of just
> who it really was, that it had left a husband and three
> children. This came gradually, because the person was
> not deemed really strong enough to take it all at once.
>
> The first grief of loss had been passed among the
> survivors. Provisions had been made for the children,
> especially the new baby for whom had been found a

temporary substitute mother who had lost her own baby and who could nurse the little one. The villagers worked together and considered themselves a unit in many ways.

So the excarnate phase of that personality life was given a good start and was in one sense more important than the incarnate phase. The experience of living in that place in that time had been had. The soul had successfully guided its incarnate personhood through that experience. Now it had an extended experience on the excarnate side. It dwelt for quite awhile in astral England. It was not hurried. Its consciousness was accustomed to incarnate physical England, and only gradually were the new excarnate dimensions revealed and experienced.

The personhood proved able to progress quite extensively, although it did not go beyond the lower astral, or possibly the middle astral range of experience. The nature of the person was not such that it was potentialed to go beyond that. Its spiritual education while incarnate had been of a limited nature. So it went as far as it was potentialed to go. Within it was instilled on that excarnate side a knowledge that there was more, that even as when in the little village it had learned there were other villages and the annual village fair in a sense had paled a bit beside the annual whole shire fair in which there were more people, more contests, more booths, more excitement, and so forth. So on the excarnate side, it learned that there were greater dimensions as well.

This was an important accomplishment, and this and other things feed into the greater spiritual search of the present Mabel person.

The after-death experiences of a person do not always feed into the totality of soul-knowledge elements which will emerge in subsequent incarnations, but at times they do, and in this case this one certainly did. In that after-death state there was, of course, a continuing interest in England. This was about as far as the expansion was going, and the expanded knowledge was knowledge of what was happening in England, and the latest gossip as well.

The expansion was of being an English person. Not particularly reaching to other countries. They didn't really play much part in that life, nor did the excarnate person really reach that far. That would have been a bit presuming for one of her status, you see. But the knowledge that there was more, has helped the present incarnation of that soul to 'presume' to go beyond a social status, the limitations of which could have been accepted. (A1821:6, 7)

WILLIAM

Dr. John does not always answer every question put to him. There are times when the client is not allowed to have that particular information. Other knowledge is "unlawful," or too advanced, for Dr. John to give. At other times, the question does not fall within Dr. John's area of ability or knowledge. He has often said, "I am not God! I don't know everything!"

William asks about his father who had recently died of cancer:

> Dr. John: There was a closeness there, but it was apparently deemed by the guides and teachers that it would be good for him to be taken out. Or possibly it was simply another experience of some one of the 'thousand ailments to which mortal flesh is heir to,' to remind the boy again that there is much to be conquered in life, and that history will not end and the Kingdom of God will not be brought on earth solely by the next coming of Jesus the Christ, but that the millennium of a thousand years is only the start of the true human era on earth, when problems can be resolved to the point where the human society can be redemptive and intelligently redemptive of the lower kingdoms, the

animal and plant and such.

So I do not quite know. But within the framework of what I have said lies at least a major portion of the answer.

The father is back into the general stream of its own soul's incarnations. The soul had not conquered certain unworthy qualities and had allowed certain negative qualities to be embraced by its personhood; certain temptations, certain weaknesses. This may have led to the cancer. I rather believe it did. But that is beyond my ability to answer.

Conductor: William next asks about his mother. He is wondering how he can help her, console her. She is still in deep mourning, and it is now eighteen years after the death of her husband.

Dr. John: It may be that she will be comforted by the knowledge that life goes on. This is the basic comfort that religion brings.

It may be that really she does not want to meet him again, fearing that he is in the same condition of limitation in some way or other.

Or it might be that she has religious training which will lead her into grave doubts as to whether or not her husband was 'saved.' As to that, the guides and teachers tell me that the husband upon his death had gone through some sobering experiences, and was reached on the other side by those who were quite constructive, and has gone on in a very constructive way, making good use of his time and opportunities and abilities. If his wife wishes, he will be the one there to meet her when she comes over.

It may very well be that she will speak his name, for instance, before she herself lets go of the final tie, her hold upon the body. I am not sure, but this is suggested that it may be. In which case, it could be taken as a sign that he is there, and in light, in accomplishment not in weakness, in strength not in lack, and will come for her. (A4276:13-15)

MARJORIE

When Marjorie asked about her youngest son, Don, Dr. John reported the immediate prior 1800 life they shared in England:

Dr. John: This is interesting. The immediately prior lifetime for Marjorie was in England in the 1800s and early 1900s. Again in the feminine, and again in a time of upheaval and war. This son was one of her sons who was too young for World War I, at the start, but got into it in the latter stages. He was born at just the turn of the century, maybe 1901 or 1902.

He did get to France in the last year of the war, saw some action, but was not killed, was not even wounded, and returned.

She (the mother) died shortly after his return. He was her youngest, or at least he was young, and had been born when she was a little older than usual for bearing a child. So she was at a ripe old age, probably of fifty or so. He returned. He did not live too long. I think he died in 1922. I do not see just why. At which time he probably would have been about twenty-one years old or so, maybe twenty-two. He married. He lost his life I believe in an industrial accident, or some way in some accident.

They are cosmic cousins and close. The war experience had brought them closer. Actually, the mother's love reaching out to him, and his knowledge that her love and her prayers followed him, established a rather unrecognized, unconscious psychic bond between them. They were in communication even though they didn't know it. At night sometimes one would leave his or her body and visit the other one. Sometimes they would meet as projected astral personalities, knowledgeably, and converse. This did not carry through into their conscious personality awareness, however.

A very interesting thing – the mother had not gone

over very long before the son came. She was told on the other side that he would be coming. So she was the one who met him when the accident came to him, and he knew there was this accident because it did not develop in a moment, but over a period of several minutes, maybe up to a half hour. She was the one who came to him as he was leaving his body, and caught his attention.

He was conscious enough to realize, 'That's funny! Here's Mama, but she's dead, but here she really is.' Of course, their meeting astrally during the war had helped prepare the way for this, so he knew it was she, and it was. She very quickly got him established on the other side, and helped him to see his little family, because he had married and had a child and his wife was pregnant again at the time of his death.

She helped him to see two things: That he could 'elp them better as he learned how to operate from the other realm, and not be caught in grief. Secondly, that there was provision that would be made for them. I do not see just what that was. Doubtlessly, it was a provision of her family or his family, probably hers, and probably she married again later. He may have influenced her to the right kind of man to be a good husband, and a good father to his children.

Conductor: Marjorie inquires about another son, Roy:

Dr. John: I must probe this a bit. He was a son, but older than the son I have mentioned, of that life. He was killed in the war in 1916 or 1917. He was wounded and he lay where he fell, and death did not come for five or six hours. He had quite an outreach to his mother. He was in quite some pain. He was just a young man and called out for her. He realized he probably would die, and he called in fear.

Someone came to minister to him, not incarnate, but excarnate. No incarnate came. It may have been that they could not come out into the field because it was covered by gunfire. Or it may have been he was simply not found in the course of the activity of that particular day. Later his body was found and given burial.

The fear stage was alleviated as someone from the Other Side came with a certain amount of anesthesia. The consciousness dulled and there was a brief coma or state of unconsciousness. The person was disengaged from the body, and taken over. There was only about an hour and a quarter or so of full consciousness after he had been dropped by shrapnel that tore a rather frightening wound in his body, into the abdomen.

Even though the body still continued to live he was gone out of it as soon as the vital forces were expired, and he was taken away onto the other side. He was taken back home. That had been his outreach, to his mother, so he was taken back there. But when he came in, of course, she didn't recognize him.

He could come to her and talk to her and put his arms around her, but she did not respond. She did not even know he was dead, and he did not know he was dead either. That was when those who were with him – I believe it was a grandfather in that life – could get through to his consciousness that he had made his transition, and could take him over to the other side in consciousness.

He visited back to her several times, more than just a few. Then he made the adjustment to the fact that he had made his transition, and went on into that excarnate side. He met his mother then when she came over. When she met her younger son, this one was right behind. She made the first contact with the younger son when he died, but then very quickly she could establish the contact with his older brother, too. (A617: 24, 25, 32)

KENT

Kent asked about a young woman, Susan, with whom he had had an unusual experience. His question concerning her brought to light a carry-over force from a prior death experience, coming out in this lifetime with an interesting twist:

Dr. John: This is an interesting life. It's in the late 1100s and early 1200s. The then incarnation of the Kent soul was in the masculine expression, and Susan was in the feminine. He was about two-and-a-half-years older, two years and a little less than five months. They lived on the seacoast in a seaport town. Not just a village, but a town. Of course, towns and cities and such then had less population, fewer people than now.

They did not grow up together. They met at a social affair which may have been a church parish affair, but they were not in the same church. When they met, he was sixteen and she was not quite fourteen. She took his eye immediately. His eye was roving and questing and looking. She interested him right away. There was not the cosmic or karmic recognition. They may have been together in the past, but it was more peripheral, if they had been together before then.

He got to know her. He approached her, as was quite permissable. In fact, these occasions were somewhat designed so the young people could meet each other. Every society has such. They danced in the folk dance of that occasion, and they shared some refreshments. He had a rather heavy mug of what was served in heavy mugs there, because he was now a man, and could partake of the stronger refreshment. He gave her a sip of it, too, when others were not looking.

She was rather impressed by this older young man who was good looking and strong and well dressed, who would take notice of her. They found topics of common interest. They arranged to meet again, and they did, in a public situation. They met a third time. But then he died in a storm at sea.

The whole boat wasn't lost, but it was a bad storm, and he was swept overboard. The boat was endangered, and he was not being foolhardy. He was doing something to help secure the boat in the storm, out at sea, and he was swept overboard. He and the boat were separated by the wind and the waves of the storm, and the others had no way of bringing the boat around to pick him up. They grieved. There was a father and an uncle on the boat, maybe an older brother.

They grieved, but things like this did happen. Not very frequently, because they wouldn't have survived if it had happened too frequently. They were a people who were stoic, and had to be.

The young man knew he drowned, and yet he wasn't dead. He found himself walking really above the surface of the ocean, above the surface of the land, and he simply walked home. No entity on the spirit side got through to him. He had not really had any training in the matter of life after death. He had not thought much about it. He had enjoyed life. He was a strong, fairly intelligent young man, and he had enjoyed the adventure of life and the experiences of it.

He had not really thought about death or the life after death. So he had no opening in consciousness that could be used by those on the other side to reach him. So when he found himself still alive, he just walked home. For him, the storm had ceased to exist, and he didn't think of himself as walking on the water, and he wasn't. He was walking above the water. He walked home.

He was somewhat dazed by the drowning. The drowning, of course, had dulled his consciousness as the oxygen was denied the body, denied the brain. The functioning of the brain had diminished, and the consciousness he had was not as sharp and full as when he had been in the body. Nevertheless, he was surprised that no one there saw him or gave him heed or anything to eat or drink. He got some for himself. Of course, it did not diminish what the others had.

He was somewhat dazed, you see, and so when the family didn't pay him any attention, he remembered the girl. He went over to her home. As he was going over, he came to a decision. You see, he hadn't quite made up his mind before he died that he was going to ask her to be his wife. He was considering several, very definitely. But she was the front runner.

Now, after death, in his somewhat clouded condition as he was walking from his house to her home, he decided that she was the one he would ask to be his wife.

It is an unusual type of situation, as you see, and a little hard to read, because in a sense he wasn't all there, and there isn't that good an imprint upon the akashic records of this portion.

On the way over to her, he was reached by those on the other side in an interesting way. As he walked along, his path changed. Of course, his path was a thought-form. He wasn't walking the actual streets, but it being his thoughtform of the streets, it could be changed more easily than an actual physical street could have been changed. As it were, he went south and came into a warmer climate, and the sun began to shine more bright-ly. This was actually the light of the other realm breaking through.

The sun began to shine more brightly, and he was still dazed enough so that he simply noted it as the sun shining more brightly and he felt warmer. Then he came upon some other people. Those, of course, were spirit beings who were designed to catch his attention, to find a way into his consciousness, then having reached his con-sciousness, to take him on into the astral realm, the postdeath realm.

So this was how it was done. He never did get to his girl's house. The thought had been strong in his mind, but then he noticed the sunlight, he noticed he was warmer. He came upon some other people. Pretty soon he recognized one of them as being – well, it may have been an elder brother who had died, but I don't think so. I think it was an acquaintance who had died when they were boys together. The other one had died when he was maybe nine years old or so. But he recognized him, and that was the opening wedge in consciousness.

The dazed quality gradually worked through. He saw this person, recognized him, called to him. The other one came over, of course, he was coming anyway. They got to chatting about old times and his mind cleared up, but in terms of back when he and this fellow had been together when they were about nine years old or eight or seven. But that was the way his attention was caught. From there the others worked with him and took him into the excarnate phase of his beingness, his personal expression and experience. Is there a question?

Conductor: Dr. John, let me read this to you. Kent writes, 'Two years ago a young saleswoman phoned me. I was busy, but believed I owed her the courtesy to meet and dismiss her. She was located two floors below my office. As I was going down the stairs, I had no way of knowing that she was a most delightful person. I wouldn't have cared, because I was traveling to dismiss her. On the way down, before seeing her for the first time, I heard a loud, commanding voice which said, "wife." We met, and there was sixty years difference between us, but we did become friends. I'm wondering about the significance of this voice that said "wife".'

Dr. John: He found her, he's seen her again. Of course, when he was looking for her before, he intended to ask her to be his wife, so 'wife' was probably in his mind. So that's been expressed now, the force of that in consciousness has been expressed and completed. It is not that she was his wife. If he had lived, she might have become his wife. It is not that she is intended to be his wife. It is not that he is to propose to her in this life, and he certainly was wise enough to know that.

You see, there was a seeking which had not found, but since that seeking has now resulted in finding, the force of it is probably ended, and they probably will not be together in any future incarnation. It does not close the door, but there is no seeking now to bring them together. (A3601:21-25)

* * * * *

Thank you, wise Dr. John, Dr. John Christopher Daniels, reader of the akashic records from high spirit planes, for tracing through the past-life death and life after death of these life reading clients. These are but a few of the thousands you have brought us, and we learn from them all.

And thank you, Religious Research, and all who have worked in the discovery, development, and research of the Loehr-Daniels Life Readings, for these multiplying illustrations of the death experience as seen from a higher perspective.

CHAPTER SEVEN

THE ASTRAL EXPERIENCE

How long do we live on earth? Most of us would turn to the Biblical "three-score years and ten, perhaps four-score" as a good average length of human life. In previous generations and other cultures the average was often less than half that, even for the half who survived infancy. (That was when a heavy breeding rate was needed.) But major advances in science — nutrition, agriculture, sanitation, medical knowledge — have lengthened the lifespan in most advanced countries to around the seventy-year average, and still creeping upward.

We think of this, our incarnate lifespan, as being the most important period of experience and expression of life for us. *It is not!* If we are intelligent, spiritually aware, and of a strong and good character, we live much more of our personal existence as a non-earthbeing than as an earthbeing. The incarnate stage of our personhood is the start, and this start is very important, for if we do not get a good start we may not go very far. But if we live the incarnate (earth) part well, then the astral plane we enter upon at death can be immeasurably larger, longer, more important, and with a greater and more abundant life and awareness, than we ever experience on earth. It is in the excarnate phase that we truly come into our own, where we are actually ourselves, expressing and growing in a depth and scope earthlife could never bestow, nor could we even envision while on earth.

In various life readings, Dr. John occasionally gives us brief glimpses into this glorious higher ascension. In one such he reported, "There are seven levels going straight up, each with seven planes. This is symbolic," he hastened to add, "not mathematical." So there is a tremendous progression open before us as we leave earth and earth concepts, the earth way of thinking about ourselves, behind.

This is not so strange, since we are aware of covering a wide range of experiences during the seventy to eighty years of our incarnate life. What must it be like to go on for another 500 or 5000 years!

It is fitting that the immediate next world would bear a great resemblance to the earth world we just left. This paralleling of worlds is the wise and loving provision of God in assisting the newly dead to make a gentle transition in consciousness from being an earth person to being an astral person. Because of this similarity of worlds, "crossing the line" can even become blurred as one steps into a world much akin to the one just left. The earth concept of the post-death state as being without a body can be misleading to the newly dead persons. They find themselves very much in a body, a body they at first perceive to be their own familiar one. It looks, feels, and functions in the same way. At first, the person may be puzzled when his spoken words no longer reach loved ones' ears, and they no longer respond to his touch. There may be feelings of dismay as he watches treasured possessions turned over to others. Often, however, this state of bewilderment and dismay is useful to the Other Side in order to catch the attention and bring awareness to the newcomer that he is no longer an earth being.

So as the physical body dies we do find ourselves in another body, an astral body which looks like an exact duplicate of the one we just left (but actually made of finer stuff), a vehicle by which we know ourselves and still identify as the self that survived death.

There are three classifications of excarnate entities, each relatively small, who remain close to earth longer than the usual time: The first group are the unfortunate earthbound persons who are held here either by ignorance or earthy appetites or by a complacency with their status quo. The second group are the teachers, guides, etc., who stay close to earthbeings for extended periods because it is part of their service, their purpose, their spiritual destiny. These persons often were fine spiritual teachers while incarnate, and received wide recognition, which is helpful in opening earth doors for their excarnate psychic ministry. Indeed, this may be a major purpose for being given earth prominence. The third group are the excarnate entities whose communication back to earth is part of their particular training in learning how to reach back from the astral threshold to the incarnate plane. Earth psychics are actually serving these recent dead who have been given this particular learning assignment and we need more, not fewer.

The mere death of the body does not make entirely new persons of us. We are still the same person, yet with a definite difference. Certain forces we had while in the body are no longer a part of our personality. There is a division of energies: certain faults, fears, unpleasant and nagging traits expressed on earth, are immediately or progressively dropped off with the body. Certain of the problems which perplexed or plagued us are dropped away. Certain traits that made some people difficult, even obnoxious, may no longer be part of that excarnate personality after the death experience. There is a simple, logical, necessary reason for this: certain problems, forces, and growth require a physical body and a physical environment in order to be worked out. It is the unfinished earth business — requiring an earth body and an earth environment — that is laid away from us at death, becoming the "karma on the doorstep" for some new birth.

So there is a certain difference brought about by the death of the body. We do not enter the next life exactly as we leave this one, *but we are the same person.* And death, the transition from an incarnate to an excarnate person, does bring us into a certain judgment of the incarnate life we have just lived. Some of our ideas and beliefs are seen to be inadequate for this new plane. Here character, not social or economic status but what we truly are, is determinative.

Within the framework of those traits not dropped at death, we pick up and carry on from the knowledge, consciousness, and interests we have built before death. Our character and our consciousness are what we really are, and we take this with us into our new estate.

The lower astral is an intermediary state where desires can be expended and let run down in preparation for the greater planes of spirituality and the new nature and experiences that lie ahead. Here in the lower astral we can experience and express many unfulfilled earth yearnings. On the astral, our minds can be more immediately creative, limited by our taste and understanding. Here can be expressed much of the goodness missed on earth, the goodness we still want, and we are allowed the necessary duration for that fulfillment.

In the lower astral are many who do not want to progress. They are content to live out their excarnate existence in this lower astral area. And there are those who are not potentialed — in either intelligence or spiritual growth — to go into higher planes. They never progress beyond the lower or middle astral, and live out their excarnate phase in that state until the soul-forces within the person are drawn back into its higher self. The astral is the threshold to the higher dimensions of life, but it is still in many ways an earth plane.

A person ejected by death from the body he knew as his

home and his vehicle of expression, is now faced with a major adjustment. Consciousness is the key in making that adjustment. The adjustment is dependent upon the ability of the newly dead to literally find himself in this new world. He must first perceive it, and then learn how to operate within its nature. If we continue to think of ourselves only in earth terms, we will remain earth shades, and will gradually fade away. Somehow our new estate must be brought to mind.

Not everyone ascends equally in the spiritual planes, nor equally long after the earth death. Some end their existence on the lower astral plane, that first step away from earth. Others go on a little way beyond, others a long way. If we do not catch the larger vision of what we truly are, we perish at the level of our lower vision. If we do not possess a strong lifeforce, or if we allow our lifeforce to be dissipated and diminished and not re-supplied, we simply do not go as far as those whose vitality is stronger.

My careful research of the Loehr-Daniels Life and Teaching Readings deals majorly with the threshold area of the astral plane. But at times we are given brief glimpses into the higher dimensions and these higher planes bear but little resemblance to the world we now know. In these higher planes we have a "body of light," far beyond our concept of the earth body or its astral-counterpart carryover. Further guidelines into this high adventure beyond the astral will come when we are ready for it but one thing we do know, whatever these experiences and expressions will be, it will be *you*, the person of you that will be having them.

The excarnate stage for each person is individually unique, as both the incarnate and the excarnate expressions lie within the structure of our personal life purpose. Our life purpose has its earth beginning with the conception and the "custom-making" of the person, and follows on through both the incarnate and the excarnate phases of our life as a person.

The incarnate stage has its "human condition," a condition common to us all. Death has its core experience, common to all. The astral experience also has similarities for all. But within the similarities lie differing individual personal experiences, and this uniqueness makes for interesting and some widely varying astral adventures as you will see from the following cases.

In one of our teaching sessions the question was asked, "On your side, let us say you have a steak dinner: Do you visualize the steak of your choice, and it is just there?"

Dr. John: This can be done. I haven't had a steak dinner for about 4,300 years. This can be done but this is more in the lower astral dimension.

May I diverge a few minutes now with your permission for some teaching. The lower astral threshold ground between the earth and the spiritual is really more like unto earth than unto the spirit realms, because progression in consciousness is a step-by-step affair. If a totally new stage or step were to be presented it would be completely incomprehensible. Unless there be some phase of comprehension within the present consciousness to which the new can attach as an expansion, we would not make the contact with consciousness of the new idea. I may not be expressing this too well. So the immediate next stage which we call Post-Mortemia, meaning just after death, is the lower astral ground which is very much akin to the material realm because this is where the consciousness is of those who have just come over. Now there are some who have in their earthlife the consciousness which enables them to fly over Post-Mortemia and 'over the mountain' — this is the figure of speech we use — 'into the Land of Lights,' the higher astral and then the succeeding, the more etherealized, spiritual realms.

Before the excarnate entity is ready to proceed beyond the lower astral, there must be the attainment in consciousness of an ability to drop thinking of itself within earth terms. The lesson which I give in *Diary After Death* and which we have used in classes for some years, as I brought it through some years ago, is a rather simple one and I will repeat it here because it will bring a certain amount of enlightenment, I believe, particularly of that which I am saying:

You can – after you have died and after your going-away party on earth and your welcoming party in Heaven are over so you can get off by yourself, and after you have been rested if need be – you can get off by yourself and think of having, say, two thumbs on your right hand. Close your eyes and think of yourself with two thumbs. Now this is something you can do on the Other Side where mind is the creator more directly than it is when it has to work with the structured physical realm. But then as you have thought of yourself with two thumbs and you open your eyes to see, you will have two thumbs.

If you haven't done it the first time, try again. And then think of yourself, say, with three legs. It takes a bit of training and skill to accomplish this. Then open your eyes and you will see you have three legs. Remember this is on the astral realm, it is not in the incarnate realm. What would you do with the third leg? But the point is, you don't need the first two. And so then think of yourself with no legs. Sit back and take a firm grip on the chair if need be and think your legs away, open your eyes and look. If it scares you, quickly close your eyes and think your legs back again. But the point is to learn not to think of yourself in earth terms, but as a bundle of energies perhaps best understood at present in human consciousness as a collection of light, a bundle of light. This is, of course, what Henry and Gertrude were taught to do in Post-Mortemia as a preparation for going 'over the mountain' – these are figurative and symbolic words now – 'into the Land of Lights.' I shall let it rest at that at the present.

I trust this will illustrate how the immediate after-death state in the lower astral seems very physical. People go fishing and they catch fish and clean them and eat them there. Then they're pretty much as they have been. And some never develop the consciousness to get beyond that stage. So their excarnate personality existence will pretty much end at that stage, and this is where the second death will come to them as persons. This is as far as they are energized or capacitied to go. Others with a little greater expansion of spiritual consciousness while they are incarnate are capacitied to go further. This is one reason why the basic teaching that each person, each human being, is a living spirit, is so important. It gives us on the Other Side the beginning point with which to work with an entity as it comes over. (A8006: 1,2)

ALICIA

Alicia asked about a special friend, and a lifetime was reported where she was the then wife of this friend. It was a short marriage of five years, and the wife died. Because she was unaware of a continuing life, she remained earthbound and focused on her earth experiences and relationships, and remained in that state until the energies of her being ran down and she was then absorbed back into her higher self, her soul.

Dr. John: Here we go back to the era when Rome was extending civilization. We find this other one as a professional road builder. He was quite good at it, too. He understood the principles of road building, he understood the engineering of roads, he understood not only the need of the substructure of a road but also how different types of soil required different substructures or foundations for the actual road surface upon which the people walked and the horses and the vehicles moved.

The then incarnation of the Alicia soul was his wife, but only for five years, and then she died. At her death she missed him as well as he missed her. She stayed rather close on the astral plane to him, reaching out to him. She was rather young, he was a little older, and she had not been enlightened as to the nature of death and of the soul and of life after death, and her consciousness was still centered upon him and upon material things and the incarnate things of life. So that she never quite realized that she was in another dimension. Well, she came to realize she was in another dimension because she could not make herself heard or seen or felt by him.

But she did not become aware of the nature of that other dimension. When she could not reach him, it was as though she just was withdrawn more and more and more, and became smaller and smaller until she was non-existent. At which point, of course, all that had been accomplished in that person was absorbed into its soul, including the fact that her consciousness had not been prepared while incarnate for excarnate existence. So the excarnate existence had not contributed anything, had not continued very long, and had come to a real death.

The soul does have in its own experience a very graphic illustration of the importance of bringing into the consciousness of persons while incarnate a knowledge of the possibility of life continuing. This is quite important. (A4520:13, 14)

AMANTE

Amante inquired about a pastlife relationship with her sister, and Dr. John tapped into a 1700 masculine incarnation of the Amante-soul. This was in Spain, and the then person was quite a gay young caballero. This brings out an interesting earthbound experience where the person was focused on earth for about six weeks until his attention was finally caught by the Other Side:

Dr. John: A quite vigorous young man. He was not very religious. If he had been it would have definitely restricted his style, especially with the ladies.

He was born in sort of a rural village, but as soon as he could he went to a seaport where life was much less religious, more free, and the women appreciated him more. Well, the girls in his hometown appreciated him also but simply could not – because of their inhibitions and the restrictions upon them – open themselves to receive his attentions in quite the same way and to appreciate his young manly talents. (Chuckling)

This was not altogether a 100% constructive lifetime. It lacked certain elements of responsibility, particularly in relationships. He was much more interested in making conquests than in what he could do for any woman in his life. If a woman presented too many problems he rather quickly learned how to avoid her, and evade those who had designs on capturing him.

But it was a delightful life and certainly a type of earth experience which the soul at that time handled very well. It was an enjoyable lifetime which extended to the setting as well. He liked who he was, and partly because he liked who he was and what he was doing he liked where he was.

He did not marry. He had something to do with the sea, but he was not really a professional sailor. He was more a professional – if you call it a profession – opportunist. He had a quick mind and fairly good one, although not deeply profound. He could see opportunities for profit.

He was a middleman who put various things together, not all of them completely legitimate. He made enough money to support his lifestyle. He transgressed some of the customs and expectations of some of those with whom he had certain dealings, and at the age of 27 he very quickly made his transition by means of a sword or dagger exercised by one of those who emotionally disapproved of what the young man had done to him.

The body was found the next morning in the side street against the wall where he had fallen. Death had

been instantaneous. Some vital organ had been punc-
tured, run through. The young man was really quite
surprised at the event. He realized what had happened
but it took him a while to realize that this event was
his key, his password, his open doorway, to another
plane. And so he remained there in the city. It may have
been Cadiz, I believe. I am not certain.

He remained in the city for some time. He walked the
streets. But he became more and more aware that people
did not see him, didn't hear him, didn't respond to him.
The girls' eyes did not brighten as he approached or when
he called to them. The older women and the others did
not see him. He then discovered – and this is one way of
a person who has not had much training or enlightenment on life after death, to discover there is a difference
– he discovered that he could walk several feet above the
pavement just as well as he could walk on it. This was
quite new to him and he rather enjoyed experimenting.
He found that he could walk quite a bit higher than
that. He found that he could move just by thinking
about it. He found that he could either rest upon a roof-
top or he could perch equally securely ten feet above it.
He then – and this was an idea fed to him by some from
the Other Side who were seeking to reach his consciousness and find a contact point within it for bringing to
him an awareness that he had come into another realm –
got the idea of trying to go through a wall. And he found
he could. Thus in a period of about six weeks earth time
he was reached by some on the Other Side, someone
whom he recognized – I do not see just who it was –
and gradually made aware of life on the other dimensions.

Here on the astral plane he found the seriousness
which he had not found on the material plane of earthliving. Actually, as I have stated before, the lower astral
and the material planes are really both of them earth
planes, with the lower astral being of course the transi-
tional plane, the threshold for taking the excarnate

person into more spiritual areas. He found there was a great deal more responsibility and seriousness along with definite joy and real living on the other plane. So here through the excarnate phase of that personality, a more balanced view of personhood, of person expression, personal experience, was brought to that soul. (A3213: 6-8)

BERYL

Beryl received a life reading as she was nearing the end of her present incarnation, and Dr. John was preparing her for the journey into this new and interesting country of the astral plane:

Dr. John: Now it is not just the soul that survives. It is the person, the person of Beryl, who will survive the death of her body and go into the out-of-body or excarnate phase. She is still a person. She is still herself. She will be the same, or almost the same, the day after she dies as she is the day before she dies. That is, she will be the same person. She will be free of the physical body and its aches and limitations. She will be in a different setting.

She will appear to have a body and all the aspects of herself she has known on earth. But she will be in a plane which has a greater freedom to it. She will meet loved ones, her parents and others, as she leaves the earth behind. It will be either a person or a light which will guide her when the time comes for her to step across the invisible line from the incarnate and material realm into the excarnate and astral realm.

The soul still watches over the person of Beryl in the excarnate realm. The person is still an expression-point of some facets of the soul. The person is still the experience-point by which the soul of Beryl gains the experience of the lower astral realm. And the soul still guides the person of Beryl through the lower astral realm, eventually into the higher astral and then into the more spiritual realms. Even as the soul had the responsibility and the learning experience of guiding the Beryl person through the incarnate phase, the earth phase.

Sometime up ahead the soul will have another person. This will be its new incarnation. It will not be Beryl come back to earth. It will be the soul having a different incarnation. Even as the second child of parents is not the first child come again, and even as the birth of the second child does not require the death of the first child, the excarnate Beryl will continue on its progression as far as it is potentialed and energized to go. It probably will not even know of the next incarnation of its soul. It will have so many other things to do: learning, experiencing, and enjoying. The incarnations − in other words, the various personhoods − of a soul are quite separate, and seldom does one know of another while either is in the earth phase or in the lower astral phase.

The Beryl person in its immortality will have an interesting life. The meeting at the time of death will be interesting. The establishment in the lower astral realm, which we sometimes call 'Post Mortemia,' will be interesting. The gaining of strength and of mental agility and emotional wholeness will be gratifying and enjoyable, and rather exhilarating. She will be young again, and with all the fine qualities that youth has. She will go on the adventure of her new stage of life after death. (A4860:2-4)

CARL

Carl asked about his wife who had died a painful and prolonged death the year before. He wanted to know if there was any way he could help her now or be of any service to her.

When Dr. John first came into her records, he perceived a confused situation with the wife. The explanation for that became clear as he probed further:

> Dr. John: Yes, they were together in a rather well-developed civilization in Mexico. This was in the first century A.D. I believe it was not the Mayan, but in the general area now associated with the Mayan. For there were people there before and after the Mayan time. This was a nicely civilized place, where people were interested in things beyond mere food and security and shelter.
>
> They had developed enough strength and sophistication that they had secure borders. They had a certain momentum of endeavoring to learn more about the stars and the seasons and God or gods and relationships of people to the God or gods, and of the immediate to the ultimate and the finite to the infinite. In their own way, you see, they had a civilized mind, inquiring for more knowledge.
>
> At that time, the then incarnation of the Carl soul was in the masculine expression. This other one became the wife, but not right away. The Carl soul had been married, and his wife died in pregnancy but not in childbirth, before the child was born. But it was a death associated with the pregnancy. When she died, he rather quickly turned to his wife's younger sister, who was the then incarnation of this one.
>
> They married and they grew closer together in their own right, and the younger sister really grew into her own rightful position as wife on her own, although it began as sort of a carry-over from her older sister, the first wife.
>
> I do not see them in any other past life. There are forces between them now, for Carl has been compassionate, and there are also outreach forces from the other one which will bring them together rather soon.
>
> She was in a mixed-up state. I see quite a lot of motion, as it were, where it would have been much better if there had been stillness. There was commotion, there

was uncertainty, there was a little melting of the boundaries of her personal beingness. This is perhaps not a good way to express it, so let me put it in a little different way.

The aura is an energy envelope customarily around the body of a living being. The skin of the body and the outside edge of the aura can define the boundaries of that person, each in its own way. Her boundaries got blurred, and this meant that some of her beingness could seep out, but even more could become indistinct and less personalized until in a sense she didn't know who she was quite as surely as she had before. This is a way of putting it. She wasn't as well defined.

His council nods and says, 'That's it.' Well, that was it; her last period of incarnate life and the first period of excarnate life. She is more defined now, she is more quiet, she is more at peace. She had a great deal of pain, and this is what helped to bring it about. However, if she had been more of a self-contained, self-directed person, it would have been better. But she did not draw her boundaries clearly. She lacked in a certain way that discipline of precise beingness. In other ways she had it, but in some ways she didn't.

This is something which this soul is learning from this experience, because the soul must learn how to handle, handle successfully and well, a human being, its own personal incarnate and excarnate being, you see. So the soul is learning. It felt the pain the person felt, but it is learning how to bring assaugement to the pain, particularly on the excarnate realm.

Now a wiser and older soul will learn how to bring assaugement to the pain of its person in the incarnate stage as well. So this is pretty much the picture.

Conductor: He says, 'My wife's health had been worsening for several years.' Then several things in the family affected his wife's mental and emotional condition and she developed arthritis and then later emphysema. She had been in the hospital several times and then a final terrible and prolonged hospital stay of four months, three of those months in the intensive care unit.

Dr. John: Her lack of definition, as it were, helped to render the pain a little less personally experienced.

Conductor: He's concerned, of course, about her now. As he says, 'Is there any way I can help or be of service to her?'

Dr. John: Yes, he can. He can reach out. When he is quiet, he can reach out and speak to her; speak of his very real love for her, his continuing concern for her. The words of the master, 'Speak ye peaceably unto Jerusalem' can be his guideline, and he, as it were, can himself evolve how to do that to his wife.

Conductor: He asks, 'Is she happy now and near me at any time?'

Dr. John: Yes and no. She has quieted a lot. She is more clearly defined in her own beingness. She knows who she is, where she stops and the not-she begins. The pain is over, although it took a while for the excarnate entity to realize the pain was over and to drop the consciousness of pain. She has been reached by someone very maternal. It may have been her mother or grandmother, or sort of a maternal cosmic family member possibly who is working with her, quietly and competently.

She is not with Carl very much, but he can reach out in his thoughts and even in his words, maybe several times a week, just to speak to her, perhaps to reminisce about something which they had done which was good, some good time they had. Assure her that the not-so-good times are understood and not held in consciousness. By that I do not mean not held against her but simply not held. Recognize that they exist, but now hold attention on the good times when he thinks of her. (A1738:15-17)

CHARLENE

The 'cosmic relationships' mentioned in the next teaching is in reference to the cosmic family relationship. There are groups of souls small enough — three dozen to fifty or so — who maintain the same kind of personal knowledge with each other, the same intimate concern, we find in an earth family. Cosmic family members will incarnate together more frequently than with other souls. There is no father or mother in this family group because the father and mother of every soul is God. But here are older and younger members, some close and some not so close, some 'graduating' out and some new souls coming in.

The Charlene soul was a bit anxious since this was the first time it had come into incarnation without the support of a cosmic family member. But she learned a good relationship in earthliving could be built with souls of similar qualities and beingness even though not cosmic family members:

> Dr. John: No, there is no past-life acquaintance. There is no cosmic relationship. They were introduced before being incarnated, but not really made known to each other. The mother graciously accepted, saying that whoever was sent to her in the plan of their guides and teachers under the mastership of Jesus the Christ would be most welcome.
>
> The Charlene soul, knowing that it was to be on this particular type of an adventure in this life, was happy to hear this from the one who had been chosen for it as mother. The Charlene soul had a bit of trepidation, as in the past it had known more previously about those with whom it would incarnate, in the immediate family that is, and it had more of a hand in that selection.
>
> Now that soul was to put its hand in the hand of God — through the agency of its guides and the goodness of the great cosmic process — rather than rely upon goodness already established in cosmic relations and

acquaintances.

It worked out very well for both of them. The relationship, I see, was one of an unusual amount of spiritual growth for each. This growth included, as Charlene could tell you, personal support, personal closeness, a joy in each other. She has lost her mother, hasn't she? Yes. The mother is here. She has a rather strange message.

The mother is a very gracious person, a person of much light and spiritual substance. She's greeting her daughter in a rather colloquial way. It's not with the dignity that you might expect of a spiritual greeting. She's saying, 'Hi babe,' or 'Hi baby,' or something like that. This may be a code message. Hi babe, or baby. 'It is unbelievably, it is incredibly wondrous over here. I do not want you to in any way short-circuit your earth stay, and I do not want what I say about the adventure and beauty and unbelievable music over here to make you discontent with earth.

'But when you do come, you will find the' − here I must try to get her precise word. This is telepathized to me, and I am picking up the thoughts, but not quite as clearly as with some who have been over here longer. In essence, she does not want Charlene to lose the fine edge of appreciation and enjoyment of her many earth experiences by knowing that they will be topped on the other side.

That mother 'dances on air,' which is a neat trick. But, of course, can be done in the spirit realm. As it were, she ascends into the air off the astral floor in the lower astral realm, and in the air she dances. Not ballet, but sort of swaying and twisting to music. She is a beautiful, artistic person, and is very happy to be reaching back to her daughter.

This illustrates in a very fine way the fact that if two souls − and, of course, in this case two persons − share certain qualities of God-likeness, they find a great fellowship together. These two are not cosmic family, they are not cosmic cousins, they do not have past lives together. But they shared in some things of God in the realm of beauty, music, deep feelings, giving to those who would receive, and receiving from those who would give.

They find in this a common bond greater than simply having a cosmic relationship or a past-life acquaintance. The mother will contact the daughter occasionally in the months and years ahead, and probably will be there to meet her when she comes over. I say probably, because it is possible that someone else of very real closeness will also come over with less of a time span between his or her death and Charlene's death, and hence be closer timewise to make the initial contact in consciousness.

When a human being makes his or her transition, it is a consciousness that needs to be caught and carried into the other realm. The consciousness has been associated with the physical beingness, now it must be associated with the spiritual beingness. This is one reason why all religions teaching that there is life after death really hold the key for their followers getting into Heaven. Because if there is this concept, even the concept of the possibility, in the mind of the person, the consciousness can be caught, you see, and the person carried from the incarnate to the excarnate plane of personhood. Which really is carrying the person from the material to the spiritual plane of beingness.

Conductor: She has felt cheated that her mother was taken away from her so soon, and she wants to know what's the reason for this.

Dr. John: The reason for that did not concern Charlene. Her mother had her own life, her own pattern, and there was reason in that pattern for her death. I do not see what that was, as I will stay with Charlene's records. I can speak to Charlene's feeling cheated:

God is honest and God is just and God is fair, but God works within the framework of eternity. The person works in the framework of the finite. The soul escapes the mortal. The person escapes the mortal aspect of the body and has a dimension of immortality, in that the person continues from the incarnate into the excarnate stage of personhood, and there can continue as long and as far as it is potentialed and energized and purposed so to do. (A1169:2-5)

DEREK

This person was so satisfied with being Japanese, and with what he felt was a superior status, he carried that consciousness of complacency to the excarnate phase, living out his personal life in the lower astral as a Japanese gentleman:

Dr. John: This is an incarnation from the masculine half of the whole soul so he is in his native gender expression. This is an interesting and unusual lifetime. The soul is emerging into modern times in its incarnational experience and learning somewhat what it is like. The immediately prior lifetime was in the 1600s A.D. in Japan. Japan was very provincial then. They believed themselves to be the chosen people of heaven. They didn't know too much about the rest of the world despite a certain exchange of scholars with China and its traditions. That incarnation was in the masculine and that person was very, very pleased to be exactly who, what, and where he was, with the pleasure centering perhaps upon his identification with being a man of Japan. The complacency of many Englishmen in recent centuries, which has tended to hold some of them in the excarnate stage right to the place and pattern of life they had in the incarnate, was matched by the complacent pride of this Japanese gentleman with just who and where and what he was.

And he was a success there. He was not a great success. He lived in the village, but he owned two houses. He had more funds than most. He had several wives who were stronger than most women, and who worked the land better than most. He could frequent the teahouse and talk with the finest men in the village, of whom where were two or three in his estimation, besides himself.

It may seem as though that person had become very content, satisfied, and proud, of really a modest achievement. Correct. He was very content, satisfied, and proud with himself.

The excarnate phase of that life continued in very much the same pattern. One of this select little group of three or four had died shortly before this one and the two of them got together immediately upon the other side, partly because the other one had not recognized anything else on the other side. His attention had not been caught, becasue he was not willing to give his attention to anything less than he. But when his friend stepped into view at death, they both recognized each other immediately and proceeded along a way into what they figured must be the teahouse awaiting them, and it was. It was largely of their own construction, their mental thoughtform that is, but it was sufficient. There had been four, and one of the others joined them.

The other never did; when he went over his attention was caught by someone whom he had known other than this elite circle. It, I believe, was a child, a daughter with whom there had been a strong soul-tie which had developed into really a bit of a love bond, plus the father's pride in her beauty, her being just exactly what he wanted her to be. She caught his attention, led him into larger experiences which, of course, opened him to the consciousness of the larger dimensions of the astral plane.

Now why did he not visit his old cronies? It was felt by those who were working with him that if he got with his old cronies, his consciousness might just settle there, so he was steered quietly away from them. He was the youngest of the four so a little more open to something else. Since he was not the top man of that four, he had a chink in his complacency, which was used for good.

But the first three stayed in that teahouse. Each noted that his companions were gradually aging, and he with them. All three of them did not go any further, but gradually aged on that side and came into an apathetic consciousness from which they went into a coma, and then into a nothingness. The second death. And that which they had been was drawn into the larger dimensions of their own soul, but not really by consciousness. The qualities, many of which were very fine, including a regard for the best, were drawn in. The experience of earth was drawn in. But the identity of the gentlemen themselves did not really expand to identify with the larger dimensions of their souls. They in effect lost their identity. But that was all right, because their identity had been so satisfactory to them, they did not seek anything more.

Well, that was interesting, wasn't it, conductor.

Conductor: Yes, very interesting, Dr. John, how complacency negates growth! Growth requires change, that we become more than we had been.

Dr. John: I wonder what significance that last prior lifetime, incarnate and excarnate, has for the present incarnation of Derek.

Well, the Derek soul is beginning now completely anew with quite a different situation. It does not want to have another incarnation like that. Once is enough; once was not bad, but once is quite enough. The Japanese way had become quite crystallized. So upon the advice of the guides and councils, quite willingly accepted by the soul, which had not been able to crack the shell of its previous personhood and get its own consciousness in, the soul was quite willing to accept a life in which conditions would be greatly different — the conditions in which it has incarnated now and the developments of this life. (A2179:2, 3)

DAWN

During the course of a life reading, the question was asked, "Is either one of my parents influencing my life from the other side?"

> Dr. John: Well, it depends on what she means by in-fluencing her. Certainly one would hope that Dawn, with her understanding, with her personality achieve-ments, and with her age, is immune to influence from just anyone who happens to be around. The mother has come some, although not anymore. The mother was somewhat earth-centered. I would not say earth-bound, but earth-centered for awhile. However, that is not the case at present.
>
> Earthlings should not think that an excarnate taking some interest in them has great power. That simply is not true. In general, an excarnate will have less power in the same sort of a situation than would an incarnate. The incarnate being present in person having various ways of exerting force and influence, can provide much more of an impact than an excarnate can. This as a general rule. And certainly it is true of her parents who are deceased. (A4660:4,5)

EDWARD

Edward is an elderly gentleman who has lived a long, diffi-cult life, and he has lived it with great courage and with good achievements. But the crown, the reward that awaits him, will not be his until he comes into the excarnate phase of his life:

> Dr. John: His death should be an easy transition. Actually he will welcome it when it comes. I do not see it as being very traumatic, not much in the way of pain and such. It might even be in his sleep. The transition will be fairly easy. He understands quite a bit of this.

He's had an inquiring mind, not only in the question of why, but also on the question of what happens.

So there will be more reward for him when the incarnate phase is over and he can go into the excarnate phase of his own personal life. He will like that. Certain qualities of his own will be permitted to blossom more. The principle of 'like attracts like' is true on the excarnate side and in higher spiritual areas more than on the incarnate side. Certain disappointments will be relieved, certain questions will be answered, certain disciplines will bear their fruit.

I may sound as though I am recommending death to him. Well, let those forces that guide his fate determine that. I do not. I do not know how much longer he will be on the incarnate side. I am simply saying that when the time does come for him to step across that invisible line, he will find the crown, the fruition, the reward, the larger beingness of himself for which he is preparing well now. Yes, that which he has earned in the incarnate stage will be his on the excarnate, and he will find certain companionship and love there, too. (A2381:8)

You see, there needs to be a certain fulfillment of desires before you are free to go on. These desires can be very fine, or they can be simply things which were denied expression in the earth plane. When these desires are fulfilled, then there is a greater freedom to go on. This is a general rule which Edward will find working to his benefit. (A2612:15)

EILEEN

Eileen, who is now nearing the end of her incarnation, has felt throughout this lifetime somewhat an alien in a strange land. This feeling stems from her unusually close kinship with her own soul. Dr. John promises, after her transition she will bypass much of the excarnate experience, and be drawn rather quickly into her soul-self. This is her desire. This is her aspiration, and it will be done:

Dr. John: Interestingly enough, when she does step across the line, make her transition, yes, she will find there and renew acquaintance with the persons she has known in this life. But on the whole she will not stay with them very long. It will simply be that she will be different than they, and she will have a different soul greeting. A soul greeting is not the same as the excarnate-person greetings on the astral realm for the personality as it comes over. She will be greeted more by her soul, and taken into different mansions prepared for her.

However, she will say hello to the others. They will reminisce and they will be friendly and then they all will go on their own ways. Her way is different. The Eileen personality will not have too extensive an excarnate existence. It will be drawn more quickly into its soul, which is to be drawn into the biggerness, the greater largeness, because there won't be really much point in this personality going through the usual astral and then gradual spiritual advances of other types of persons. It will be drawn more quickly into a higher type of beingness, to which she now aspires, and for which she has made herself ready.

From the person standpont, what is the purpose of this life? Well, that can be pretty much as she will. She feels the impulses from the soul to which she has been given, and she feels a kinship with the soul much more than with her social and hereditary and marital and family level of beingness. This makes for a certain divine discontent.

It is understandable. Once one sees the full picture, it certainly is understandable. We trust Eileen will understand why she has not been at ease, and will not be at ease, even with the persons she loves. Not one of them really is from a soul that is on the level of maturity of her soul. It is not to say that her soul is superior in the eyes of God. But it is superior and in fact it is a twelfth-grade-soul intead of a fifth-grade-soul, so to speak. Even though Eileen herself may be a fifth-grade-person, just as the others in her life, she is from the higher-grade-soul.

We trust, and we warn her, not to get trapped in either of two reactions to this. One: do not get trapped in a feeling of despair, that she is not worthy of her soul, and why in the world would God or life or her guides and teachers or anyone permit her, who is really entitled to being born on the other side of the tracks so to speak, on a higher status and a higher station, why did they permit her to be born where she was and live her life where she has? There was reason.

On the other hand, do not become smug and snobbish and say, 'Well, I know that I am really of a much superior soul to these others around me.' Let her avoid both of these. Let her continue to be Eileen, seeking the best of which she is capable.

Now the best of which she is capable in this life, as an incarnate person, is not going to measure up to what she wishes it could be. She would like to have a larger capacity for doing good. She would like to have a larger opportunity of living. She would like to have greater mental abilities, greater understanding. She would like to be of a finer level of wifehood and motherhood and personhood in general. Ah, yes. But even as the soul had to take Eileen as she is, so must Eileen accept herself.

Eileen can feel and be inwardly very happy with the higher levels and forces of being which are from her soul, and which are increasingly extending from the soul into and throughout her being. But Eileen is still Eileen on earth. She is still Eileen, and will be, until she dies.

The purpose of the Eileen person was to live the Eileen life. This may sound like a very simple and even silly statement. The purpose of the Eileen person was and is to live the Eileen life. To be a child in the family and to the parents where she was born. To marry whom she married, to be a mother of the children whom she bore and reared. To have the problems, the experiences, the setbacks, the dreams, the achievements, the happinesses,

the frustrations, the failures. All of that that Eileen has
had. (A2801:4, 5, 6)

FREDERICK

Frederick inquired of his present brother, and learned they
had shared a lifetime together during the 1700s American
Revolution. Both were in the masculine.

The importance of the Revolution escaped them at the time,
but on the excarnate side they were given teachings on the
real significance of the United States in world history.

This excerpt follows the Frederick person through most of
the 1700s incarnate life and the death experience. After that
death, his guides allowed him to stay close to earth for awhile
to comfort his wife and family. Then, when his wife finally
made her transition, they progressed together through the
various stages of the astral and beyond:

> Dr. John: They were together in the 1700s life, the
> mid-1700s life in America. They were in the American
> Revolution. They were young men together and farmers.
> In the Revolution they were actually in several battles
> where shots were fired. They did not join the army of-
> ficially, neither got hit and neither hit the enemy with a
> bullet. But it was sort of exciting and they were patriots.
>
> That sort of enlivened the long hours of subduing
> the fields, the acres, cutting down trees and grubbing out
> stumps and burning out stumps and carrying stones and
> plowing and turning up more stones and carrying them
> over and making stone walls and stone houses. If they
> had had a good market for stones, they would have been
> rich. It was in the Massachusetts area, coming into Ver-
> mont, if I place it correctly.
>
> But they found ways of adding some spice to their
> lives. They courted. The war came before they married.
> Their general response, even though they were patriots

and were in it a little bit, was that each of them married and went a little farther north. Not particularly to get away from the war, for they were not caught up in the war too much. The went a little further north to open some new land of their own.

They each built a little log house and cleared some more land along a creek. They had adjoining portions. Their wives were good friends, so the foursome really did quite well. But the foursome very quickly became a fivesome, a sixsome, a sevensome, an eightsome, and they made quite a family. One had only three children who grew to maturity. The other had seven or eight.

They sort of treated it all as one family, and there were a lot of good workers in the children. They cleared land and planted their corn and other crops and raised their food animals. They were quite good shots. One was quite a good shot and the other didn't have quite as good eyesight. They would go hunting together, and although one killed twice as many game, they shared it. Simply carrying it home was more of a job than shooting the game, if they got an animal like a deer or a number of smaller animals.

So it was a happy life between them. Not too much accomplished, excepting that they had an earthlife in that type of experience-framework, and at a certain hinge-point in history, when history was being made. They had a touch with it, even though not a very big touch. Of course, when the war was won they were among the people who had helped to win it.

The difficulties in the early formation of the Union of States did not concern them too much. They were quite amenable to it, and it was fine when it happened.

We follow the Frederick one into the after-death state, since you said that is one of his interests. In this life he lived to be into the forties, or I believe he died at fifty-one. Again there was nutritional deficiency, or maybe it was an internal organ that was naturally deficient; that is not too consequential, because fifty-one was a pretty good age, more than the average certainly.

Frederick went into the lower astral realm at death and stayed quite close to earth, and at first was not aware of being dead. It took a while to awaken, and when he did he found himself right still there. And it *was* right still there. But after being ignored by the other people and not heard when he spoke, he got a bit disturbed and reached up and struck one of the children, and his hand went right through with the child paying no attention. This sort of jolted him.

There had been some religious instruction there in the community, so there was a dawning realization that he had come into a different state of experience. At this point the religious instruction was helpful, in that some from the Other Side reached this one and they gradually told him he had died and that it was quite all right. He said he'd like to stick around there for a while, and they said that was quite all right, 'just don't forget you are in a different state of being now, but it's quite all right to stay around for a while.'

He said he wanted to stay and see if – there was a girl who was seven months pregnant, one of his daughters whose name was or may have been Elizabeth or Susabet, or that may have been a nickname – so he wanted to stay and see Susabet's baby. Susabet was what he called her, but I think that was a nickname. They said that was quite fine.

Several months later the baby was born and by this time he had seen that the family was going along pretty well. He was out during the time of his own funeral, so the grief of his widow and his children at the time of the funeral did not reach him. He was still in the consciousness of whatever it was that caused his death. Even though they continued to grieve for him some, life went along and they had to keep at work.

He was with his wife quite a bit and brought a lot of comfort to her. In the night hours he was right there with her, and would be in bed with her and holding her at times and talking with her and telling her he was all right and she was all right and the children were all right. Once or twice he brought her a good bit of advice about one or more of the children. Not in any great critical situation, but he brought the counsel that was good at that time.

So she had a feeling of his presence with her, which was good. Even after he did withdraw then into other realms and into more activity in the astral realm, he kept open to her, so that if she thought of him or needed him, he could return and be with her. She did not remarry, and outlived him for less than three years, by which time he was well acquainted over on his new plane and met her and brought her over with a lot of gracious happiness.

They stayed on that new plane, but there they were given further instruction in the purpose of this country. They had not really been too concerned with the Revolution. They were all for it and glad it took place and glad they won the war, but now they were given further information that this was to become a very significant country and have quite a place in history.

This was sort of their general education, and gave them both a deeper appreciation of that lifetime, of some aspects of the lifetime, than they had had when they actually were incarnate in it. They saw that added significance to that life. Then they went on into the more spiritual realms. I do not follow them after that. But after a relatively short while, within several years after the wife had come over, the two of them went on, and I believe are still in existence — that is what I seem to pick up from their trail — but in quite some different realms.

They were capable individuals, capable persons, and their souls are still making use of them to experience in those advanced spiritual realms open to the person, and to express through them within that milieu. (A2524: 20-22)

FELICIA

This teaching brings knowledge of what happens to a person coming to the Other Side with much negativity, how evil is handled. The presenting question was, "Can a soul regress — like after it seems to be going along fine — and then it has a net regression in a life?"

Dr. John: Yes, in two ways. There can be energies sometimes characterized as ticking time-bombs within the consciousness when a person is incarnate. Sometimes such energies will suddenly erupt and spew forth in a way quite destructive of the personality. This does not happen often and when it does happen, it usually is under guidance by those higher ones working with that individual. You see, it's a way of clearing that pocket of psychic infection, using 'psychic' here in the sense of personality forces, in the incarnate realm. This is not common, for usually the problems are worked out in gradual, positive growth rather than sudden, destructive explosion.

A second way of answering your question is to say, yes, an excarnate entity can have a net regression in its excarnate experience. This usually would be by the will of the entity itself, but at least a minor responsibility would rest with the soul of which the entity is an expression-point and experience-point, and with the council of that entity, that personality.

Now, usually the entities that come over with a great deal of negative force are gathered (partly by the like-attract-like principle, and partly by deliberate design of those who have responsibility for the lower astral realm and the new excarnates coming over) into a certain area. Is there a fence around this? Is this a prison? Yes, to an extent. It's a hospital to an extent. There may be no walls, no fences apparent, and yet they are — partly by their nature and partly by the control exercised by the custodians of this realm — held within that area of beingness, that area of existence, that area of duration, that area of a lower astral realm. I bring these contributions toward an answer to your question. Would you like to ask further?

Conductor: Felicia was especially interested in the fate of Adolf Hitler. Does evil to that extent eventually work its way out of that area of encampment?

Dr. John: I do not know what has happened to that entity. His was an exceptional case of evil. Perhaps I will find out and will bring that information at some future time.

Conductor: What about that question in general? Can a person confined because of its evilness be changed and work out of its astral prison or hospital?

Dr. John: Yes, sometimes the evil ones can either expend some of their negativities and then rise to the light, to some extent anyway, sometimes to quite an extent, on the lower astral level. Yes, sometimes they can. Sometimes they continue to expend the energies of their beingness in the negativities to which their consciousness has become so accustomed while incarnate until all the energy of their beingness is expended and they slowly lapse into apathy and then into nothingness.

Now when that happens, it very often happens in this rather interesting way: The being that is becoming de-energized drops into a beginning apathy, lethargic beingness, and then his world seems to drop away, other people will drop out of his lessening consciousness until finally he is all alone and he is too de-energized to really care. And then he falls into a sleep, a coma, that is second death, and that entity is no more.

Now you may ask, what happens to the soul in such a case? That is entirely dependent upon the soul itself, particularly with young souls. Though sometimes with souls that are a little further along a person, an incarnation, will get out of control and be handled in this way. It may be able to be brought back into control on the excarnate side; it may not be. And so this may be the best way to end up a rather sorry, unsuccessful chapter from which the soul will learn, hopefully, and do a little better job when later on it must handle a later personality with many of those forces. (A8006:3,4)

MR. GILBERT

Usually the concluding meeting of a Religious Research seminar is a teaching session with Dr. John, with various questions being asked from the floor.

One of the seminar students asked, "I have a three-part question, Dr. John, and all three parts deal with God. (1) Does death change our perception of God and bring us closer to the light? (2) Do we meet God in person, so to speak? (3) Are we aware of a dramatic difference once we cross over to the Other Side?"

Dr. John: The day after you die you will not be much different from the day before you die. This is one of the important things to know about it. When someone dies, sometimes they think they have great wisdom, and they will try to come through and they will speak as a great master possessing great truth. Quite possibly they don't know much more than they did before. They do know they are still alive after passing through the experience of death, and that is a great knowledge. But it does not make them very wise in itself.

The meeting with God. What do you mean by the meeting with God?

Student: Do you see His face? Do you see more light? Do you feel more that He hears you or sees you? Is there more of a dialogue?

Dr. John: Not necessarily. When you go from the first semester of kindergarten to the second semester of kindergarten, you are still in kindergarten. The whole soul stage is a young stage as the God-child. The instrument of consciousness of the person is quite definitive here. If it is still possessed of growing, it will grow, but there are no shortcuts. Growth is a step at a time. One enlightenment gained, assimilated, then another enlightenment approached, hopefully gained and assimilated, as long as you are potentialed and energized to grow. God you can 'see' at any stage to the extent of your growth then, but He does not become totally known or 'seen' just because you die. (A8034:28, 29)

GLORIA

Gloria asked about her ex-lover. She mentioned that when they first met, the emotional and sexual electricity flowing between them was remarkable. This was something she had never experienced before. They were lovers for about two years, and then came a painful goodbye and parting of the ways:

Dr. John: This is interesting. In the early 1300s they were both together in Greece. Both masculine, but lovers. The then incarnation of the other soul was older, and introduced the younger man into homosexual love. But the younger was homosexual in inclination. It was quite a fine relationship for almost six years. It was accepted. They had to move from their native village to a larger town and into a certain section, as it were, where they were accepted. It was a good relationship.

Then the older man fell sick and within about ten days died. Whatever it was that he had was contagious or infectious, because the younger person got it likewise. But his body was stronger, was younger, and it was almost two months before he died.

When he died he was met on the Other Side by his friend, who by that time had enough knowledge of the lower astral realm, the beginning of the excarnate life of the personhood, that he could be the one to meet his friend, to catch his attention, and then to introduce him to some other friends, some new friends of the older

man on the Other Side, who could take them both farther into that life.

They had an interest in aesthetics, in beauty, and this
was used as a potential to carry them really quite a little
way. They went from the lower astral, where they experienced beauty and were shown more forms of it and
given more teachings, into the higher astral where they
had more understanding of the essence of beauty, of the
mystical bounce of beauty, the mystical nature of
beauty, of which the material manifestation is drawn or
from which it is drawn. I think the both of them went
into higher spiritual realms as well. I do not follow them
there. (A1155:19,20)

HYACINTH

Hyacinth asked about her yoga teacher. They had a good
guru-chela relationship, and she has been his disciple since
seventh grade. This brought out an interesting situation in
that he had also been her guru on the Other Side following a
past-life transition. This brings another example of how our
earthly desires can bring fulfillment, or development, in the
excarnate stage. In this case it was a development which
carried over and bore fruit in this lifetime.

The following excerpt brings out this particular past life,
past-life transition, and the astral teaching with the guru —
a soul relationship which carried over into this life:

> Dr. John: The father had a home a little better than
> the general run of homes, and he had an interest in
> spiritual things very genuine and intelligent. So the
> traveling holy men who occasionally came to the village
> often stayed at his home.
>
> He shared with all his children, the daughters as well
> as the sons, their teachings and his interest in spiritual
> things. This particular daughter was more interested
> than any of the other children. Partly because she was a

young soul. The souls who have a deeply spiritual nature anyway, as they come into earth incarnations tend to carry that spiritual beingness with them as sort of a special radiance not perceived by everyone.

This kindness on the father's part, who did perceive it in his child, although he could not quite have explained it, resulted in that child on the excarnate side going into a study of the holy things as understood and presented within that culture. So she went to school, she went to the ashrams set up on the Other Side by teachers from that tradition, and learned there their understanding.

When she went over, her father met her, introduced her to the guru whom he had chosen, and she was happy to accept his choice and become a chela of that guru and learn what she could. (A4554:18, 19)

* * * * *

Up to this point in our study of death, we have taken the person from its prototype, pre-conceptual beginning, through the "custom-making" of the new personality (usually accomplished during the first three months of pregnancy), following through the incarnate and then the excarnate phases of its personhoods — going as far as the person is potentialed and energized to go — until finally the excarnate personal-self, fully expanded or self-realized, is again absorbed back into its true total self, its own soul.

The different kinds and degrees of astral experiences one has are initially dependent upon his/her spiritual progression while incarnate. To the degree one grows and develops here, to that degree is she/he potentialed to progress further in excarnate experience and expression.

In the chapters ahead, we will closely examine some areas of human problems and suffering in the general field of death and dying, problems and suffering usually caused by ignorance.

With this ever-growing body of advanced spiritual knowledge pouring into earth consciousness, we are now able to
approach these age-old problems with new insights, directly
and honestly, and with a greater degree of intelligence.
Mankind can now take mastery of these problem areas, and
with this taking dominion, "light a candle rather than curse
the darkness."

Death with understanding is a lighted way.

CHAPTER EIGHT

THE DEATHS OF INFANTS AND CHILDREN

Why should an innocent child be taken in death?

If man were an animal, attacks upon young life would be understandable. Predators usually find the young easier to kill. But man is a spiritual being, operating under spiritual laws as well as physical. There is a soul purpose in human birth – and there is a Divine Purpose in human death.

When finally there is knowledge that there can be, and is, simple and logical reason – not merely accident – in the death of infants and young children, the sharp pain of loss can be alleviated, comfort is at hand. And I am not speaking of what we so often hear at funerals, "God wanted this child with Him in heaven." Comfort (which is a Latin word, from *cum* plus *forte*, meaning *with strength*) – when finally we see reason that makes sense to us, we can be comforted. I shall give more illustrations in this chapter than a general reader may want, because those who have lost an infant or young child may be looking for that reason which speaks to their loss.

The first and most frequent reason is simply that the loss of life when young, the loss of an infant or child by its parents and friends, is one of the earth experiences for each and every soul. Souls come into earth to undergo and cope with the experiences earth holds. Death is one such experience. Young death is a difficult experience to master. Simply to know the purpose behind it does not remove all the hurt, but does help a great deal. Young death is to be as all other life events, a learning and growing experience for the souls involved.

HEATHER

Dr. John reports an 1800 feminine lifetime of the Heather soul, where the then-person suffered the loss of three children:

> The woman bore two children. Let me probe this a bit. She bore three. One died very early. Possibly lived a day or so. But the other two died before either of them reached the age of eight. These were very, very definite losses to the mother and to the father, although his suffering was partly because he saw his beloved wife suffer.
>
> But these accomplished for the soul qualities of strength, maturity, and character. One of the accomplishments in this case was personally seeing that even though they were living in a time of advanced civilization – this was in the 1800s – there still was much knowledge to be gained. There was born within the woman's loss, grief and anger, a determination which permeated the soul, for the increase of human knowledge and mastery of earth. (A4276:12)

HELENA

A father asked about his youngest daughter Helena, and Dr. John reported that this daughter had reached a stumbling block because the soul in several past lives had proved unable to handle grief in a positive way. So her soul (through the persons) was being held in a pattern of loss until this lesson was learned:

Here is a soul who has hit a snag in its ongoing. Let me probe for this. This is not the daughter's reading, and I am not dealing directly with her akashic records, and to open any soul's records is quite a procedure and I can not do that now for her. So I am resorting to another method, of gaining general impressions as it were.

I see this other one came into some difficulties in handling earth experiences that involved trauma, particularly involving the difficulties happening to loved ones and the loss of loved ones.

The soul incarnate as the daughter, Helena, is farther along than the souls of the rest of her family, and thus is coming into coping with more difficult earth experiences. So in two of the last three incarnations, it came into experiencing injustice and harm done to those whom it loved. This was very difficult, and the soul did not handle it well.

So it has been kept in this general area until it does handle it. However, in this lifetime it is not expected that injustice and harm really will come to any whom it loves, either of its present family or of the husband and the children as it is expected that this young woman will have up ahead. She is now approaching the whole subject from a more academic point, learning more about such conditions as conditions rather than as personal experiences of her own.

Conductor: Her father mentioned that Helena is a psychiatric nurse who has been suffering for three years from a nervous breakdown. But she hopes to go back to work soon. She is very interested in spiritualism.

Dr. John: If she's interested in spiritualism it may be that she would be open to the concept of reincarnation. Her father will know. If she be open to the concept of reincarnation, possibly what I have brought through may be of some helpfulness to her, providing reason for difficulties. In this life she is coming into more of a professional and, as it were, a one-step-removed way of dealing with some of the difficulties that humans experiience. (A123:10, 11)

INGRID

In a prior lifetime the Ingrid-soul faced the loss of her children and successfully transcended those learning experiences:

> There were four children who lived and several who did not. She grieved over the ones who died, but not unduly. This happened. You produced a child and you didn't know at the time you were carrying it if it would live or not. You hoped it would and you didn't think about it too much. If it did, that's fine, you rejoiced. If it did not, you accepted the fact and laid the child away with a few days of tears, then went on with life. (A2001:14)

IVY

The Ivy-soul's first touch-down into earthbeingness was a conception that somehow got botched and ended in a miscarriage. This young impulsive soul was quite annoyed with the person not coming to a live birth.

In the next conception, the soul had its first live birth, and within its native feminine gender. With this soul-force of brashness flowing into the person, by the time she was four years old she was very assertive. She knew exactly what she wanted and what the soul behind that little girl wanted, which was a full earthlife. But that incarnation was carried through only to the ninth year and then terminated, because the guides and teachers felt that puberty would put too much strain upon this young soul. The Ivy-soul was furious. She refused to believe the ending of that incarnation was for its own good.

For the following third earth experience, the soul asked for and was granted permission to tackle a full earthlife. It got a little more than it had bargained for in learning how to cope with the death of a child. But the person did achieve mastery of this difficult earth experience with the help of three wayshowers, though with little help from her own soul. The person had to achieve the growth largely on her own.

The following is that third earth experience:

The next life actually was close to a hundred years later. It was in the 2000s B.C., again in India. It was agreed that this time the soul's wish to carry right on through to becoming a wife and mother, to having a more full earthlife, would be granted. So this time the present father-soul, the sponsor soul, incarnated in the feminine gender and was the mother of the daughter.

The daughter, moreover, was given two older sisters. So there were three wayshowers for her in that life. I do not see details on the two older sisters as yet. We may not find them among her present acquaintances.

This daughter carried through. She was a little quieter. She did not have to be quite so self-assertive because she knew more now of herself. She wasn't reaching out and taking new land. She was already possessed of the experience she had had, and the education and training between earthlives, and the knowledge that there were three more experienced souls incarnate now with her in the feminine expression to help her.

So she was a more pleasant person, really, and still had enough vivaciousness and liveliness. In this life she did go through puberty, then courtship, and her responses were somewhat guided by the suggestions of her older sisters and particularly her mother.

She was married. She had two children who were quite healthy. Then a child which sickened and died. This nearly threw the soul, because it had not planned on such a thing happening. The person of herself as the bereaved mother had to endure that grief without any help from the soul, for her soul was more upset by it than she was.

The husband was helpful. The older sisters were helpful. The mother, who had seen other children die, was helpful. So the girl came through that experience saddened, a little more quiet, but not deeply upset. The fact that that incarnation really mastered the experience of losing a child was very helpful to the soul.

Death came at the age of twenty-six. There were several other children, and she was a young grandmother. (A1192:5)

JENNIFER

Jennifer is a nurse, and she is disturbed when she sees little babies die. She says, "I see babies born into the world, and I can assure you that if they live for fifteen minutes they have a personality. Then they die. Not very many, thank goodness, but a few. What happens to these tiny, new, innocent helpless personalities?"

Dr. John: With some there is only a spark of life, a 'soul breath.' If the soul knows that that incarnation is going to be very brief, it may not invest very much of itself in it and that personhood may be terminated rather soon. The racial experience of infant death is an experience of humanhood for parents and for children.

On the other hand, those infant deaths for whom there is greater purpose and potential may be received on the Other Side and brought along. Their growth will not be restricted to the stages of body growth of incarnation. It will be more a growth in consciousness. But growth in consciousness must begin with the consciousness where it is. A baby just a few weeks old, yes, it is a little person, and the personhood may be developed. But it begins with the consciousness as it is at the time it is received on the Other Side. This is a rather specialized department in 'Post-Mortemia' (the lower astral). You say she is a nurse?

Conductor: Yes.

Dr. John: Her question shows a concern for babies. Would she like to volunteer?

Conductor: Yes, that is part of her question. She says, "If they survive on the excarnate plane, who cares for them? Because I would like to apply for that job if I can.'

Dr. John: Then let her apply. I'm not the one to whom to apply. She has already made this known to her Council, and so it is known to those who will have supervision in that area. Also, mature personalities coming over have a great deal of freedom of choice of what they would like to do for such time as they would like to do it. After death, if one wanted to play chess, one might play chess for a year or for ten years, you see.

This is a fine service, to work with the infants who come over. It is not only the matter of a desire. There is a need for intelligent, loving beings on the Other Side, excarnate persons, to work with children and the little ones who come.

Conductor: May I ask: The ones who do not survive in the excarnate, are they taken to, as Jennifer puts it, 'the great pool of life,' the reservoir of God-beingness? Or are they taken into their soul?

Dr. John: That which has been gained is taken into the soul. With any personality, when the time on the excarnate plane of personhood comes that its potential and its purpose have been achieved, fulfilled, expended, then whatever energies are left over go back into the great pool of God-beingness. But mostly they have been drawn into the soul. This is how the soul grows and is enriched. (A2612:15, 16)

There are astral nurseries but they are for excarnate persons who died as young children, and have to be brought along in consciousness from that start. An old soul who incarnates, then dies as an infant, can be brought along quite quickly in consciousness here. Another, in whom the human race earth-consciousness is stronger, will tend to gauge his growth here by reference to some earth-child and so the equivalent of earth years is required. There are nurseries here for such. (July 1976 Journal "Spirit Children" VI:10-br)

JASON

The next case brings out an interesting astral experience for this little boy Jason. This is an experience of personality fulfillment of desires denied the little boy while in earth-living:

Dr. John: The son and the mother are closer than the son and the father. They were together in the immediately prior lifetime, which was in the 1800s, the late 1800s, and for the mother coming into the early 1900s, but not for the son. The mother was in the mother position then and the son was a son, even as now. He was a son but sickly and could not get outdoors and run and play. From the very beginning he was always indoors and with the mother. It was frustrating for the little fellow. There were two older sisters and he was just indoors with them whereas his older brother, he had one older brother, got outdoors with the father.

They were farmers. It was not in this country. This was somewhere in Central Europe. It was pretty close to the eastern border of France, probably close to either the Italian or Swiss border, and the outdoors was quite interesting. There were hills and there was snow. This little boy had a respiratory trouble, a type of asthma, and he would look out and get a bit excited and then the asthma would pick up and he could hardly breathe and they would have to quiet him down and his sisters would pay him a lot of attention. But he wanted to be outdoors with his older brother and his father. It was quite a frustrating time and the little youngster died when he was, well, he lived to be more than five years old but not six years old, and he died appropriately enough in an asthmatic attack where he simply could not get his breath and he was fighting for this breath but it ran out and he died.

He was met on the Other Side by, I think, a great-grandmother. He didn't recognize her but she knew him pretty well and got him over the consciousness of asthma. That took some doing and some time, but then he went on quite happily in the astral realm and climbed the mountains and slid in the snow and things like that. It was good and he enjoyed it, and he said, 'This is the way it should be when next I come into the physical plane, and, by golly, it's going to be!' So even though he did get outdoors in the excarnate side of that life, in a way it reinforced rather than diminished the desire to do so on the physical plane, and so that desire carried over to the present. She's got a very interesting little fellow on her hands. But he should be a very rewarding son to rear, too, especially in these early years. (A3188:11)

Many deaths of infants and children can be attributed to "touch-down" experiences for souls new to earthliving. Many new souls have a certain trepidation, and even fear, coming into personhood expression in this strange new realm of earth. This apprehension is understandable when we remember that souls are native to spirit and alien to matter (by "spirit" we simply mean non-physical, non-material planes of expression and realms of beingness), and as such these anxious new souls may actually be given just a quick dip into earth beingness the first time or two.

When you next hear of a child's death, know this may be a new soul perhaps getting cold feet and pulling back into spirit, and this pulling back into spirit is not such a great mistake, With some souls it may take two, even three, brief touch-down incarnations before that particular soul feels confident enough to settle into a full earthlife.

Not all new souls are apprehensive toward earth experience. Some are more adventuresome, and eagerly anticipate this new and exciting adventure. They come in and live a full earth life as soon as they can. Others come for varying lengths of time, depending upon their own individual choice or that of a higher decision.

Then there are those new souls who have a definite attitude problem. They will not listen to their guides and teachers, but will insist upon jumping into an ill-advised and premature incarnation. Often this jump is blocked by the guides and teachers, but at other times the incarnation is allowed to take place for the soul to learn the error of its ways by a painful learning experience. The next time, hopefully, when its guides and teachers speak this foolish one will listen.

KIRSTIN

Kirstin inquired about her father and Dr. John reported he was a Cosmic Family member and sponsored her into earth-living in the 2100s B.C. in India:

In a sense, this was not quite the first. There had been a conception, but somehow it got bungled and ended in a spontaneous miscarriage in about the eleventh week. This was prior to the incarnation of which I speak.

The person, in a sense, had been brought together, that is, the different forces of it, by that time. So the soul had a little taste of personhood and was quite put out at there being a miscarriage instead of a live birth then. This soul can be rather impetuous at times. So on the Other Side its forces were regrouped, its guides and teachers worked with it, and the second time it came not only into live birth but came all the way into puberty.

This means it experienced being itself, separate from the mother's body. It learned it had an identity of its own, as it was given a name and others called it by its name and responded to it when it spoke to them. It learned identity also as it learned to walk, learned to take care of its body and its bodily functions. Then learned to express a will of its own. The little girl by the time she was three or four had become a bit imperious. She knew she was a person and she demanded her place in the world. The family alternately thought it cute and found it a nuisance, to have the little girl so assertive.

But such she was, and carried on until approaching puberty; just a week and a half or twelve days before the ninth birthday, the soul's touch with the body was broken. The soul was taken away, and this caused the quite sudden death of the little girl. The soul was furious. It refused to believe that this was in its own good, that it was not really ready to go into puberty, courtship, marriage, motherhood, and so forth.

But it was somewhat molified by the guides and teachers, and it was shown the reasons why. It was told that it had made good progress, and they did not want the progress gained to be lost. The soul more or less accepted this. There wasn't much it could do about holding the life grip onto the body. The guides and teachers, although recognizing that this quality of forwardness had certain irritations, did not let that bother them as they worked with this attractive, eager young soul. (A1192:4, 5)

KENT

Kent is an unusual case in that the soul-person born into his first earthlife lived only three years, and then came back into the same family as the sixth child:

> Dr. John: This was not the first incarnation to show on the records. There had been one into which the soul had lived to be three years old, almost three, two years and nine or ten months. Let me probe this: The two incarnations were very close together. They were both within that same family. The first time, the child was

the firstborn. Death was a part of the plan of that life, an early death, and was brought about.

But the soul had taken so well to that household, and under the careful spiritual tutelage of the father and the careful physical provisions of the mother had come along so well, that they allowed it to come in as the sixth child, the sixth pregnancy that was carried to birth. Two of the older siblings had died. Let me see if this one was one of them. No, there were two others, so there were two older siblings who continue to live, and this one also.

This time this one, under careful watching from its Council, lived not only to puberty but through puberty and into young manhood and manhood. He became a husband and a father, and carried through. Partly by the strength of its then father. This is interesting.

Conductor: Unusual too, isn't it, Dr. John?

Dr. John: Yes, and thank you for saying that. It is unusual. I see that the father supplied not only encouragement and protection and fine direction, and provided the culture and education and training that made it worthwhile to continue that life, but also supplied strength in a spiritual flow of strength. He supplied strength by example but also he exuded some of his own strength into the beingness of the other to help solidify it, as it were.

Because one reason for early death in a very young soul is that the soul has not yet learned how to really solidify, crystallize, give substance to, the energies of its own being. There are times when a person will be etherealized and not even incarnated, as an early attempt or an early first step for a rather timid soul, let us say, toward incarnation.

This soul was not really timid. It was not brash, and it had certain fears. But it also has courage, and it has an eagerness and enthusiasm about it. So that first life, that starting life, that was a double-life in this unusual way, and carried through. This gave the soul a good start on its incarnations. (A4126:3)

LANCE

Lance asked about his mother, and it was brought out that she sponsored him into his first four earthlives. A sponsor soul, as the name implies, is that other individual soul who sponsors us into earthliving, or into some particular phase or cycle of it. The sponsor soul is at least a little farther along than the one it sponsors, and usually but not always a cosmic family member. The sponsor soul will appear most frequently as the mother of the incoming one but sometimes as father, brother, sister, uncle, aunt, grandparent, teacher, or close friend.

The sponsor soul usually maintains an interest in its protege beyond the sponsored lifetime, and the two will usually incarnate together more than only that one time:

> She sponsored him into his first earthlife, which was a succession of three lives in the same tribe in Africa. It is on the African plains, and not in the treed area. There is a river which flows regularly. They did not suffer a drought. They had a certain amount of civilzation for that time. This was back about the 2200s B.C., and he was in the masculine, his native gender expression.
>
> It was not a small tribe. It had enough size to defend itself. They had some animals which they controlled, food animals. They had customs in which the survival knowledge of the tribe was preserved. They were endangered at times by wild animals, but knew how to protect themselves and their food animals. They did some crude agriculture. They had some culture in that the older men, some of the older men, and some of the women, could tell them stories, the myths and legends of their tribe, in which the tribal history was preserved in a somewhat embroidered fashion.
>
> They had their religion in which they endeavored to

relate their lives and the life of their tribe to the super-
natural forces which they recognized as being at work in
the universe, because they knew they did not establish
the place where they lived, and they did not establish the
sun and the moon and the stars. There was Something
Else that did. So to establish the correct relationship of
them and of their tribe to that creative Something Else,
certain explanations, certain theology, had grown up
along with certain rites and practices which they believed,
rightly or wrongly, and with quite a bit of rightness, put
them in a correct relationship with the 'Powers That Be'
beyond themselves.

The first of these lifetimes was a pregnancy to the
sponsor soul as mother, which came to live birth. The
child lived from forty-eight to seventy-two hours and
died in the third day. There was something wrong with
the body. The body could not function outside of the
womb, could not take nourishment, could not take
fluids, and so death came. This was rather purposeful.
Simply to give the soul new to earthliving an introduction.

The next incarnation was within about fifteen to
seventeen years. He came again as a baby boy, to a
former sister, a daughter of the sponsor soul, so the
sponsor soul was the grandmother. This time the life
did not last much longer, about eight or nine days, going
into the tenth day. It had been thought this one would
last longer, but the vicissitudes of life there were such
that something happened and the baby simply did not
survive.

Then there was a little more time taken on the Other
Side, a period of about fifty years, and then came to the
same mother the sponsor soul, who, of course, was then
in another incarnation. This time the child carried right
through into the tenth year, into the eleventh year,
past the tenth fall. The baby had been born in the fall,
so his birthday was in the fall. That was really a rather
good start.

Further into the Reading, Dr. John brought out the fourth earthlife of this soul, still in the masculine, and the sponsor soul came in again with this one in a mother-son relationship:

> I find them then in the sixth, seventh or eighth century B.C., in that period, in Babylonia, again as mother and son. This is, in a way, a most undistinguished life. They have low intelligence, and a low economic status although they don't go hungry. They have a low response-quotient to life. One might say, 'Why is that life in there at all?' But it adds substance, it adds quantity, and it gives the soul experience with one type of earthliving which was much more prevalent then than now.
> In this life the mother died early. The mother died when the boy was in his seventh year. The boy felt grief, felt loss even more, but continued. The ranks of the adults closed, as it were, and some woman who lived nearby and had a husband and children of her own sort of moved in to help take care of the children and the household of this one. Death came in the latter teens. By that time he was a man in that culture, and a father, and was recognized as a husband in the rather informal way of marriage there.
> By the time the soul came into another incarnation it was well acquainted with the fact that life in different areas imposed different requirements for survival. The four lifetimes got the soul adjusted to earthliving in an earthbody. When the soul came into this next incarnation, in the 200s A.D. in the feminine in South America, it had settled in fairly well into earthliving. Here there were new and different necessities. Survival in a hot place had demands different from survival in a cold place. There were different ways in which food was procured, there were different explanations of the universe, different religions, different theologies, different cosmologies, different philosophies. Each society had its own established methods and more. So here was another experience. (A2023:7, 8)

MARCUS

The next reading brings out a fascinating history of a soul whose first three personalities were formed experimentally on the astral plane but not incarnated. The patterns were formed and then dissolved. After three proto-incarnations, a fourth personality pattern finally came into a physical conception:

> Dr. John: Its first incarnation was in the 600s A.D. It was in the masculine expression. This was in China. The setting was in a peasant community with farming, but in a village where life was really not too demanding. Oh, they had to work but they raised enough food. They paid taxes but they were spared the depredations of marauders, by the strength of their overlords. They had a modest religious teaching form of the philosophy of life, which taught a cosmology of the world and their relation to the world.
>
> There had been several previous proto-incarnations, as it were, where a personality had been formed experimentally on the astral plane, and just temporarily, so the soul would know what it could be like. It rather liked that, and then that pattern was dissolved. Another pattern was formed and still a third pattern, to teach that eager, bright-eyed, enthusiastic soul how there are different personalities, different personhoods. It did not come into the first one. It did not identify with it. It was not linked up with it with a vital life cord. Nor with the second. Nor with the third.
>
> This was a good teaching. I would commend the council who did that. In fact, I would pass the suggestion on to other councils that they show the souls in their care, if the soul is intelligent enough and interested enough, how different personalities can be formed and dissolved.
>
> Finally a fourth was formed and a soul-breath of life linked with it. This came into conception, and the

Marcus-soul was quite fascinated watching the process of the first trimester, the first three months, of conception wherein the personality and the body were formed.

This was not brought to live birth, but the pattern was sufficiently well thought out and well accomplished that with a few changes, it was used for the next incarnation, which came to live birth and the soul continued to inhabit that body up to the age of one year, seven months and two or three weeks I see.

By this time the person had begun to really establish its own sense of identity. It knew who it was. It knew the sound of its name and responded to it. It had attained a certain mastery of its own body functions. It was toilet-trained, almost, and it could walk, so the accomplishment of identification as a person was well begun.

Then it was withdrawn and a new personality was formed, because the other person continued in the astral realm for awhile, giving the soul that experience more by observation than by life identification.

Then a new personality was formed, and still in the 600s A.D. it was born as a boy with the sponsor soul as the father in this peasant community in China, as I have mentioned. Here the eagerness, a characteristic of this soul, carried it well through the preteens, the puberty stage, into young manhood, and it lived what was really a rather full life. He was married. He had two children, a son and a daughter — well there were two daughters, but one died in infancy. When he was 19, before he was 20, before he reached his 20th spring, he died. This was not unusual, and really for the soul it was quite an accomplishment. (A4130:7-9)

God is androgynous (both masculine and feminine). The soul, made in the image and likeness of God, is also androgynous. In the higher spiritual realms the soul functions as a whole. But as the soul prepares for its earth lessons it is polarized into what we call the masculine and feminine "halves". These soul "halves" are true soul-mates. Much of the urge to completion within us, much of the striving that we know, is to once again find and be united with our other half to make us whoe again.

The androgynous nature of the soul extends into the masculine and feminine soul halves. Each half must incarnate in both its native and non-native genders. Gender change — from masculine to feminine and feminine to masculine — is one of the most difficult early learnings for a soul. One of the major contributions of reincarnation to human progress and welfare is that each one of us, as souls, must spend enough lifetimes in both feminine and masculine to get the experience provided by life in that framework, and to become proficient in both, and at ease in making the transition between them.

When the soul comes into its integrating experiences — some in earthlives and some elsewhere — it must have deep content and easy mastery of both the masculine and the feminine phases of personality life.

Early gender transition lives can be difficult, and in many cases the first (and sometimes the second) such life is brief. Indeed, a first other-gender life may well be counted a success simply if the soul accepts any expression within the other-gender body for any length of time. If such an one is met with a great deal of love and acceptance by its parents, it is encouraged to come back later for a longer stay in that valence. So a gender transition infant death may be permissibly, purposefully and graciously soon. As Dr. John has often said, "Where there is a change in gender, the soul does not always make it the first time" — as is brought out in these following six excerpts of early death:

MALVINA

This is a feminine soul in a feminine lifetime with only seven incarnations behind it. In its brief soul history, there were two touch-down masculine lives. The soul is slated for a masculine cycle of lives up ahead:

Dr. John: I believe she has not had a masculine expression except for — well, there are two infant deaths, boy babies, involving the soul. In one of them it was simply known that that child was going to die in infancy, and the soul made very little investment in it. So this life could be counted as a pastlife or it could be just dropped out of the picture and not counted at all.

The other one, which was masculine, was more dubbed in. It came later, and the soul knew it was to be in a masculine body, but very briefly, and so it quite knowledgeably watched and had some hand, a small part, in the formation of the body, the guides and teachers doing most of it. So it experienced life in a masculine body even though it died when it was nine days old; but it had accepted it, you see.

For a young soul simply to accept a birth and a body of the non-native gender is a step, usually a rather difficult step. It was not difficult here in that the soul was willing, but that incarnation was terminated very quickly. That was in the 1400s. The place was so meaningless that I do not decipher it. It was not purposed that the person live, you see, and the place where you live becomes more significant as you grow up in it. (A1570:18)

NADINE

This is a first full incarnation in feminine living by a basic masculine soul:

Dr. John: They were in a mother-daughter relationship at that time, with Ann as the mother and Nadine as the daughter. This was a tryout of feminine living for this basic masculine soul, and it did not stay long. The daughter died in her third year, and the mother grieved deeply at the loss of her little one. But the love she had given the little girl, and the fact that its first incursion into earth in feminine expression had been so well received, even though brief, gave this soul the necessary reassurance and experience so that in its next try, it stayed on. (AB597:16)

NATHAN

When a mother inquired about one of her present sons, Dr. John reported he had been a son also in a 1400 lifetime in Italy. In this lifetime, the little fellow was lost at the age of three, literally lost. He just wandered away when no one was watching and got lost in the woods and perished. The reading went on to explain the mother's overprotectivenss of the son in this lifetime as a carryover of uneasiness caused by her grief at losing him previously. Her overprotecting attitude was causing problems in their relationship now. Dr. John reassured her:

> She isn't going to lose him in this lifetime, so that should lay to rest the subconscious uneasiness and fearfulness for him. (AB2254:12-13)

A year later a Life Reading was given for this son, now a young man of 21, and additional information was given:

> He comes from the basically feminine half of the soul. This is not the first time in masculine living. . . the first time was when he was before with his mother. He was her son in the 1400s in Italy, and wandered away at the age of three and perished. . . that disappearance of the three-year-old little boy in that lifetime was the outer expression of the feminine soul wandering away from one of its masculine expressions, and returning, looking for, the feminine. It did not stay with that masculine expression very long. Very often where there is a change of gender, the soul does not make it the first time. (AB2504:3, 4)

OPAL

Opal asked about her mother who had made her transition at age 54. Dr. John reported that the mother-soul had sponsored Opal into her first feminine lifetime. The mother's death was also a planned event in her own ongoingness:

Yes, the mother brought the Opal soul into its first feminine expression, in a lifetime in the 900s in the Middle East. This was in the nature of being an in-again-out-again life. It carried the Opal masculine soul through the experiences of being born into a feminine body, through childhood, until the personality was seven years of age. That was all that was needed then in the learning experience. That was as much as the masculine soul was ready to learn. So that earthlife was accomplished at the age of seven, and the girl died.

Now that little girl and her mother had a good relationship. The mother loved the little girl, and the little girl knew it. But at the same time, not all of the mother's love was wrapped up in this daughter, and the little girl knew that, too. The mother had a husband whom she loved very much. She had her own mother and her own sister whom she loved very much. The little girl had an older brother whom the mother loved very much. The circumstances of daily living in that lifetime were such that the mother had many responsibilities, many duties, many interests. So although she gave time and love to her little girl as was needed, and sufficient to anchor that masculine soul well in that feminine expression — still it was not an overly close bond. They were not too tightly interwoven.

So when the time came for the separation, it was accomplished without too much of a wrench. There was pain and suffering on the part of the mother, for it was a difficult experience to lose a child. But it was not what you might think of as a major catastrophe in her life. The mother met it creatively and positively. There was this quality of impersonal love as well as a very deep personal love.

This present lifetime saw a carrying of the relationship through a longer span of years. There are still years of experience in the relationship between a mother and a daughter which these two have not had. They will have these, in time. The mother-soul, because of her earth-rooted love for this one, and because of this quality of nonpossessiveness, was given the opportunity of taking part in the soul-growth of the Opal-soul by taking a major role in one of the experiences of this personality-life. The mother-daughter relationship and the daughter's early loss of her mother contrived to deepen the feeling tone of this soul. At the same time the departure from earthliving of the mother-soul was also in tune with her own cosmic planning and purpose. It was not merely that this early death was for the Opal soul's sake; it tied in also with the mother's own next stage of learning.

So the mother's death was not a happenstance. It was not an accident. It was not done by an unfeeling universe. A great deal of love and protection and care has surrounded the various stages of progress in Opal's life. (AB2598:5, 6)

OWEN

The Owen-soul, a masculine soul, is now going into a serious cycle of feminine lives. The experiencing of life within the native gender is easier than the experiencing of earthlife within the non-native gender. A masculine soul will have an easier time attaining masculine success in earth schooling than it has in attaining feminine success. A feminine soul will find feminine success comes more naturally and more easily to it than masculine success. So the early incarnations of a soul are usually in its native gender. It is a much harder job going into the non-native valence and making a success of that. But this harder job provides a greater opportunity for soul-learning and growth. Dr. John briefly departs from

Owen's soul history to bring in a basic gender-change teaching:

> The Owen-soul is experiencing a transition period which is one of the difficult transitions. This is a masculine soul, but going into a feminine cycle of experience. It has had several feminine lifetimes in the past, but these have been excursions or visits rather than serious stays. There has not been in the past the serious development of feminine qualities.
>
> There are many purposes for incarnations in the nonnative gender, the foremost being that the two halves do not become so polarized and so crystallized that they could not come back together into a homogeneous, let alone congenial, whole. A second value is that this way they each gain more experience: it is a very definite earth experience to incarnate and live in the non-native gender expression!
>
> A third very major value is that in this way each learns more about the other, the other side of itself. So it comes to understand itself better. The soul grows in its own consciousness, in its own awareness of its true beingness, you see. It can look at the other side of itself through its own experience.
>
> Here you come into the picture of Owen. Think of the Owen-soul as being a fine young river coming into the great river of God's Plan, not at a right angle, but on the oblique angle. The Owen-river, and the river of God's Plan, is carrying the Owen-soul into feminine expression and development at this time. (A2039:2)

PAMELA

Pamela is from the feminine half of her soul with seventeen or eighteen past lives on earth, three of which were touchdown lives in the masculine, as Dr. John brings out:

> I would add here that it has had three masculine

excursions, but none of them of major import. One baby
boy lived for twelve days. This was enough for the soul
to really grasp the fact that it had come into masculine
birth and had held the birth. Then it was withdrawn. It
really could not have gone much farther without undue
strain, nor with any competence. It may seem strange
that twelve days is an achievement, and three months
would be an undue strain. Earthlings do not see particularly how this could be, since an 'infant is an infant is an
infant' in much earth understanding.

But it is not so for the soul. The very act of coming
into an incarnation, particularly of the non-native gender,
is an achievement. To hold that for twelve days is more
of an achievement than to hold it, say, for just three
hours or three days. In fact, to hold it for twelve days is
to signal that it has achieved masculine incarnation.

The second masculine incarnation, which followed
the first in point of sequence but not immediately, went
to the age of three years. By this time the infant person
had achieved selfhood as a small child. In other words,
it did not have to be carried around, it could walk
around. It did not have to be toileted, it toileted itself.
It could speak. It recognized father, mother and siblings.
It even had a younger sibling. In fact, it had two younger
siblings. It knew its place in the family. It knew itself to
be one of the family.

The third of the masculine experiences came in the
mid-1800s. I see these are all quite recent. In fact, the
immediately prior lifetime was this 1800s one. This one
was designed to take advantage of — let me back up a
bit and say it a little differently: This one lasted through
the ninth year, almost to the tenth birthday. Since this
did represent a further incursion into masculinity, an
additional element which was already established within
the soul was introduced into this life to be an added
element of strength and support.

This was a religious element. . . . This 1800s incarnation was in India. The boy was born into a very devout

family. There was a test thrown at the soul. Not a great test but a little test. In the second week, near the end of the second week where the first death period had taken place, there was an illness, a gastro-intestinal illness that came upon the baby. If the soul had waivered or weakened or had been uncertain in its determination to continue, it might have pulled out at this time.

But it was determined to continue. It didn't even realize that this was a test, and that was nice. It simply held on a little tighter and without worry, held onto the body, kept the life within the body. . . There was not a similar test at the age of three. . . It lived into the beginnings of puberty. It saw its own body begin to change. It saw the male genitals enlarge in size. It began to feel certain different feelings as the biological processes began to ripen. It met these with a quiet interest and a bit of curiosity rather than fear.

Then why was the soul withdrawn from that experience when it was not fearful? Because it probably would have become fearful as puberty developed and as the body ripened into that stage of maleness where it could become a lover and a father. The soul was not ready for that. (A3263:3, 4)

PHILIP

Simply not being wanted is another reason for some infant deaths, as we have long suspected. Since babies do respond so favorably to love, it is not surprising they respond unfavorably to a lack of love. True, if a soul really wants to come in – or if there are other strong reasons holding the soul to that life – the lack of parental love will not cause an early death, but may in fact be used as a strengthening influence. The end result in any situation is caused by whatever forces are at work in that situation, the person's own decisions being usually the most decisive.

In the case of Philip, rejection was sufficient to cause the soul to withdraw from a life already begun:

> Dr. John: They (the present aunt and nephew) were
> together in a lifetime in the 1300s. This was in England.
> She was in the mother-role to him at that time. However,
> she on the soul level was very rejecting of earthlife in
> general and of motherhood in particular at that time. The
> consequences were that he stayed with her only three
> weeks and then was taken out of life.
>
> The present aunt, the previous mother, did experi-
> ence a certain contrition from the former experience –
> after all, losing a baby is one of the devastating experi-
> ences of life – and so in this life was allowed a certain
> closeness, as the aunt, with this one who had been re-
> jected previously when a son. (AB1973:8)

QUETTA

The next example is another infant death by rejection, but
in a rather selective way. It was in the immediately prior
lifetime, in Italy in the 1800s. The then-mother, because of
her own strong masculinity, favored her sons and wanted
no daughters.

> Dr. John: The Italian mother had three boys and
> then had a little girl whom she lost after ten days. And
> then she had two more boys, and then another little
> girl.
>
> Personality-wise, that Italian woman did not par-
> ticularly like women. She was one herself, yes, but
> remember this was a masculine soul running that fem-
> inine lifetime and feeling that the feminine personality
> ought to line up with the masculine. So within that
> Italian mother there was a very strong force of rapport
> with men but not with women. She was very happy in
> the birth of her sons. She never wanted a girl. She said
> each time she was pregnant, she did not want a girl. Her
> attitude when the first girl was born was, 'Oh, no! Not a

GIRL! What will I do with her?' She was really quite disappointed that she had a girl. And that little baby's soul knew it; and when the mother was not won over to love for the baby, the soul simply withdrew after ten days.

She was given another opportunity, by having a second daughter born after some more sons. The second daughter was not the first daughter returned, it was another soul. It met the same element of rejection in the mother. But this soul that came in as the baby was a little older than the other soul and decided that this attitude of the mother was not going to chase it out of its earthlife, it was going to stay!

It stayed. And the mother took care of the child, but never established really very close bonds with it. She did not neglect her little daughter; the girl was fed and clothed and she was certainly disciplined when she needed it. But the mother's warmth and tenderness and gentleness, what there was of it, went to the boys.

A little later in the reading, the Conductor asked about the Client's present childlessness. She had two miscarriages in this life, but no live birth. She wondered if there was any past-life relationship with those two she lost. And the answer:

Dr. John: These were two souls seeking entry into earthliving through the opportunity thus opened, but because of the lack on the part of this masculine soul preparing the physical body in this lifetime, and because of the soul's former rejection of baby life in the Italian lifetime, they could not get in. (AB1823:8, 9)

QUANN

An early death was brought about by this soul's ineptness in handling a full masculine life, which is understandable in that this was only the second masculine experience for the feminine soul:

> Dr. John: The second masculine expression was in
> the 1600s. It was a rather brief expression of eleven
> years. The personality was an Indian boy, a North Ameri-
> can boy who established himself well with his family
> and with the members of the tribe around him, had a
> good rapport person-to-person, but who did not fit in
> very well in the activities required of him. The body was
> somewhat disjointed. He was awkward. He was left-
> handed. He stuttered and stammered. He had a lot of
> fears; he was afraid of hurting himself, he was afraid of
> thunderstorms, he was afraid of being lost.
>
> Now of course back of this physical ineptness, and
> back of all these fears, was the feminine soul adjusting
> to masculine living without the quality of ease and assur-
> ance that it needed. Because of the native outgoing na-
> ture and happiness of the personality in relationships to
> those around him, his family and the members of his
> tribe liked him. They recognized that he was not very
> good material for an Indian Brave, so they just took him
> good-naturedly and didn't bother him too much. It was
> a good enough lifetime on the human relationship level.
> And before it came to be too much of a problem what to
> do with him, the earth life was ended.
>
> Conductor: The early death was all right then?
>
> Dr. John: Yes. (AB547:15)

QUENTIN

A recent previous-life suffering can produce a carryover of
soul-resistance and result in infant death. The following
example has two points of interest: one, a child which died in
infancy returns to the same family; two, the reassurance
given the reluctant one by an intervening child with whom
he has strong ties.

Quentin is the middle one of three boys. His older brother,

William, died twelve days after birth. Quentin asked if he had past-life ties with this brother who died:

> Dr. John: Yes, the older brother is the same soul as the younger brother. That soul had some reticence about coming into earthliving, and withdrew the first time. Then it was the fact that the Quentin-soul was here which drew the other in the second time, and secured him in earthliving. This brother is basically a masculine soul and has had more earthliving than has the Quentin-soul.
>
> Conductor: Then it was neither newness to earth-living, nor a change in gender, which produced this infant death?
>
> Dr. John: There have been lives recently of quite some strenuous activity, and the soul allowed some negative forces to develop. In a sense it might be said that earthliving had turned sour for the soul; he just didn't want any more of it.
>
> But Quentin is a Cosmic Family member, and with a close bond of companionship on the other planes of life. This helped to persuade the other one to come when he found the Quentin-soul had come and was in expression. (AB1956:6)

RENEE

Child deaths can be the result of soul failure, rebellion, weakness, purpose, or mistake. There is no set rule. The following is a case of a soul rejecting a life experience, and cancelling out that incarnation:

> Dr. John: This was in the latter part of the 12 or early 1300s. This was in France. This was not really a wine area. It was not specialized in wine although they grew grapes and made wine and their wine was just as powerful in its effect upon the drinker, its raw effect, let us say, as the wine made in the other areas with more

class and taste.

They were agriculturists, farmers. They were keepers of cows, makers of cheese. The daughter died when she was nine, nine years and about six weeks old. There was an accident with the cows. I believe a cow brushed her over and stepped on a leg, breaking the leg between the knee and the ankle and some bacteria got into the wound. The end of the bone did not protrude. The skin was rather deeply broken. Bacteria got in and got into the blood stream.

The bone was set according to their best knowledge at that time and splinted, but it would have been a misshaped leg, and the soul rebelled at that, the soul of the daughter. Now it is becoming clear why the death. The soul rebelled at having a misshaped leg.

It had been planned that it would have the experience of a slight crippling and the soul had accepted it but with trepidation, and when the girl just approaching young womanhood, and being quite an athletic and active girl, slightly large for her age, came to the time when there would be a broken leg, a misshaped limb, with quite a period of convalescence, and then with an inability to laugh and run and romp as before and with a lessening, you see, of her marriage value – well, the soul became frightened and became obdurate, expressed its own will contravening what it had previously accepted, and simply used the occasion to end that incarnation. The bacteria that got into the wound were allowed to set up quite a blood infection and in a period of at least a week, about eight or nine days, the infection which should have been thrown off by the healthy young body, if the soul had poured in the life force instead of pulling it out, the infection brought about high fever and death.

The after-death experience is quite interesting. The personality there was involved, but actually the greater guilt lay upon the soul, and the soul would have to work out some of these negative qualities in incarnations after that one. The personality was brought over to the Other

Side. The high fever of the last several days, with its hallucinations, was used to establish consciousness of some of the beings on the Other Side, and the actual time of death was unnoticed. It was a gradual transition of consciousness, and of consciousness of companions, from the earth side to the astral side. There she was met by some relatives she had known. Probably a grandmother. I see — well, first I see two women. Maybe a grandmother and an aunt, or two grandmothers, or a great-grandmother and sombody. Then a religious figure who came in somewhat later, with other children pretty much her own age, several of them. So she came in and she came in without the consciousness of the leg having been broken, and it was not broken.

Now the council had quite a little decision to make, and they conferred with their supervisory council whether to bring over the girl with a consciousness of the broken leg and the crippling that would have resulted, so that the experience which the soul was now rejecting and cancelling on the incarnate side could have been had on the excarnate side of that personhood.

But it was felt that without the soul's assistance in this, because the soul is still the vital life force of the personality in the excarnate as well as in the incarnate side, this would not be accomplished in any satiisfactory or positive way. The negativities, in other words, were made into what we call 'karma on the doorstep' to be picked up as the soul stepped back over the threshold into some future incarnation, and the excarnate personality of that girl was allowed to go on in a more normal experience of development, and then swung gently into the larger aspects of the higher astral realms. It was not potentialed to go into the higher spiritual realms, the etheric realms, but it did go from the lower astral into the higher astral. (A3160:14-16)

During a Public Teaching Session with Dr. John, which is

usually the concluding session of Religious Research gatherings, the question was asked from the floor, "If God exists, and is a loving God, why does He allow so many innocent people, especially children, to suffer and die, even more so today than in the past?"

Let me answer that. Suffering is no more so today than in previous generations. There have been some generations of less suffering, but the proportion of suffering has been far too high in every generation. But God, in making a being after His own kind, had to give freedom. That freedom will involve mistakes. If these mistakes did not bring pain, the individual would not recognize them as mistakes. This is a great general principle which must not be lost, and must not be glossed over. Mistakes should bring pain, so that we learn from them and withdraw from them and find the better way.

You may say, why bring pain to children? This is a good question. This is a compassionate outreach. Pain brought to children should be felt by the adults who have more chance of making changes.

Then in earth we do have the conflict of good and evil. This is a subject which has not been asked, and is too big a subject, the subject that would take a day simply to broach. But there is the conflict of good and evil, and evil does find energization apart from God in the hurts that feed evil. (A8034:29)

How many times have we heard the question, "Why does God allow suffering, especially to children?" This is a large question, and the ones asking usually expect a simple answer easily understood. There are no simple answers. The soul must learn not just to endure, but to successfully endure and cross, this area of experience.

It is interesting to note that some accidents are just that, *accidents*, with no cosmic cause or purpose. This a dangerous realm we live in, and accidents can not always be prevented or predicted. Dr. John brings this out in the following teaching:

> It is true that in earth there are many difficulties, many hurts, many illnesses, many causative factors of illness and injury which are native to earth. Earth is a realm where evil and good are in conflict, and this is more than only symbolism. It is a realm in which accidents can occur. Not as many things are accidents as may be called accidents. But there are accidents in the aspect of the causative forces being within the earth but not really deserved by the individual to whom the accident comes. You are in this type of environment. (A8034:21)

Here is one of those accidents:

ROBERTA

Roberta asked if she and her father had a past-life relationship:

> Dr. John: Yes, he was the father in the immediately prior lifetime, which was in this country in the 1800s. She was in the feminine expression, and he was one who went west, not clear to the coast, not seeking gold, but going out to where there was new land to be had, purchased for, oh, some very small amount per acre or per something. And she was scheduled for a life in that framework, and then she died.
>
> She fell from a wagon, I think from the covered wagon they were taking on this trip, and a wheel passed over either her body or her head — no, it was her body. She was, of course, quite injured; her ribs were crushed. She was conscious but in deep shock, and just her eyes could see. And her eyes looked at her parents who, of course, rushed to her, and they, with great love and tenderness, spoke to her, brought her reassurance which carried her through the death process.

I wonder how she fell from the wagon to fall under the wheels (Dr. John probed further): She was sitting on a seat, a wide seat, a bench type of seat, in the front, and had somewhat leaned forward, quite happily, and something jolted, maybe the wagon struck a rock or something which jolted it so that the father and the mother, the mother was holding a smaller baby, were both shaken. I can see them shaken forward and back. But the little girl was shaken forward and tumbled over.

Death came quite quickly. It was in a matter of between 30 to 40 minutes. They buried the little body there. They were with others, it was a party going out and the party stopped their trip, I think it was, well, it was the rest of that day and all of the next day. Then they started again, on the morning of the third day, because life had to go on and their journey had to proceed. But she was buried in, I believe it was southwestern Pennsylvania, or possibly across the line into what is now Ohio. A little wooden marker was placed on the grave in the form of a cross, and her name — well, I don't get what her name was but it was left on the grave in some way. It was a little arrangement of stones that spelled out the name. The name also was written on a piece of wood. This was an attempt by the parents to, as it were, preserve her beingness a little more beyond that early three years at which she died. Of course, the rain washed away the stones, and the wood — something happened to it, it weathered, and the grave become indistinguishable within a few years. But the real immortality, of course, was that the little one went on to the Other Side.

Here she was met by some who deal particularly with children who come to the Other Side. They caught her attention much as one would catch the attention of a child, probably by some moving object, possibly a pet or something that would catch her attention, maybe a doll — and having caught the attention she was 'safely over', because they held her very closely, they gave her a great deal of love. The trauma of the accident was rather quickly healed because it had happened so quickly and unexpectedly.

And this was an accident. It was not intended. There are accidents. True, the accidents are effects brought about by adequate causes. True, also, that evil in this world — which feeds upon human grief and suffering and other negativities — itself is a cause of many accidents. I say 'many' meaning a fair-sized percentage. But the mere fact that the earth itself is as yet an imperfect place means that imperfections will come. So there was no karmic reason for this early death, and it was not an intended part of the pattern. It was part of incarnations, of earthliving.

. . . The father and the mother both were very happy to find their daughter as they made their transitions some several decades later. So there was a certain healing there. Then, since the healing of a traumatic event, or the completion of incomplete business, on any one plane, or in any one realm, is usually accomplished finally upon that same plane or within that same realm, they were brought back for the present life together, which was the larger healing of the prior life lost. (A4186:3, 4)

* * * * *

Grief of a deep and prolonged nature is one way in which we "feed evil." This is one way in which we add our energies to the force of general evil in the world, rather than to good. In knowing this, we would not, indeed we must not, feed so destructive a personal grief with the full energies of our being.

The understanding now being gained as to the various causes leading to the deaths of infants and children can now be used. This new knowledge can go a long way in reducing the devastating effect of the loss, and in the evil-feeding duration of the grief in such loss.

In our understanding of the larger purpose of God; in the knowledge of our immortality; in knowing there are successive incarnations open for every soul; and in learning the orderly framework of our spiritual nature – in all these we find a definite strength to meet and transcend every loss, but most importantly for this chapter, the deep sorrow in the loss of a beloved child.

This can bring comfort, and this can bring the strength to endure what we as yet cannot change or control. The soul that lies behind that child will have many, many opportunities to express and experience all that earthlife has to offer. There is a plan for that soul that is indestructibly good, planned by a tremendously wise and absolutely loving Father-Mother God, in whom the death of a child is cradled in law and in love.

CHAPTER NINE

DEATH CONTROL

I had my first opportunity to talk with Dr. John during the 1971 Religious Research Seminar in Princeton, New Jersey. Knowing that final seminar sessions are usually question and answer sessions with Dr. John, I had come from Chicago for the express purpose of asking him these two very important questions:

    1. If I ever become terminally ill and in constant pain, would I have the right to take my own life?
    2. What about the helpless elderly patients who are mistreated, or those lingering on in a non-human state? Are these conditions spiritually necessary?

For many years I had watched the elderly-ill and other hopeless cases, sometimes lingering on for years, a heavy burden to themselves and their families, and a drain on public resources. I would then look ahead with dread to my own old age and wonder if I would end up in a similar state. It was important for me to know if, under those distressing circumstances, I could in good conscience take my own life. I needed an authority I could trust for definitive answers. By the time of the 1971 seminar, I had studied Religious Research material and had carefully "tested" Dr. John for three years, and when I finally had the opportunity to ask those questions, I knew I could believe the answers:

Dr. John: The prolongation of life in general to the last possible gasp is a rather new development in earth affairs, and poses still some problems for those who have that area of general charge on This Side. We think a person should be allowed to die in dignity. And incidentally we would say that very often these older persons have lost the keen edge of consciousness, have lost perhaps most of their consciousness, and do not feel the treatment they get as being an insult as someone else looking upon it might feel it to be.

The right to control the time you die requires still a little more knowledge than the masses have, the right of an individual to choose his own time of death. The soul chooses its time of birth. And the soul can choose when to withdraw, but on the whole it is left to the body itself to some extent. To the extent that the body holds onto life for some additional years, all right, the soul will leave its life principle, although it may withdraw a great deal of its content so that only a soul-breath is left in that body. There needs to be greater spiritual understanding before the right of an individual to choose his/her own time of death could be considered a universal right. Those of you here, most of you, know now that you could choose your time of death if you did it preferably in consultation with several others. It's good to check with ones guides, with others, and that it be not an emotional or impulsive thing.

Question: You are saying if I am terminally ill and in great pain, a burden, I could with impunity and in good conscience, take my own life?

Dr. John: If the pain is prolonged, if the good that was to be gotten from the pain has already been gotten, there is no point in prolonging the experience. Now to know whether or not the good has been gotten will require quite a depth of spiritual insight, and is a decision that should be made gradually. But then, yes, it would not carry the usual penalties of suicide.

You see, the usual penalty of suicide is simply this:

There is a pattern which has been established for this life. That pattern has its own ongoing momentum. If you commit suicide, you don't have the body in which to accomplish it. You are still on the job, but one of your major tools has been stolen or thrown away. If the life pattern is completed, and then you choose to die, choose carefully, gradually, thoughtfully, prayerfully, and perferably after talking it over with several others (probably not your doctor), then there would not be the usual penalty, the usual result for suicide. Often it would give you fewer years of misery, and a little earlier start on the progression of glory ahead.

Question: What about the mistreatment of the elderly I've seen in private homes, in hospitals, and in some nursing facilities for the aged?

Dr. John: Don't feel as badly about it as I think you are feeling, because they are not feeling it as keenly as you are feeling it. Now wrong treatment is wrong treatment anywhere, of course. But sometimes a human has lost so much of the soul content that it is more of an animal, and must be treated mostly in that framework. (1971 Religious Research Seminar)

Every day 5,000 people celebrate their 65th birthday, and 3,500 people over 65 die. This is a daily gain of 1,500 in the ranks of the elderly, bringing a host of aging problems that will test the country's resources as the elderly population increases.

More and more local, state, and federal funding will have to be used for the care of the elderly, especially the poor and sick who can no longer care for themselves. Some hard choices will have to be made for the types of long and short-term care facilities America will turn to in the decades ahead.

In many third-world nations the life expectancy is only 32 to 35 years. Even in this country, at the turn of the century most Americans died long before they reached 65.

As medical technology keeps advancing, it brings a steady torrent of new and ever more sophisticated and expensive equipment. The already high cost of medical care has literally laid siege to our entire economy. Health-care is a $285 billion-a-year business. Nearly 10% of the U.S. Gross Product in 1984 went to medical care, compared with only 5.4% in 1960, and the run-away costs are surging ahead. Says Federal Reserve Chairman Paul Volcker, "We appear to have turned the corner in most areas of inflation, but health costs have shown very little sign of improvement."

Uncontrolled medical costs are like an illness that infects prices everywhere. General Motors spent more than $3,300 per employee on health insurance in 1985, or double the 1976 outlay. GM estimates that its health-care bill added about $370 to the cost of producing each car it made. Payments for insurance claims have shaken the nation's insurance companies. The Prudential Insurance Company, the nation's largest private health insurer, abruptly announced that it would stop issuing health insurance to individuals. The cost of health care has played havoc with the federal budget. Officials of the Mayo Clinic in Rochester, Minn., offer the startling calculation that it cost as much as nine million dollars to add one additional year of life to the seriously ill patient through such ultra-modern technologies as kidney dialysis and organ transplants.

The cost to the families involved is equally overwhelming, both emotionally and financially. There is the grueling aspect of caring for the victims as they lose the ability to care for themselves, becoming incontinent, unruly, destructive. To the emotional toll of a terrible sense of loss there is also the feeling of guilt when that person must finally be institutionalized. The cost to the family unit is catastrophic. The following examples are taken from United Press International releases:

A 79-year-old man in Fort Lauderdale, Florida, Hans

Florian, loved his wife Johanna to the end, even as he put a pistol to the demented woman's head and pulled the trigger. The motive was not jealously, revenge, or profit, it was done with love and mercy. The woman was suffering from Alzheimer's Disease.

Hans and Johanna had been married for thirty-three years, but Hans could no longer wish life upon his wife whose mind started unraveling in the late 1970s.

First, she started panicking whenever he would step away from her, wanting to know where he was. Then her handwriting declined and within a few months she couldn't write at all. Then she couldn't drive, she'd drift into the oncoming lane.

As the disease ravaged her brain, Hans and his son bathed Johanna, pried open her teeth at feeding time, woke to her screams, picked her up when she stumbled, and changed her clothes five or six times a day as she wet and soiled them.

For most of the last two years, friends said Johanna screamed constantly, howling like an animal unless heavily drugged.

Florian learned all he could about the disease, and the reward was sorrow in advance. He learned scientists are far from discovering the cause of Alzheimer's Disease, let alone the cure. They only know the results, the brain withers and fills with bubbles.

The Broward County Grand Jury, which could have indicted Florian on first degree murder charges, understood the pitifully senile state of his wife and refused to indict him for any wrongdoing.

It was once thought that severely demented patients could not live very long. Today we know, says Chicago Neurologist Jacob Fox, that they can survive for upwards of fifteen years. "We've gotten better at preserving lives, but it's not clear we're doing the person a favor."

Medical research has made tremendous strides on many

fronts, and the human race has come a long way from the days when nomadic tribes, crossing a river, would leave their old and sick behind to die. But we have not reached a good answer for our hopeless sufferers.

In Houston, Texas, Billy Clore, age 25, shot to death his hopelessly comatose father. Billy's dad, Robert Clore, had already told his family, if he ever got in a 'bad way' he wanted to die. 'I felt he was suffering, and I wanted to stop his suffering', Clore told police. But unlike Fort Lauderdale, Houston indicted Clore for murder.

* * * * *

In January, 1979, George and Jeanine Loulousis of Mokena, Illinois, watched anxiously as their three-month-old son Jonathan developed a sudden and rapidly-rising fever.

Three years later their son was dead. He died of a rare and incurable form of colitis. This left his emotionally shattered parents to face an equally catastrophic economic problem, a staggering $400,000 in medical bills incurred in the futile fight to save their son.

* * * * *

Dr. Marcia Angell, deputy editor of the New England Journal of Medicine, wrote that the present administration has proposed 'Baby Doe Rules' based on the idea that 'all life no matter how miserable should be maintained if technically possible.'

Currently, parents decide whether doctors should struggle to save their handicapped babies when the chance of a normal life is gone.

'For the government to think that it can do better with a set of general rules, which are of necessity insensitive and vague when applied to a particular patient, is both arrogant and foolish,' she wrote in an editorial.

The administration proposed the rules after the highly publicized case of a retarded infant, dubbed 'Baby Doe.' The child was born April 9, 1982, in Bloomington, Indiana, with Down's Syndrome and a food pipe defect that prevented him from swallowing. His parents decided to withhold corrective surgery and intravenous feeding, and the baby died six days later despite a prosecutor's efforts to require treatment.

The rules would require every handicapped infant to receive all possible treatment unless death is inevitable or the risk of treatment is prohibitive. Hospitals that defy the regulation could be denied federal funds.

* * * * *

Mrs. Rannazzisi is a 65-year-old stroke victim, unable to speak or move. Doctors say there is nothing they can do — a diagnosis that has taken the family months to accept. But there is one indignity the hard-working middle-class family still cannot come to terms with: There is no place for Mrs. Rannazzisi to die.

Long Island Jewish Hospital, where Mrs. Rannazzisi was admitted nearly a year ago, wants to discharge her because officials there say they can no longer justify the $450-a-day expense of custodial care. More than thirty nursing homes near her home on Long Island have rejected her, because they say they do not have sufficient staff or beds. Nearly everyone agrees she is too ill to go home.

Mrs. Rannazzisi is one of thousands of chronically ill patients who remain in hospitals long after they can benefit from such expensive care. It cost hundreds of thousands of government dollars to keep them there.

These cases present the dilemma of our times. On the one hand is the futility and suffering of life's continuance. With the logical argument that if it's all right to terminate life at its beginning, why it is not equally right to terminate hopeless cases at its end?

On the other hand are those who argue in reverence that nature has the right to decide the time of death rather than leaving it to human decision. Our generation has seen the change of abortion from an act of homicide to an act of expediency. No similar new approach has yet been reached about death, but progress is being made.

During the two decades of the 1960s and 1970s, death moved out of the shadow of cultural taboo and onto the agendas of medical professionals, educators, clergy, and public policy-makers. Society is beginning to recognize its enormous health and dying problems. Ethical, legal, financial, personal and social procedures are yet to be worked out, but the recognition is dawning that these problems lie within the larger framework of the welfare of all society. This, for our time, is an important step in taking mastery of earthlife. And there is a growing recognition that many earlier societies were more realistic, and not more cruel, in their methods of dealing with the elderly and the terminally ill.

From the prestigious *Science News* (October 9, 1983 issue), Kathy Fackelmann's article "A Question of Life or Death" presents the present dilemma of doctors in making a decision to continue a life-support system or to "pull the plug" on terminal or comatose patients. This is an excerpt from that article:

> Late one night I was called to a ward by a nurse to see a patient breathing his last. My knee-jerk reaction was to do a tracheotomy. Immediately he began to breathe again and signaled for a note pad lying on a nearby table. He wrote, 'Why did you do this to me?'
> George R. Dunlop, a surgery professor at the University of Massachusetts Medical School, told this story to members of the President's Commission for the

Study of Ethical Problems, a group of medical, legal, and ethics experts who met in Washington, D.C., to discuss problems doctors face when making decisions to stop medical treatments for dying patients. Dunlop, disturbed by the incident, which occurred fifty years ago in a Cincinnati hospital, said he felt it was wrong to save this patient's life because it only prolonged the man's suffering.

Joel Feinberg, a University of Arizona philosopher, told commission members another story about the dark side of medical technology. His 90-year-old mother's heart stopped, and the hospital emergency team broke her ribs during resuscitation. 'She never said a word, but moaned in pain the whole time after that. I think this was a moral abomination.' Feinberg's mother is not an uncommon occurance. Patients in intensive care units often die ten or twelve times during the course of a night, only to die again, finally, hours or a few days later. Often these patients are revived just enough to be conscious a little longer of their pain.

What does Dr. John have to say about the use of heroic methods of resuscitation in inappropriate situations? The question was asked, "Does the soul experience trauma when life is extended by life-support systems?"

In general, yes. Part of the trauma being that when the pattern for that life is over, why should the physical instrument be maintained? When the time of purposefulness has ended, then there is a certain vacuum, a certain lack, in that which lies ahead, and prolongation of the physical instrument is a painful process, part of the pain being its purposelessness. A person without a purpose is an anomaly in this purposeful creation and this purposeful world. That is part of it.

Another part is that it is just a stupid thing to do.

Question: If it is widely known that there is soul-trauma in the senseless continuation of a life-support

system, then we as a people can become strong enough
to insist we will not have this for ourselves or for those
we love. Is this not true?

Dr. John: Correct. I would applaud. Also, let us remember that the high regard for human life is a fairly
recent development, and that is to be applauded. But it
has carried over a little too far in some excessive manifestations. I said excessive, not expensive, but it is both.
There are many factors involved in this. The individual
doctor could be subject to very devastating and destructive criticism and withdrawal of his livelihood if he
were to step outside the accepted practice, you see.

So the pioneering work must be done by such as you,
a valued friend and comrade. The human understanding
of this must be carried forward. Part of that being the
understanding that life is of the spirit, that only temporarily do we inhabit our bodies, and there comes a time
for not paying the rent any more. (A8034:22)

Question: When it is evident that a person is never
going to come out of a coma, does the soul stay in the
body?

Dr. John: This is a yes and no question with quite a
little gradation of percentage points on each end. Long
ago I mentioned that with the young woman Karen
Quinlan, the soul had wanted to pull out, was not supposed to, and was being held in. That soul is being held
in because the soul itself has to learn. There are other
cases where the soul is almost entirely out during a long
coma, out of the personality, out of the body. But as
long as there is some life, there is some soul touch. As
long as there is a soul-touch and the necessary body organs are intact, there is some life in the body. Yes.

Question: One of the psychics, I think it was Jane
Roberts, brought out through the Seth material that
sometimes a person will be trying to prepare for what's
in the afterlife by going into a long coma. Is there anything to this teaching?

Dr. John: Well, that sounds logical. I really do not

have an index file, a card file on coma cases, but this could be possible. It would not be so much the soul as the personality. And really not very many personalities have the wisdom to know that. I'm not sure it would be considered very wise, to keep a toe-hold in the physical but venture out a ways into the lower astral on purpose. It's an interesting question. I really do not know. I have not watched. I have allowed them their privacy.

Question: If it is known on the Other Side a person will not come out of a coma, then where is that person and what is that person doing?

Dr. John: Well, a coma is a matter more of the personality than of the soul, and a coma is brought about more by physical factors than by soul factors. The soul will not have to devote as much of its being, nor as much of its attention, its consciousness, to a personhood in coma as to one not in coma, and so the soul — which perhaps had thirty percent of its beingness vitally engaged in that personhood may now in coma have only five percent — and will find other things to do with the additional twenty-five percent, and shift its weight of attention to what some of the rest of the soul is doing, or perhaps is on something new. Yes. (A8045:3)

For major changes to come about in the official policy of health-care professionals in care of the terminally-ill and hopeless cases, there must first be public understanding and opinion. This support is necessary before the laws and policies are updated. And it is growing. Beginning in the early 1960s, a tremendous amount of scientific data has come forth on death and dying. Public consciousness is beginning to shift. For example, this survey by the American Hospital Association has reported in the March 15, 1982 issue of the Chicago Tribune:

A majority of Americans appear to be in favor of 'pulling the plug' in cases of hopeless illness, according to a survey conducted for the American Hospital Association.

Seven out of every ten people polled in the nation-wide survey are in favor of discontinuing expensive life-support systems for patients who have little chance of survival. The biggest surprise of the survey was the over-whelming number of people in favor of stopping life support in hopeless cases as a means of reducing in-creasing hospital and insurance rates. Seventy-one percent favored the termination of extraordinary life support.

The right to take one's own life when faced with a hopeless physical condition is another matter, more controversial than 'pulling the plug' on terminal cases. Mankind has not yet reached the level of spiritual discrimination to support the individual's right to practice death control. The concept, however, is being gradually introduced into human con-sciousness, and in some cases with a growing acceptability.

A recent well-publicized case in support of "self-deliverance" is that of the prominent intellectual and writer Arthur Koestler:

> On March 3, 1983, the bodies of Arthur Koestler and his wife Cynthia were found in their London apart-ment. The couple had committed suicide. At the time of his death, at age 77, Koestler was suffering from leukemia and Parkinson's Disease. Cynthia, age 55, was not known to be ill, but a friend said, "Their marriage was very close, and she was completely devoted to him."
> The Koestlers belonged to an organization called "Exit" which supports the right to die with dignity. Arthur Koestler wrote the preface for the organization's manual *A Guide to Self-Deliverance* (distributed to the 8,000 members of the British Voluntary Euthanasia Society). The preface reads, "There is only one prospect worse than being chained to an intolerable existence: the nightmare of a botched attempt to end it." For the growing number of proponents for "self-deliverance",

the Koestlers' suicides seemed to summarize a more gentle way out for the terminally ill.

In the United States assisting a suicide is a crime, but under the First Amendment, how-to-do-it manuals detailing methods of suicide may be published. Thus, *Let Me Die Before I Wake*, put out by a Los Angeles-based organization called "Hemlock", has been sold freely in bookstores.

Another death-by-choice case stands out for its gentleness:

> Vinoba Bhave, a disciple of Mohandas Gandhi, was regarded after the Gandhi assassination in 1949 as his spiritual heir, and in his own right was one of India's premier social reformers.
>
> Following his policy of 'passive resistance' to the end, Bhave when he became ill at age 87 and knew death was close, stopped all food and medication in a voluntary move to assist his death. He died in November 1982, refusing to continue bodylife whose purpose had been served out.

There is a healing in death, and there is comfort for those who come into the larger understanding that death brings ultimate healing.

Here is a beautiful case where the court recognized the right to death-by-choice. The case is extreme, but that is where principles are most clearly recognizable. And the soul is so much better off! Now, it can have a decent incarnation, perhaps with the twin who was stillborn.

> TAMPA — The parents, two lawyers, a doctor and a nurse looked on in tears as the respirator was unplugged. Forty minutes later, 14-month-old Andrew James Barry died in his mother's arms.
>
> 'Mama and daddy just held him, rubbed him, patted him and kissed him the whole time,' said Leroy Merkle,

Jr., court-appointed guardian for the child who was removed Wednesday from the life-sustaining machine at Humana Women's Hospital.

The 2nd District Court of Appeal ruled January 27 that Andrew, born Christmas Day 1982 with a severe brain defect, had the right to die. Lawyers in the case say it was the first time in Florida that an Appellate Court has allowed a child to be taken off life-support equipment.

More than 90 percent of Andrew's brain function was gone. He was blind, had no memory or speech and could not sense, feel, or touch. But he was not legally dead. Doctors detected some reflexes in his brain stem. They said with a respirator Andrew could live from six months to five years. Without it, they predicted he would live no more than two hours.

Andrew was the younger of twins born in the Tampa hospital on December 25, 1982. The older twin was stillborn. Andrew was put on a respirator within hours of his birth.

After seeking the advice of doctors and priests, the child's parents Mark and Laura Barry, obtained court permission to turn off the life support.

The Appellate Court in upholding a state court ruling from October, said the parents' decision 'overrides any interest of the state in prolonging their child's life through extraordinary measures.'

'The parents' informed decision is backed by uncontroverted medical evidence that their young child is terminally ill, and that his condition is incurable and irreversible,' wrote Judge John M. Scheb for a three-judge panel.

Doctors testified they would not have put the child on the respirator had they realized the severity of the birth defect. But once they did, they were concerned about the legality of turning off the machine and insisted on a court order.

In granting permission, the court said that doctors

need not worry in similar cases in the future. A court order would be necessary only if 'doubt exists, or there is a lack of concurrence among the family, physicians and the hospital, or if an affected party simply desires a judicial order,' the three-judge panel said.

Chief Assistant Hillsborough State Attorney Tony Guarisco had argued for 'the preservation of life,' but called the 2nd District Ruling 'a correct decision.'

Since a losing party has 15 days to ask a court to reconsider, the Court Order did not become final until Sunday. Marchese advised waiting until Tuesday to ensure that the Order would not be challenged. It was not.

'It's a very emotional time for all of us,' Marchese said. 'We won, but the reality hit us all.' (Associated Press release 2/7/84)

The subject of taking one's own life in a terminal illness came up during a Staff Teaching Session with Dr. John. The question was, "Will the time come when a person may choose his or her own time of death?" His answer:

It is true that the time will come when the time of death can be chosen. There are times when the taking of a life by the individual is really a spiritual advance over a continuation of a life that is meaningless, and is a detriment to others as well as to itself. But to discern which is which and the proper timing is a level of discrimination and discernment not yet reached on earth. On Our Side too, the guides and teachers on the whole do not as yet know enough, do not have enough spiritual principles, for reaching the right answer to counsel self-release, except very rarely.

However, the needless prolongation of a life that really has ended is the pendulum swinging the other way, and 'pulling the plug' in such a situation is not suicide and is not murder. It is a going along with the natural order of things, which natural order and right order of things had been violated by the needless prolongation of purposeless existence. But discrimination is the key, and discrimination is a large problem in this area.

Question: How does terminal illness fit into someone taking his own life before going through the purposed agony of a slow death? Is there any karmic imbalance caused by this?

Dr. John: There can be a long terminal illness which may be an opportunity to experience the love of others in the care given, and the progressive love of society providing care. Having said that, this is but one general consideration, and each individual case is an individual case. It is not possible to make a set rule in this area, and it is difficult to reach an individual decision in many of the cases. (A8034:27, 28)

My own personal feelings on death control were and are that for society to insist that physical life be lived to the uttermost gasp no matter how hopeless the illness, no matter what degree of pain, is a presumptous and self-righteous imposition on a fellow human's right to self-determination. I agree with the British physicain Elliot Slater, "A man's life is his own, and if we say it is not we are saying that he is a slave and not a free man. Slavery is still slavery no matter how kind the intentions, nor if it's from those near and dear to us." "A man's life is his own" means that in the larger framework of God's purpose, God gives us the right to make free-will decisions how we will live our lives, and we carry full responsibility for those decisions. We do not turn our free will or responsibility over to someone else. If we make mistakes, and we will from time to time, God's loving correction will make of those mistakes learning experiences for us. He will gently nudge us back onto the right path. As Dr. John has often said, "There is nothing wrong with a person that reincarnation can't cure."

Under the law, what are your rights while a hospital patient, especially if you are terminally ill or in a coma?

Psychologists Dr. Dorthy M. Gaev and Dr. Sean R. Bezalel are two of the many professionals actively engaged in a wide dissemination of legal information on patients' rights while hospitalized, and the rights of the terminally ill to die in a more natural and gentle manner. Both Dr. Gaev and Dr. Bezalel have kindly made their legal research available to me personally for this book, as follows:

It is essential that you understand all your rights before going to the hospital, and especially your rights in the Intensive Care Unit. You must speak to your doctor in advance. It is advisable to type out exactly what you will and will not consent to in ICU, and have the whole paper notarized for your chart.

While in a hospital, you have the right to refuse all treatment, medication, a medical test or procedure, surgery, or a machine, including a life-support system. The admission form you sign is a blanket consent form, but legally it is almost worthless. It does not give the hospital the right to do anything to you without your consent.

You will be required to sign a special consent form for your doctor for any procedure to invade your body with tubes or probes. Do not sign this until you know exactly what you're consenting to. There is a law called 'informed consent', which means your doctor must tell you everything about a procedure before you sign the form. Many don't bother to tell the full truth. If your doctor doesn't answer all your questions, you would be wise to refuse to sign and get another doctor.

You have the right to leave a hospital any time you want. Keeping someone in a hospital against his or her will is false imprisonment. First, however, it might be wise to check with your insurance company to see if they will pay the bill if you check yourself out.

You should know that any doctor or nurse who does something to you against your will has committed a crime called battery under civil law. Treatment without permission is battery. If you have a terminal illness and don't want to be kept alive by machines, you can refuse transfer to the Intensive Care Unit.

Filling out a 'Living Will', a document saying you don't want to be kept alive by machines, does not guarantee that you will be allowed to die with dignity in a hospital. Many doctors and hospitals do not respect Living Wills.

MADA

Mada is terminally ill, and she came to Dr. John with some anxious questions. Her first, "There have been many people brought to my home in the last stage of their illnesses, needing my care. This placed quite a burden on those caring for them. I am wondering why life must be prolonged in this hopeless way?"

Dr. John: She has had, then, opportunity to see that a chosen time of death in comfort, in love, in faith and not in fear, would be preferable and spiritually more advanced than some of the barbaric deaths which must be suffered as long as man feels he must maintain every possible instant of life within the physical body. Oh, my goodness, if man only understood that on the excarnate side of life there is so much good waiting for you! However, the excarnate should not be undertaken until the incarnate has yielded its full fruitage. And the judgment involved in this is not a light matter. But it is not a matter beyond human ascertainment. Yes.

Conductor: Mada's mother died in her home of cancer, and Mada took care of her until the end.

Dr. John: Well, if she took her mother into her own home in the terminal stages, and took care of her there, I would say she has done two things: She has certainly served the mother well; and she has seen what an uncontrolled death, left up to the determination of a painful ravaging disease only, has been like. This is hardly the highest human way to die.

Mada has a devastating form of multiple sclerosis, diagnosed ten years prior to her life reading, and she shared her feelings on death control with her Conductor:

> I would gladly welcome death. I have 'hung in there' raising three children, and I now believe my mission is done. I speak of suicide freely to my friends and family, and if my condition deteriorates further, I have the will to take my own life. I understand the consequences of such an act, but I am still adamant.
>
> Over the years, I have seen the old and the terminally-ill die. I have seen the traumatic savagery of terminal cancer. I simply see no purpose in continuing as a useless burden. I need whatever comfort Dr. John can extend. I ask this in the name of Jesus the Christ, whom Dr. John serves.

Here is Dr. John's compassionate reply:

> Now let us address that possibility of suicide. As I have said upon various occasions for many years, the time is coming when the time of birth and the time of death, both, will come under direct human control, and this is good when done rightly.
>
> Certainly the control of birth is one of the most basic requirements now of human progression. Likewise, it marks another step forward in man's wisdom necessary for the success of human life upon earth, and for man's growing compatibility with God. God does not permit cosmic idiots into real companionship with Himself. Youngsters, yes, honest mistakes, yes. Even a repeated mistake if not repeated too often, yes. But one who simply does not grow in knowledge, in wisdom, is recycled, is among the many who are not chosen. To be compatible with God requires a great increase in our intelligence and ability, and I say 'our' because this applies to the Individuated-God-Being on any stage as well as upon your stage. And it requires the discovery,

and the voluntary complete alignment of ourselves, with the structuring of God's universe and God's will as expressed in that structuring, and in other ways as well.

So every bit of intellectual mastery taken over all or any of the processes of life is a step forward when done correctly. Birth control falls within this, and the control of the time of death does likewise. Certainly the great advances in nutrition and medicine and other understandings of the body have given man a great new control of the time of death.

The development of the correct understandings which are spiritual, as well as the assessment of physical factors, can lead into a correct and rightful and spiritually-progressed choice of the time of death.

Man really has not come into that state of knowledge very extensively as yet, but more and more people are carefully thinking about and exploring the various concepts and understandings required. If Mada and her husband and possibly the other members of her family come to a time of agreement that the condition of her body and the completion of the positive aspects of her life really indicate spiritually and logically that it would be good for her to make her transition, and if it is done with sufficient time so that all concerned come to an emotional acceptance of it as a good and glorious step out of limitation into greater health, into more life, into even a greater companionship with them, her loved ones, then if such a decision is made, well, I for one certainly would not speak against it in any way. I believe it could be a step of spiritual progression to reach such a stage. (A2046:7, 8, 10, 12)

*   *   *   *   *

As we draw to the conclusion of this book we all know there is a great deal more to be learned about death. Hopefully these pages will have helped prepare you, the reader, for your own personal experience of this great transition of life from one plane, the incarnate, to the far better and vaster plane of the excarnate personality. There you will learn yourself more than anyone here on earth could tell you!

Dr. John's words of understanding, of compassion, of wisdom and guidance, are my conclusion to *Death With Under-Standing.* But let me add these from that delightful and insightful book of a generation ago, *The Days of Our Years,* by the Chinese author Lin Yutang. He is saying the same thing:

The symphony of life
should end with a grand finale
of peace and serenity,
of material comfort and spiritual contentment,
not with the crash of a broken drum
or cracked cymbals.

INDEX

RELIGIOUS RESEARCH BOOKS

Science and Religion
THE POWER OF PRAYER ON PLANTS (Loehr, 1959, 1969)
DEVELOPMENT OF RELIGION AS A SCIENCE (Loehr, 1983)

Life After Death
DIARY AFTER DEATH (Loehr, 1966, 1976, 1986)
DEATH WITH UNDERSTANDING (Writers Group, 1987)

Reincarnation (Soul Progression)
DESTINY OF THE SOUL (Roberts, 1986)
KARMA, THE GREAT TEACHER (Roberts, 1985)
DR. JOHN: HE CAN READ YOUR PAST LIVES (Hussey & Sherrod, 1983)
CROSS-CORRESPONDENCE AMONG THE LOEHR-DANIELS LIFE READINGS (Amidon, 1985)
INCARNATION AND REINCARNATION (Roy Smith, 1976)
THESE CAME BACK (Webb, 1976)
Reincarnation Quickbooks
   1. KARMIC ROOTS
   2. KARMIC JUSTICE FOR WOMEN

Mysticism
MY FATHER WITH THE SWEET NAME (Goulding, 1982)

The Loehr-Daniels Life Readings are still (1987) available.
Write for information

RELIGIOUS RESEARCH PRESS
Box 208 Grand Island
Florida 32735 U.S.A.